The Persistence of Victorian Liberalism

**Recent Titles in
Contributions to the Study of World History**

The Maori and the Crown: an Indigenous People's Struggle for Self-Determination
Dora Alves

Shamanism and Christianity: Native Encounters with Russian Orthodox Missions in Siberia and Alaska, 1820–1917
Andrei A. Znamenski

Neville Chamberlain and British Rearmament: Pride, Prejudice, and Politics
John Ruggiero

Philanthropic Foundations in the Twentieth Century
Joseph C. Kigor

The Politically Correct Netherlands: Since the 1960s
Herman Vuijsje
Translated and annotated by Mark T. Hooker

Continuity during the Storm: Boissy d'Anglas and the Era of the French Revolution
John R. Ballard

Ambivalent Embrace: America's Relations with Spain from the Revolutionary War to the Cold War
Rodrigo Botero

Paper Liberals: Press and Politics in Restoration Spain
David Ortiz, Jr.

Triumph and Downfall: America's Pursuit of Peace and Prosperity, 1921–1933
Margot Louria

Philadelphia's Enlightenment, 1740–1800: Kingdom of Christ, Empire of Reason
Nina Reid-Maroney

Finance from Kaiser to Führer: Budget Politics in Germany, 1912–1934
C. Edmund Clingan

The Uncertain Friendship: The U.S. and Israel from Roosevelt to Kennedy
Herbert Druks

The Persistence of Victorian Liberalism

The Politics of Social Reform in Britain, 1870–1900

Robert F. Haggard

Contributions to the Study of World History, Number 77

GREENWOOD PRESS
Westport, Connecticut • London

Library of Congress Cataloging-in-Publication Data

Haggard, Robert F., 1968–
　　The persistence of Victorian liberalism : the politics of social reform in Britain, 1870–1900 / Robert F. Haggard.
　　　　p.　cm.—(Contributions to the study of world history, ISSN 0885–9159 ; no. 77)
　　Includes bibliographical references and index.
　　ISBN 0–313–31305–9 (alk. paper)
　　1. Great Britain—Social policy—19th century.　I. Title.　II. Series.
HN385.H3175　2001
361.6′1′0941—dc21　　　　00–035320

British Library Cataloguing in Publication Data is available.

Copyright © 2001 by Robert F. Haggard

All rights reserved. No portion of this book may be reproduced, by any process or technique, without the express written consent of the publisher.

Library of Congress Catalog Card Number: 00–035320
ISBN: 0–313–31305–9
ISSN: 0885–9159

First published in 2001

Greenwood Press, 88 Post Road West, Westport, CT 06881
An imprint of Greenwood Publishing Group, Inc.
www.greenwood.com.

Printed in the United States of America

The paper used in this book complies with the
Permanent Paper Standard issued by the National
Information Standards Organization (Z39.48–1984).

10　9　8　7　6　5　4　3　2　1

Contents

Acknowledgments	vii
1. Introduction	1
2. The Idea of Progress during the "Great Depression in Trade and Agriculture," 1873-1896	9
3. The Revival of the "Condition of England" Question, 1883-1893	27
4. The Purification of Philanthropy and the Reform of the Poor Law	53
5. Socialist Theory, the Labour Movement, and Social Reform	83
6. Conservative, Liberal, and Radical Responses to the Social Question	117
7. The Limits of Governmental Intervention during the Victorian Era	141
8. The Strange Vitality of Liberal England	175
Bibliography	183
Index	203

Acknowledgments

One of the pleasures of finishing a project such as this is that it gives the author an opportunity to thank all of those who provided help and encouragement along the way. The archivists and librarians at the British Library and at the British Library's Newspaper Record Office at Colindale furnished me with many of the raw materials for this study in a prompt and professional manner. The interlibrary loan staff at the University of Virginia's Alderman Library proved invaluable in locating and obtaining for me a large number of obscure titles both before and after my research trip to Great Britain. Professors Nicholas C. Edsall and Lenard R. Berlanstein of the University of Virginia's Corcoran Department of History afforded me with constructive guidance and helpful advice throughout the research and writing process. Stephen G. Hague and Christopher L. Pepus, in addition to participating in many enlightening discussions of my project's problems and possibilities, reviewed the manuscript carefully on two separate occasions and, in the process, favored me with a wide-ranging critique of both content and style. Finally, the anonymous reader at Greenwood Press and professors Mark F. Thomas and Stephen D. Arata of the University of Virginia supplied me with a combination of kind words and insightful comments about my work. Although these readers have saved me from a multitude of sins, both large and small, none of them is responsible in any way for those failings which remain.

On a personal level, I would like to thank my parents, Paul Wintzel and Doris Jean Haggard, for the inspiration of their example; my wife, Mary Maclin Weems, for kindnesses too numerous to mention; and our daughters, Ann Catherine and Lauren Elizabeth, for helping me to keep it all in perspective.

Chapter 1

Introduction

The following analysis of British social theory addresses the issue of where to locate the fundamental ideological break between the small-government liberalism of the past and the principles which underlie the modern Welfare State. The common view among historians of nineteenth-century Britain is that such a shift occurred prior to 1900. Liberal political thought is most often seen as an uncomfortable—although perhaps necessary—interlude, growing out of the Industrial Revolution and, gradually, into the twentieth-century Welfare State. While providing a viable political alternative for its time, nineteenth-century liberalism existed only upon sufferance. Once British public opinion possessed the imagination, will, and political power to demand a massive expansion of the social services provided by the State, classical liberalism was doomed. Consequently, the only question worth pondering is where to place the "origins" of the Welfare State prior to 1900.

A handful of historians locate the first stirring of the Welfare State in the distant past—following Henry VIII's dissolution of the monasteries in the 1530s, with the passage of the Statute of Artificers in 1563, or upon the establishment of the Elizabethan Poor Law in 1601.[1] A larger, but still small, number of historians argue that the Welfare State was conceived during the first half of the nineteenth century. For them, the industrial, communications, and bureaucratic "revolutions" which occurred in Britain between 1750 and 1850 provided the State with both the incentive and the means to extend its protection of the poorest, most vulnerable

---

[1] See Karl Schweinitz, *England's Road to Social Security* (London, 1943); J.R.T. Hughes, "Henry Mayhew's London," *Journal of Economic History* 1969 29 (3): 526-36; and Maurice Bruce, ed., *The Rise of the Welfare State: English Social Policy, 1601-1971* (London, 1973).

classes. According to the noted historian George Kitson Clark, in order to "master the forces which their society had engendered, to do something for the myriads who thronged their streets, to respond at all effectively to the demands of justice and humanity, they had to use increasingly the coercive power of the State."[2] For Clark and other like-minded historians, the factory, sanitary, housing, education, and municipal reform legislation of the early Victorian period heralded the arrival of the intrusive governmental regulations and expanding professional civil service of the modern era.

Furthermore, by 1850 the State had proven itself to be willing to search for national solutions to the social problems inherent in a modern, urban, industrial economy. For historian David Roberts, the British government and bureaucracy had realized by the first decade of Queen Victoria's reign that although "local authorities were not unwilling to improve institutions and end social abuses . . . they needed the stimulus, advice, and sustained energy of experts from Whitehall"; as a result, "however limited the responsibility, however meager compared to the responsibilities assumed by Whitehall today," the period between 1830 and 1850 "did mark the beginning of the welfare state."[3]

While recognizing the importance of both ideological and legislative precursors earlier in the century, historians of late Victorian Britain have, not surprisingly, tended to consider the final decades of the nineteenth century as being of preeminent significance to the rise of the Welfare State. Although parliament passed little substantive social legislation between 1878 and 1908, the late Victorians established, according to many historians, the ideological framework for the massive State expansion of the twentieth century. The "idea" of the Welfare State—a mixture of utilitarian, evangelical, Radical Liberal, and socialist thought—was, in their opinion, conceived during the late Victorian era; the simultaneous democratization of the British political system between 1867 and 1884 made the birth of the Welfare State a matter of historical inevitability.

Therefore, as the historian Asa Briggs has noted, the "long intervening period" between 1880 and the 1940s "was a period of intermittently intense struggle to secure objects which had already been defined before the beginning of the twentieth century."[4] Legislative inactivity in the realm of social reform during the late Victorian era should not, consequently, be interpreted as a sign of the continued strength of classical liberal ideology. After all, according to Anthony Wohl, it was necessary for the late Victorians to pass "through an essentially negative or pessimistic *fin-de-siecle* reaction against the 'sacred' doctrine of laissez-faire before they could move on to formulate coherent new social and

---

[2] George Kitson Clark, *The Making of Victorian England* (New York, 1972), 280.
[3] David Roberts, *Victorian Origins of the British Welfare State* (New Haven, Conn., 1961), 315. See also Kathleen Woodroofe, "The Making of the Welfare State in England," *Journal of Social History* 1968 1 (4): 303-24.
[4] Asa Briggs, *The Collected Essays of Asa Briggs* (Brighton, England, 1985), 192.

Introduction

political programs."[5]

Historians have used various arguments to prove that the ideology of the Welfare State originated during the late Victorian period. Many insist that a new political culture emerged after 1880. Increased competition from overseas raised fears that demoralization and industrial inefficiency within the British working classes would result in inevitable economic decline. The desire for stability in an increasingly democratic age and the emergence of new political rivals—the Independent Labour Party and the various branches of the London socialist movement in particular—combined to ensure that future British politicians would be far more disposed to seek legislative solutions to the Social Question than they had in the past.[6] Finally, improved living conditions for the majority of British workers after 1870 and the availability of more reliable information about the plight of the urban poor made poverty seem less tolerable than before.

The impressive studies conducted by Charles Booth, Seebohm Rowntree, and others after 1880, which did so much to educate the Victorians about the "Condition of England," are important for another reason as well. For many historians, they are proof that the Victorians had finally come to the conclusion that character did not play so large a role in poverty as had been previously thought. If the poor were merely the helpless victims of a grinding, industrial system, should not the State actively intervene to alleviate their misery and provide them with the opportunity to become productive, responsible citizens?[7]

In addition, historians often argue that the late Victorian middle and upper classes were quick to discard their former belief in the efficacy of economic progress, private charity, and local initiative. Thus, for Anthony Wohl, the "sheer magnitude" of the Social Question "made nonsense of the mid-Victorian reliance on traditional methods of social administration."[8] "Once traditional philanthropic capitalism and individualistic efforts" had been found wanting, the "late Victorians

---

[5] Anthony S. Wohl, "The 1880s: A New Generation," *Nineteenth Century Studies* 1990 (4): 2. Although historian Walter Arnstein notes that during much of the 1890s public "preoccupation with social reform gave way to preoccupation with empire . . . the ideological shift that was to cause Britain to establish the fundamentals of a welfare state in the early years of the twentieth century had already taken place" (Walter Arnstein, *Britain Yesterday and Today*, 6th Edition [Lexington, Mass., 1992], 197).

[6] For example, see Maurice Bruce, *The Coming of the Welfare State* (New York, 1966); Gaston Rimlinger's "Welfare Policy and Economic Development," *Journal of Economic History* 1966 26 (4): 556-71, and *Welfare Policy and Industrialization* (New York, 1971); Jerald Hage, Robert Hanneman, and Edward Gargan, *State Responsiveness and State Activism* (London, 1988); and Peter Baldwin, "The Welfare State for Historians," *Comparative Studies of Society and History* 1992 34 (2): 695-707.

[7] See Abram de Swaan, *In the Care of the State* (New York, 1988) and David Cannadine's article in Lenard R. Berlanstein, ed., *The Industrial Revolution and Work in the Nineteenth Century* (New York, 1992).

[8] Anthony S. Wohl, *The Eternal Slum* (London, 1977), xiii.

could comfortably accept the necessity for state or municipal socialism."[9] From that point on, such historians argue, the floodgates were open; all that was left was for the "collectivist" tide to roll in.

Those interested in the connections between poverty and public policy in Britain during the final decades of the nineteenth century have never had to look very hard in order to find evidence of both a disenchantment with contemporary Victorian responses to the Social Question and a willingness to resort to increased governmental intervention in the economy. Reverend Samuel A. Barnett, for example, in 1883 proposed a pension of between eight and ten shillings per week for all those over sixty who had never received Poor Law relief, the transformation of workhouses into industrial schools, and State control over all dispensaries, infirmaries, and hospitals.[10] The following year, Arnold Toynbee issued his famous statement of middle class contrition: that "we have neglected you; instead of justice we have offered you charity, and instead of sympathy, we have offered you hard and unreal advice; but I think we are changing."[11] In 1890, a writer for the *Westminster Review* argued that "If all the sums subscribed in charity now, together with the poor-rates, were properly consolidated and administered by businessmen under Government control . . . some real headway might be made against this tide of poverty."[12] Nine years later, W. B. Columbine predicted, with remarkable prescience, that in fifty years

when the colonies are full, and when our export trade has seriously declined through the growth of foreign manufactures (which is already rapid), Englishmen will, perhaps, be driven by the pressures of a suicidal competition to seek relief by means of the municipalization or nationalization of industries.[13]

Unlike many of their contemporaries, these writers did not fear the prospect of increased governmental regulation of or intervention in the economy; they believed that the British people would be willing "to accept and support every measure which seems likely to promote the well-being of the community," especially those that increased the education, leisure, comfort, and refinement of the working classes.[14]

While agreeing upon the existence of an ideological "climacteric" during the final third of the nineteenth century, historians have had a great deal of trouble defining precisely when the moment of critical mass was reached. Many refuse to

---

[9] Anthony S. Wohl, "Octavia Hill and the Homes of the London Poor," *Journal of British Studies* 1971 10 (2): 130-31. See also Richard Rodger, *Housing in Urban Britain, 1780-1914* (Basingstoke, England, 1989).

[10] See Samuel A. Barnett, "Practicable Socialism," *Nineteenth Century* (April 1883).

[11] Arnold Toynbee, *The Industrial Revolution* (London, 1884), 53.

[12] "The London Poor: Suggestions How to Help Them," *Westminster Review* (March 1890), 273.

[13] W. B. Columbine, "Social Problems," *Westminster Review* (April 1899), 376.

[14] Ibid., 380.

Introduction 5

tie themselves to any one decade. David Owen posits a "perceptual revolution" in the way the Victorians viewed charity and the State between the 1860s and the outbreak of World War I. James O'Neill believes that the Welfare State of the twentieth century represented the culmination of a long, complicated historical process beginning around 1870 and completed, in ideological terms, before Victoria's death in 1901. Eric Midwinter—closely following the interpretation expounded by Albert V. Dicey in his *Lectures on the Relation between Law and Public Opinion* in 1905—describes the period between 1865 to 1901 as the era of the "Collectivist State." M. M. Sankhdher argues that the emergence of the concept of the Welfare State occurred between 1889 and 1914. Eric Evans states that Britain moved decisively away from self-help and local initiative between 1870 and 1895. Peter Flora and A. J. Heidenheimer associate the "take-off" period with the final two or three decades of the nineteenth century. Finally, Jens Alber locates the birth of Welfare State ideology between 1880 and 1914.[15]

Other historians focus their attention on a single decade. Helen Lynd, Gertrude Williams, Gareth Stedman Jones, J. Roy Hay, and Jose Harris cite the 1880s as the crucial period. At that time, they argue, the unthinking Victorian belief in economic progress collapsed and poverty was first recognized as a national problem requiring the intervention of expert administrators.[16] Noted political scientist Samuel H. Beer agrees with the idea of a decisive transformation in British political thought during the 1880s. In his opinion, the Liberal/Radical policies which had dominated Britain between 1867 and the 1880s were set aside for Radical/Collectivism after 1890.[17] A far smaller number of British historians assign paramount importance to the period between 1895 and 1905. The "Efficiency" movement, industrial unrest, economic crises, and military defeat during the early stages of the Boer War combined, in their opinion, to inspire

---

[15] See David Owen, *English Philanthropy, 1660-1960* (New York, 1964); James O'Neill, "The Victorian Background to the British Welfare State," *South Atlantic Quarterly* 1967 66 (2): 204-17; Eric Midwinter, *Victorian Social Reform* (New York, 1968); Albert V. Dicey, *Lectures on the Relation Between Law and Public Opinion* (London, 1905); M. M. Sankhdher, *The Concept of the Welfare State* (Delhi, India, 1975); Eric Evans, ed., *Social Policy, 1830-1914: Individualism, Collectivism, and the Origins of the Welfare State* (London, 1978); Peter Flora and A. J. Heidenheimer, eds., *The Development of Welfare States in Europe and America* (New Brunswick, N.J., 1981); and Jens Alber, "Continuities and Changes in the Idea of the Welfare State," *Politics and Society* 1988 16 (4): 451-68.

[16] See Helen Lynd, *England in the 1880s* (London, 1945); Gertrude Williams, *The Coming of the Welfare State* (London, 1967); Gareth Stedman Jones, *Outcast London* (Oxford, 1971); J. Roy Hay, *The Development of the British Welfare State, 1880-1975* (London, 1978); and Jose Harris's "Political Thought and the Welfare State, 1870-1940," *Past and Present* 1992 (135): 116-41, and *Private Lives, Public Spirit: A Social History of Britain, 1870-1914* (New York, 1993).

[17] See Samuel H. Beer, *British Politics in the Collectivist Age* (New York, 1965).

interest in social reform at that time.[18]

A few authors ascribe the ideological origins of the Welfare State to specific individuals or organizations. Gertrude Himmelfarb, for instance, assigns great importance to the popular social investigator Charles Booth. According to Himmelfarb, his study of London poverty helped to "moralize" the poor in the eyes of his Victorian contemporaries. Previously, it had been widely assumed that the "deserving" poor were deserving because they did not require societal assistance; "now it was assumed that the deserving poor were a social problem requiring assistance because they were deserving."[19] Booth's main contribution was, therefore, to expand the scope of the Social Question beyond the pauper classes. As the famed economist Alfred Marshall succinctly stated, "while the problem of 1834 was the problem of pauperism, the problem of 1893 is the problem of poverty."[20]

The Fabian Socialists are also often cited as being among the "founders" of the Welfare State. Indeed, Gertrude Himmelfarb has commented that "the welfare state is inexplicable without Fabianism."[21] In addition, Jeremy Bentham, Edwin Chadwick, and John Stuart Mill often receive credit for providing the intellectual framework for the modern State as well. Benthamism, according to historian Jose Harris, was "the seedbed of the Victorian Welfare State."[22] Government by experts acting in the interest of "utility" and "efficiency"—staples of both Fabian and Benthamite thought—found a receptive audience within the ranks of the "New Liberalism." John A. Hobson, Alfred Marshall, Thomas H. Green, and Joseph Chamberlain before 1900 and William Beveridge, David Lloyd George, Seebohm Rowntree, Winston Churchill, and John Maynard Keynes after the turn of the century all used the principles of "utility" and "efficiency" to make their case for a host of new social programs.[23]

Others less often mentioned include a number of prominent socialists

---

[18] See E. P. Hennock, "Poverty and Social Theory in England: The Experience of the Eighteen-Eighties," *Social History* 1976 (1): 67-91; Ellen F. Paul, *Moral Revolution and Economic Science: The Demise of Laissez-faire in Nineteenth Century British Political Economy* (Westport, Conn., 1979); and Harold Perkin, *The Rise of Professional Society* (London, 1989).

[19] Gertrude Himmelfarb, *The Idea of Poverty* (New York, 1984), 531.

[20] Alfred Marshall, *Official Papers* (London, 1926), 199, 244-45.

[21] Gertrude Himmelfarb, *Poverty and Compassion: The Moral Imagination of the Late Victorians* (New York, 1991), 378.

[22] Jose Harris, "Political Thought and the Welfare State, 1870-1940," *Past and Present* 1992 (135): 118. See also R. C. Birch, *The Shaping of the Welfare State* (London, 1974); and Harold Perkin, *The Rise of Professional Society* (London, 1989).

[23] See Alfred Marshall, *Principles of Economics* (London, 1890); Derek Fraser, *Evolution of the British Welfare State* (London, 1973); Michael Freeden, *The New Liberalism: An Ideology of Social Reform* (Oxford, 1978); J. Roy Hay, *The Development of the British Welfare State, 1880-1975* (London, 1978); Geoffrey Fry, *The Growth of Government* (London, 1979); and Peter Weiler, *The New Liberalism* (London, 1982).

(William Morris and Stewart Headlam), writers (John Ruskin, Charles Dickens, and Matthew Arnold), and reformers (Octavia Hill and Josephine Butler).[24] The impact these individuals had on the ideology of the Welfare State was, however, limited, indirect, and, in several cases, wholly unintentional. The same might be said for the evangelical movement. Katherine Heasman's contention that the evangelicals must be counted "among the many hands which laid the foundations of the social services of the twentieth century" should not be taken too seriously.[25] Nor should Victorian philanthropy as a whole be assigned a positive role in the origins of the Welfare State. Historians who argue, as Brian Harrison does, that "the distinction between the philanthropist who alleviated misery by distributing his own money and the reformer who pursues the same objective by campaigning to redistribute other people's money, though conventional, is somewhat arbitrary" or, like A. P. Donajgrodzki, who contend that the transition from paternal, personal influences to professional governmental institutions was "easily accomplished," will not bear looking into.[26]

The same must be said for those, like Gertrude Himmelfarb and George Kitson Clark, who argue that the Charity Organisation Society was yet another godparent to the Welfare State. By "moralizing" the poor, Himmelfarb believes, the COS legitimized them as potential "clients" of the State. For Clark, the systematic, professional philanthropy practiced by the COS served as a model for the social service sector of the State during the twentieth century. To their credit, both Himmelfarb and Clark recognize the COS's contributions to the origins of the Welfare State to be entirely unintended.[27]

In sum, according to the standard interpretation accepted by most historians of nineteenth-century Britain, increased imperial, political, and economic uncertainty induced the late Victorians to discard their traditional belief in national economic progress. The revival of the "Condition of England" question in the 1880s prompted both a growing public interest in social reform and a redefinition of poverty; in the future, the impoverished—as the innocent victims of the Industrial Revolution—were to deserve aid not because of their good character but because of their material condition. The late Victorians also finally recognized that private charity was unable to cope with the mass of British poverty. The rise of the London socialist movement, the Independent Labour Party, and the "New Liberalism" after 1880, thus, reflected a profound dissatisfaction with classical

---

[24] See R. C. Birch, *The Shaping of the Welfare State* (London, 1974); J. Roy Hay, *The Development of the British Welfare State, 1880-1975* (London, 1978); and Harold Perkin, *The Rise of Professional Society* (London, 1989).

[25] Katherine Heasman, *Evangelicals in Action* (London, 1962), 295.

[26] Brian Harrison, "Philanthropy and the Victorians," *Victorian Studies* 1966 9 (4): 355; and A. P. Donajgrodzki, ed., *Social Control in Nineteenth Century Britain* (London, 1977), 24.

[27] Gertrude Himmelfarb, *Poverty and Compassion: The Moral Imagination of the Late Victorians* (New York, 1991), 203-4; and George Kitson Clark, *Churchmen and the Condition of England* (London, 1973), 274-75.

liberalism and a new willingness to entrust the State with the alleviation of economic distress. The combination of these various factors spawned a new political ideology, that of the twentieth-century Welfare State. Whether the traditional view, and its component parts, will stand serious scrutiny is, however, a question worth pondering.

Chapter 2

The Idea of Progress during the "Great Depression in Trade and Agriculture," 1873–1896

By the middle of the nineteenth century, the "Idea of Progress," the notion that a growing economy would eventually lift the poorer classes out of their present squalor and into prosperity, had become one of the mainstays of nineteenth-century liberal social theory. Because material improvement was supposed to come as an inevitable by-product of economic growth, there was little reason for the State to intervene actively in the distribution of societal wealth. Indeed, the common belief was that excessive governmental intervention in the economy would slow the growth rate and, thus, prevent or, at least, reduce working class progress. Historians have often assumed, however, that because of the democratization of the British electorate, rising imperial challenges abroad, and increased economic uncertainty at home, the late Victorians lost their faith in national economic progress. Therefore a proper appraisal of Victorian liberalism requires us to determine how far public confidence in progress had eroded during the final decades of the nineteenth century.

The democratization of the British polity under the Reform Acts of 1832, 1867, and 1884 and the Redistribution Act of 1885 caused serious concern within the late Victorian middle and upper classes. Observers from across the political spectrum concluded that as the power of men of property declined, so too would their ability to limit the expansion of the State. Socialists claimed that parliamentary reform had given them "a sufficiently powerful weapon—namely, a vote—with which . . . to work the harmless wonders we dream of."[1] From this point forward, they hoped, socialism would "be the rudder, if not the engine as well as the rudder, of the great vessel Democracy."[2] Liberals such as Richard Haldane noted that the "extension of the franchise [had already] worked a profound change in the composition and the ideas of both political parties."[3] Joseph Chamberlain, perhaps the most influential proponent of late Victorian Radicalism, argued in a speech in August of 1885 that "if there are any people who imagine that the enfranchisement of two millions of citizens can have taken place, and that these men intend to make no use of the privilege which has been conferred upon them, they will have a rude awakening."[4] Staunch individualist Lord Wemyss warned that parliament would be forced to resort to "the robbery of the rich and the few, in order to bribe and get the votes of the many."[5]

Nor were these the expectations of a mere handful of persons residing within the precincts of metropolitan London. It was commonly believed at the time that a parliament dominated or, at least, heavily influenced by working class voters would actively support the cause of social reform; popular pressure to nationalize land and certain industries, tighten restrictions on various industrial practices, and establish expensive social programs seemed, to many, a natural consequence of the democratization of the electorate. In order to prevent the radicalization of Victorian politics, working class voters and wavering politicians had to be reassured that the traditional social remedies of the Liberal and Conservative parties still provided the best way to guarantee the continued economic progress of the laboring classes in the future.[6]

As it turned out, the wealthier classes need not have worried; for a number of reasons the danger that the liberal paradigm would be displaced because of the extension of the franchise to elements of the working classes proved illusory during the late Victorian period. First, only the most respectable British workers had obtained the vote even as late as 1918.[7] All women—who were expected to be

---

[1] *The Clarion*, 16 January 1892.

[2] "Socialism," *Westminster Review* (October 1882), 372.

[3] *Progressive Review*, November 1896, 133.

[4] The speech Chamberlain delivered at Hull on 5 August 1885 is cited in Herman Ausubel, *The Late Victorians: A Short History* (New York, 1955), 144.

[5] See Lord Wemyss's speech printed in *Self-Help v. State Help: Speeches Delivered at the Third Annual Meeting of the Liberty and Property Defense League* (London, 1885), 25-29.

[6] See William R. Greg's "Strikes, Short Hours, Poor Law, and Laissez-faire," *Fraser's Magazine* (September 1872) and *Rocks Ahead, or the Warnings of Cassandra* (Boston, 1875); Charles Rolliston, "Forces of Disorder," *MacMillan's Magazine* (July 1892); and R. D. Melville, "The Present Socialist Position," *Westminster Review* (November 1896).

[7] Participation in the British political system rose sharply after the passage of each Reform Act: about twenty percent of Englishmen and Welshmen could vote in parliamentary elections in 1833, thirty-three percent in 1869, and sixty percent in 1886 (H. J. Hanham, *The Reformed Electoral System in Great Britain, 1832-1914* [London, 1968], 35).

represented by their husbands or fathers—and approximately forty percent of adult males were legally without the vote at any given time, even at the end of World War I. Domestic servants, most soldiers, adult sons living with their parents, criminals, foreign residents, lunatics, those who had recently received Poor Law relief, paid party agents, and the peers of the realm were not allowed to vote in parliamentary elections. In addition, complicated registration laws effectively disenfranchised fully a quarter of adult males who might otherwise have been entitled to vote. For example, anyone who changed residence—even if only to move from one apartment to another in the same building—had to reregister; as the registration process took an unduly long time and as a person had to be legally registered as much as a year prior to an election, it is not difficult to see how many were, at least for a time, struck off the electoral rolls.[8]

Second, among those workers who could vote in parliamentary elections, relatively few were willing to support either socialistic reforms or the establishment of an Independent Labour Party prior to the turn of the century. The stratification of the working classes—by income, occupation, residence, ethnic background, religion, and gender—helps to explain their unwillingness to desert the established Victorian political parties and their social remedies. Unionized, skilled, full-time, male workers consistently valued themselves above unorganized, unskilled, casual, or female laborers. In addition, widespread working class acceptance of the idea of respectability served to define further the differences between the various elements of the laboring community.

Respectability might be obtained in a number of ways: by earning enough to keep one's wife at home, belonging to a club or friendly society, engaging in any form of conspicuous consumption, or by maintaining a spotlessly clean residence. Refraining from swearing, from drinking to excess, or from fighting with one's spouse or neighbors might also set one apart as a decent and worthy member of the working classes. Thrift, industry, and self-reliance were, moreover, as much a part of respectable working class life as they were tenets of middle class morality. As Victorian poverty was largely associated with the least respectable class of laborers—manual, unorganized, unskilled, casual, and, often, female workers—and as it was commonly believed to be the result of their own improvidence, laziness, or intemperance, one should not be surprised that few among the enfranchised "Labour aristocracy" were disposed to raise their own taxes to provide a more complete social safety net for those in distress. As long as poverty and pauperism were defined as primarily a moral problem, large numbers of workers would continue to support the traditional social remedies and political parties of the

---

[8] Neal Blewett, "The Franchise in the United Kingdom, 1885-1918," *Past and Present* 1965 (32): 33-35, 40.

Victorian State.[9]

The late Victorians, particularly policy makers and elements of the emerging popular press, were also obsessed with imperial rivalry during the era of the "Great Depression." Still, one should not exaggerate British anxiety. Most Britons recognized that, although the "New Imperialism" of the 1880s and 1890s caused some conflict and tension in international diplomacy, it did not, at least in the short term, endanger Britain's position as the preeminent imperial power in the world.[10] Indeed, imperial expansion and federation were seen, particularly after 1890, in an increasingly favorable light. Cambridge Professor John Robert Seeley reasoned in his book, *The Expansion of England* (1883), that the channeling of British emigration to the colonies would provide both relief for industrial distress at home and expanded markets for British manufactures abroad. The eminent British historian James Anthony Froude wrote in *Oceana, or England and Her Colonies* (1886) that imperial federation—the strengthening of the economic ties between Britain and its empire—would spur economic growth, lessen the impact of the protectionist policies of Britain's industrial rivals, and exorcize the specter of national decline.[11]

Lord Dunraven, the principal author of the Minority Report of the Royal Commission *On the Depression of Trade and Industry* in 1886, likewise called for both the direction of British emigrants and investment towards the empire and preferential treatment for colonial food products imported into Britain. Ernest E. Williams, the author of the most popular book on the threat of foreign competition published in Britain during the late Victorian era, *Made in Germany* (1896), also supported the idea of imperial federation and agreed with Dunraven that Britain should reconsider the use of tariffs to ensure "Fair Trade."[12] Although Seeley, Froude, Dunraven, and Williams all expressed concern for Britain's future during the final decades of the nineteenth century, each remained confident that Britain would prosper if it made better use of its empire. In addition, an increasing number

---

[9] See John Benson, *The Working Class in Britain, 1850-1939* (New York, 1989); Paul Johnson, "Conspicuous Consumption and Working Class Culture in Late-Victorian and Edwardian Britain," *Transactions of the Royal Historical Society* 1988 (38): 27-42; Gertrude Himmelfarb, "Victorian Values/Jewish Values," *Commentary* 1989 87 (2): 23-31; and Standish Meacham, *A Life Apart: The British Working Class, 1890-1914* (Cambridge, Mass., 1977).

[10] In fact, Britain emerged from the "Scramble for Africa" with many of the most strategically and commercially important territories. See Bernard Porter, *The Lion's Share*, 2nd Edition (New York, 1984) for a useful introduction to this subject.

[11] See John Robert Seeley, *The Expansion of England* (London, 1883); and James Anthony Froude, *Oceana, or England and Her Colonies* (London, 1886).

[12] See the Royal Commission *On the Depression of Trade and Industry* (1886 [cd. 4893], v. 23; and Ernest E. Williams, *Made in Germany* (London, 1896). The questions of tariff reform and imperial preference were politically dangerous throughout the late Victorian and Edwardian periods because of their association with higher food prices; Britain did not completely abandon "Free Trade" until 1932.

of influential politicians—Benjamin Disraeli, Joseph Chamberlain, and Lord Rosebery among others—and writers, such as Alfred Lord Tennyson and Rudyard Kipling, inspired imperialist sentiment by proclaiming the virtues and usefulness of empire. By 1900, in marked contrast to the situation thirty years before, the British empire was popularly regarded as a source of strength, prestige, and pride.[13]

The most significant challenge to Victorian stability, therefore, arose neither from the democratization of the British polity nor in the colonial sphere, but within the economic arena. In 1871, few doubted the strength of Britain's economic position *vis-à-vis* the other Great Powers. The London *Times* declared that

We can . . . look on the present with undisturbed satisfaction. Our commerce is extending and multiplying its world-wide ramifications without much regard for the croaking of any political or scientific Cassandras. . . . Turn where we may, we find in our commerce no traces of decadence.[14]

As the 1870s wore on, however, more and more social critics came to the conclusion that "general and technical education, moderate wages, and frugal habits [overseas] are raising formidable rivals to us even in manufacturing industry."[15] The rapid industrialization of the United States and Germany after 1870 posed an increasingly serious threat to British markets, both at home—because of its adherence to free trade—and abroad. American and German domination of the new industries of the "Second Industrial Revolution"—steel, chemicals, and electricity—raised real questions about whether Britain would be able to compete in the technologically intensive international economy of the twentieth century.[16] Furthermore, even in the manufacture of textiles and iron goods, the staples of British industrial expansion throughout the nineteenth century, Britain faced stiff and growing competition from the newly industrializing nations in Europe and America.

The shocking realization that, after nearly a century of economic preeminence, British industry no longer commanded the field raised fears of national decline within the late Victorian middle and upper classes.[17] Even more damaging to their confidence in national economic progress was the onset of the

---

[13] The depth of imperialistic sentiment within the British working classes is, however, open to some debate (see Bernard Porter, *The Lion's Share*, 2nd Edition [New York, 1984], 136-37).

[14] (London) *Times*, 26 September 1871.

[15] Charles Trevelyan, *Seven Articles on London Pauperism* (London, 1870), 6.

[16] By 1890, American factories were producing more steel and iron than Britain; Germany exceeded British production of these items in 1893 and 1903 respectively (David Landes, *The Unbound Prometheus* [London, 1970], 269).

[17] As the popular journalist and social investigator Frederick Greenwood pithily noted in 1890: "as soon as we begin to estimate our strength by comparison . . . the truth comes out that England can no longer boast of being the dominating Power in the world" (Frederick Greenwood, "Britain Fin de Siecle," *Contemporary Review* [August 1890], 303).

"Great Depression in Trade and Agriculture" in 1873. Falling profits and prices, shrinking land values, diminished international markets, lower interest rates, and the long cyclical downswings in the economy between 1873-1879, 1882-1886, and 1890-1896—representing as they did the reappearance of the trade cycle after a generation of largely uninterrupted prosperity—heightened feelings of societal malaise.[18] Although historians now dismiss the idea of a general depression in the British economy between 1873 and 1896, the late Victorian middle and upper classes do seem to have suffered from both real economic trauma and a certain depression of the spirit at this time.[19] In addition, several sectors of the Victorian economy were especially hard-hit.

A large number of British farmers were forced off the land by the mass importation of wheat from the United States and Russia and meat from Australia, New Zealand, and Argentina. The damage inflicted upon British agriculture by foreign competition during the last decades of the nineteenth century aggravated political discontent in Ireland, induced some three and a half million British citizens to migrate overseas, and increased overcrowding in many English cities. Moreover, the rural exodus after 1870 raised a number of troubling questions about Britain's status as a Great Power. Being unable to feed itself, Britain was placing its survival and independence into the hands of foreign, grain-producing nations. In addition, if large cities, as some believed, inevitably bred "racial" deterioration, then the depopulation of the English countryside carried with it the prospect of eventual national decline.[20]

Those involved in the export trade also suffered heavily during the "Great Depression." British exports of manufactured goods between 1873 and 1899 grew at only about half the rate of the previous twenty years. As a result, unemployment in the mining, metals, engineering, shipbuilding, textiles, and construction trades was often quite heavy; indeed, the areas most impacted by high cyclical unemployment during the "Great Depression" were those that produced largely for foreign export: the northern industrial areas of England, Ireland, and, from the

---

[18] See Charles Wilson, "Economy and Society in Late Victorian Britain," *Economic History Review* 1965 18 (1): 183-98.

[19] As one respected historian has remarked, "the 1880s were the most troubled decade—for the nobles and notables of Britain . . . since the 1840s or the 1790s" (David Cannadine, *The Decline and Fall of the British Aristocracy* [New York, 1990], 25). For the debunking of the "Great Depression," see S. B. Saul, *The Myth of the Great Depression in England* (New York, 1969).

[20] See the "Report from Her Majesty's Commissioners on Agriculture" (*Parliamentary Papers*, 1882, xiv, 32-33); the "Final Report of Her Majesty's Commissioners Appointed to Inquire into the Subject of Agricultural Depression" (*Parliamentary Papers*, 1897, xv, 85-87); the Minority Report of the Royal Commission *On the Depression of Trade and Industry*; and T. W. Fletcher, "The Great Depression of British Agriculture, 1873-1896" *Economic History Review* 1961 13 (3): 417-32.

1880s, Scotland.[21]

For the nation as whole, however, unemployment was less of a problem during the late Victorian period. Although there were several years of extremely high unemployment—most notably in 1879, between 1884 and 1887, and in 1893—the overall unemployment rate for the last three decades of the nineteenth century was only slightly higher than during the preceding period.

Unemployment Rates[22]
1851-1873	4.60%
1873-1882	4.06%
1882-1890	5.47%
1890-1896	4.18%
1873-1896	5.03%

Plus, as economic historian A. E. Musson has noted, we should not "regard 5 or 6 percent as being 'abnormally high' prior to the modern 'full employment' policies: unemployment was probably higher in the period 1815-1850, and it was certainly far higher between the two world wars."[23]

Not surprisingly, most Victorian commentators agreed with the economist John Rae that "the problem of the unemployed is not ... of increasing gravity in our time" and that "even their numbers vary less from time to time than we are apt to suppose."[24] The unemployed only became a serious social problem when, as during the mid-1880s, large numbers of respectable, thrifty, and industrious artisans fell upon hard times.[25]

Nor was a low national unemployment rate the only sign of British economic health during the "Great Depression." The economy continued to grow, albeit at a slower rate than during the first half of the nineteenth century. Lower growth was, arguably, inevitable at this juncture; prior to the 1890s, "there were no new high growth industries leading the economy while the more recent growth industries, steel and engineering, were already facing strong competition

---

[21] See Humphrey Southall, "The Origins of the Depressed Areas: Unemployment, Growth, and Regional Economic Structure in Britain before 1914," *Economic History Review* 1988 41 (2): 254-56.

[22] The rate for 1851-1873 is derived from A. E. Musson, "The Great Depression in Britain: A Reappraisal," *Journal of Economic History* 1959 19 (2): 201; the remainder are from Brian R. Mitchell, *British Historical Statistics* (New York, 1988), 124, 149-50. One should, however, treat these figures with some caution as they are based upon trade union returns.

[23] A. E. Musson, "British Industrial Growth, 1873-1896: A Balanced View," *Economic History Review* 1964 17 (2): 402-3.

[24] John Rae, "State Socialism and Popular Right," *Contemporary Review* (December 1890), 881. See also Henry Tregarthen, "Pauperism, Distress, and the Coming Winter," *National Review* (November 1887).

[25] See (London) *Times*, 17 February 1886 and 6 March 1886; and Arnold Toynbee, *"Progress and Poverty": A Criticism of Mr. Henry George* (London, 1883).

overseas."[26] The shift towards lower growth consumer industries also served to limit economic expansion during the last decades of the nineteenth century.[27] Although British economic growth during the "Great Depression" suffers slightly in comparison with the period prior to 1850, it continued at about the same rate as during the largely prosperous years between 1856 and 1873.

Rates of Growth (percentage increase per year)[28]

1860-1880	2.3%
1865-1885	2.4%
1870-1890	2.4%
1875-1895	2.5%
1880-1900	2.4%
1885-1905	1.9%

Moreover, British productivity matched that of both Germany and the United States prior to 1900; only after the turn of the century is a substantial divergence evident. The perception of economic stagnation was largely created by a combination of two factors: rising competition for markets at home and abroad; and an unflattering comparison between Britain's relatively mature economy and the growth rates achieved by, first, the fastest-growing sectors of the American and German economies and, second, the high-growth early decades of British industrialization.[29]

Just as important, working class standards of living rose substantially after 1880, perhaps more than in any period since the outbreak of the Napoleonic Wars.[30] Income inequality, both among workers and relative to the wealthy classes, diminished as well, at least to an extent. As one historian has written, "While not spectacular, the egalitarian leveling up to World War I was universal: the income shares at the top fell, the shares at the bottom rose, the relative pay of the unskilled

---

[26] Derek Aldcroft and Harry Richardson, *The British Economy, 1870-1939* (New York, 1970), 116-17.

[27] For a more negative view, see William A. Lewis, *Growth and Fluctuations, 1870-1913* (London, 1978). See Sidney Pollard, *Britain's Prime and Britain's Decline* (New York, 1989); and Roderick Floud and Donald McCloskey, *The Economic History of Britain since 1700* (New York, 1981) for a more positive appraisal.

[28] Peter Mathias, *The First Industrial Nation* (New York, 1969), 459. See also Roderick Floud and Donald McCloskey, *The Economic History of Britain since 1700* (New York, 1981); and David Greasley, "British Economic Growth: The Paradox of the 1880s and the Timing of the Climacteric," *Explaining Economic History* 1986 23 (4): 416-44.

[29] Donald McCloskey, "Victorian Growth: A Rejoinder," *Economic History Review* 1974 27 (2): 275. See also Donald McCloskey, "Did Victorian Britain Fail?" *Economic History Review* 1970 23 (3): 446-59.

[30] John Burnett, *Plenty and Want: A Social History of Diet in England from 1815 to the Present* (London, 1966), 92.

improved, the premium on skills declined, and the earnings distribution narrowed."[31] The basis for this rising standard of living was the marked decline in agricultural and industrial prices after 1870.

Index of Prices (1913= 100) [32]

1870-1874	122
1875-1879	116
1880-1884	107
1885-1889	88
1890-1894	87
1895-1899	78

During a period of declining prices, one would expect real wages in Britain to rise unless offset either by high unemployment or sharply lower wages. Although money wages, after taking unemployment into consideration, remained basically stationary between 1874 and 1888, they rose impressively during the 1890s. Real wages, moreover, grew dramatically during both the 1880s and the 1890s.

Wages and Earnings, Allowing for Unemployment[33]

1850	100.0
1873-1882	149.4
1882-1890	148.8
1890-1900	164.8
1873-1896	151.7

Growth Rates for Real Wages per Year[34]

1856-1873	1.62%
1873-1882	1.03%
1882-1899	2.03%
1899-1913	-0.46%

In addition, the 1880s witnessed the highest rate of national income growth *per capita* of any decade in the latter half of the nineteenth century.

---

[31] Jeffrey Williamson, *Did British Capitalism Breed Inequality?* (Boston, 1985), 200. According to Williamson, income inequality in Britain peaked around 1860.

[32] Brian R. Mitchell, *European Historical Statistics, 1750-1970* (New York, 1976), 737.

[33] Brian R. Mitchell, *British Historical Statistics* (New York, 1988), 124, 149-50.

[34] Charles Feinstein, "What Really Happened to Real Wages?" *Economic History Review* 1990 43 (3): 330. See also Ian Gazeley, "The Cost of Living for Urban Workers in Late Victorian and Edwardian Britain," *Economic History Review* 1989 42 (2): 207-21.

Net National Income at 1900 Prices[35]

	Total (Million £)	Per Head (£)
1860	559	19.4
1870	774	24.8
1880	932	26.9
1890	1416	37.8
1900	1750	42.5

Although full-time workers obviously benefitted most during the "Great Depression," all workers—from the poorest casual laborer to the most respectable trade unionist—profited from lower prices.[36] Increased purchasing power allowed the working classes to consume a more nutritious and varied diet, including larger quantities of meat, sugar, cheese, tea, and beer after 1873.[37] Rising real wages and working class spending also spurred growth in the consumer goods sector of the economy—the clothing trades, home products, furnishings, magazines, and newspapers in particular—making it the fastest growing segment of the late Victorian economy.[38]

This generally positive evaluation of the health of the Victorian economy in no way conflicts with the conclusions reached by many of the most eminent British economists of the nineteenth century. Robert Giffen, chief statistician of the Board of Trade and editor of the *Journal of the Royal Statistical Society*, strongly supported the idea of working class progress during the nineteenth century. In his estimation, living standards and income had risen enormously between 1830 and the 1880s. Wages had doubled, and workers, because they were much better fed and housed, could expect to live longer, healthier lives. Nor were these advances confined only to skilled laborers; Giffen asserted that the poor "have gained during these fifty years [1830-1880] more than any other class, or, indeed, than all other classes put together."[39]

---

[35] Peter Mathias, *The First Industrial Nation* (New York, 1969), 457; see also Roderick Floud and Donald McCloskey, *The Economic History of Britain since 1700*, 2nd Edition (New York, 1994), 2:3, for comparable income growth rates.

[36] This fact was recognized at the time; Thomas Brassy argued in 1879—the single worst year of the "Great Depression" as far as unemployment was concerned—that falling prices were helping to eliminate much of the suffering of the commercial downturn of the 1870s (Thomas Brassy, "The Depression of Trade," *Nineteenth Century* [May 1879]).

[37] Between 1877 and 1887, the retail price of food in a typical English workman's budget fell by thirty percent—the most significant drop of the nineteenth century (John Burnett, *Plenty and Want: A Social History of Diet in England from 1815 to the Present* [London, 1966], 99).

[38] See Charles Wilson, "Economy and Society in Late Victorian Britain," *Economic History Review* 1965 18 (1): 183-98; and W. Hamish Fraser, *The Coming of the Mass Market, 1850-1914* (Hamden, Conn., 1981).

[39] "The Progress of Our Working Classes," *The Economist* (24 November 1883), 1363. Nor was Giffen alone in this contention; see Alfred Marshall, *Principles of Economics* (1890; Reprint Edition, London, 1922); and W. H. Mallock, "Statistics of Agitation," *Quarterly Review* (January 1884). See also Robert Giffen, "The Progress of Our Working Classes in the Last Half Century," *Journal of the Royal Statistical Society*

Furthermore, the poor were better educated and less subject to crime and pauperism than ever before. Workers spent on average twenty percent less time on the job, yet most were now in a position to save a portion of their weekly income. In sum, according to Giffen, the last fifty years had brought "a revolution in the quality of labour and the general conditions of life" for the working classes.[40] Although recognizing that Britain faced increasing economic competition during the 1880s, Giffen believed that the steady material progress of the previous half century could be maintained as long as Britain did not embrace a policy of socialism.[41]

A large number of Giffen's contemporaries came to the same conclusion about the extent of working class progress. Michael Mulhall, for instance, argued in *Fifty Years of National Progress*, which was published in London in 1887, that poverty, prices, illegitimacy, and liquor consumption were on the decline in Britain's largest cities. The noted novelist George Gissing described Queen Victoria's Jubilee of 1887 as the celebration of "the completion of fifty years of Progress. National Progress, without precedent in the history of mankind!"[42] George J. Goschen, Liberal politician and one-time president of the Poor Law Board, concurred with their assessments and stated further that wealth was being more widely and equitably distributed amongst the various classes.[43] Economists George Wood and Arthur Bowley agreed that both money and real wages had risen substantially since the 1860s. Both proclaimed that the poorest part of the working class, the so-called "residuum," was smaller than ever before, and that society's

---

(December 1883); and "Forty Years of Health Statistics of London," *The Lancet* (11 June 1881), 959-60.

[40] Robert Giffen, "Gross and Net Gain of Rising Wages," *Contemporary Review* (November 1889), 839. This sentiment was shared by the authors of the Final Report of the Royal Commission *On the Depression of Trade and Industry* (1886). See also Giffen's "Further Notes on the Progress of the Working Classes in the Last Half Century," *Journal of the Royal Statistical Society* (March 1886).

[41] See Robert Giffen's articles, "The Progress of the Working Classes in the Last Half Century," *Journal of the Royal Statistical Society* (December 1883); and "The Recent Rate of Material Progress in England," *Journal of the Royal Statistical Society* (December 1887).

[42] George Gissing, *In the Year of Jubilee* (1894; Reprint Edition, Rutherford, N.J., 1976), 57.

[43] According to Goschen, "while some people are crying out for the artificial reconstruction of society on a socialistic basis, a sort of silent socialism is in progress" (George J. Goschen, "The Increase of Moderate Incomes," *Journal of the Royal Statistical Society* [December 1887], 604). For a similar sentiment, see Bernard Mallet, "Facts for Fabian Socialists," *MacMillan's Magazine* (March 1890), 352. See also Michael Mulhall, *Fifty Years of National Progress, 1837-1887* (London, 1887).

resources for dealing with it had never been larger.[44]

Many social commentators also believed that working class morality had improved along with their material condition. There was, after all, less evidence of heavy drinking, sexual misconduct, crime, and pauperism among the urban poor.[45] Professor Leone Levi claimed in 1885 that he expected soon to see

> the great volume of the labouring classes slowly, yet surely . . . yield to softer influences, waste and intemperance rebuked and vanquished . . . with manners more refined and morals more elevated, leading a labourious and dignified life; and in all public questions exercising an appreciable and wholesome influence.[46]

In addition, the working classes were often thought to be more physically fit than their predecessors, and not just in the countryside. The inhabitants of Britain's largest cities were neither shorter nor did they weigh less than those living in adjoining rural districts. The availability of inexpensive food, remarkable improvements in urban sanitation over the previous quarter century, and the easy availability of numerous parks and pleasure-grounds ensured that town-dwellers had every opportunity to keep themselves in good health.[47] Indeed, the extent of national progress since 1830 caused one writer to warn that prosperity and leisure might pose a danger to British industry by inducing sloth and decay. Such threats could, however, the author argued, be avoided by a reinvigorated and watchful public.[48]

Thus, although the era of the "Great Depression" witnessed periods of severe economic distress and high unemployment, and British agriculture and export

---

[44] See George H. Wood, "Some Statistics Relating to Working Class Progress since 1860," *Journal of the Royal Statistical Society* (December 1899); A. L. Bowley, "Changes in Average Wages (Nominal and Real) in the United Kingdom between 1860 and 1891," *Journal of the Royal Statistical Society* (June 1895); and "The Progress of Fifty Years," *London Quarterly Review* (October 1887).

[45] Crime, pauperism, drinking, and illegitimacy all declined during the last half of the nineteenth century. The illegitimacy rate, for instance, fell from seven to four percent in England from 1850 to 1900 (Gertrude Himmelfarb, *The De-moralization of Society: From Victorian Virtues to Modern Values* [New York, 1995], 255).

[46] Leone Levi, *Wages and Earnings of the Working Classes* (London, 1885), 40. Levi's work mirrors Giffen's optimism about the pace of working class progress. The Final Report of the Royal Commission *On the Depression of Trade and Industry* (1886) also comments upon the increased thriftiness of the working classes.

[47] See Hugh Dunn, "Is Our Race Degenerating?" *Nineteenth Century* (August 1894); Frederick Greenwood, "Britain Fin de Siecle," *Contemporary Review* (August 1890); and Charles Roberts, "The Physical Condition of the Masses," *Fortnightly Review* (October 1887).

[48] See "Some Lessons of Prosperity and Depression," *Quarterly Review* (January 1888); see also "Degeneration: A Chapter in Darwinism," *London Quarterly Review* (July 1881), an article which warns of the demoralizing influences of leisure, security, freedom, and plenty.

industries were hard-hit during the last quarter of the nineteenth century, for most workers the period between 1873 and 1896 was a time of low overall unemployment, falling prices, stable wages, and a rising standard of living. This is not to say that economic uncertainty did not play a large role in the revival of the "Condition of England" question during the 1880s. Still, as the "wail of distress did not come from the mass of the people, who were for the most part better off, but mainly from industrialists, merchants, and financiers, who felt the pinch of falling prices, profits, or interest rates, and were best able to make their complaints heard,"[49] public interest in the Social Question may have had as much or more to do with distress and insecurity within the middle and upper classes as with the perennial suffering of the urban poor.

Uncertainty about their own economic and political outlook during the "Great Depression" caused a segment of propertied society to dismiss social harmony and material progress as an illusion. For such critics, a rising working class standard of living was largely offset by a growing sense of relative deprivation. Economist and social theorist John A. Hobson argued in 1896 that, although income poverty was falling, "subjective or felt poverty is growing with the widening gap between legitimate human desires and present possibilities of attainment."[50] Material improvement was, thus, for Hobson a double-edged sword. Once the poorer classes had been given "a glimpse of a more prosperous life," their needs would be much less easy to satisfy; the danger of poverty, therefore, increased as conditions improved because economic progress raised expectations and aspirations that might be difficult to fulfill.[51] In addition, those laborers left behind by working class progress could be expected to become more and more frustrated by the hopelessness of their position.[52]

The "legitimate human desires" of the working classes were being stimulated by a number of different factors. Better education both created new tastes and ensured that "the rising generation . . . will not tolerate what their fathers have

---

[49] A.E. Musson, "The Great Depression in Britain: A Reappraisal," *Journal of Economic History* 1959 19 (2): 200. In support of this interpretation, one can cite the Final Report of the Royal Commission *On the Depression of Trade and Industry* which states that "Complaints of depression proceed chiefly from the producing classes" (1886 [cd.4893], v. 23, xi).

[50] John A. Hobson, "Is Poverty Diminishing?" *Contemporary Review* (April 1896), 499. Hobson's views did not go unchallenged; one influential writer scoffed that his "doctrine as to real or subjective poverty, if it proves anything at all, proves real poverty rises as economic poverty declines" (William H. Mallock, *Classes and Masses* [London, 1896], 802).

[51] John A. Hobson, *The Problems of Poverty* (London, 1891), 27.

[52] See "The Poor," *Saturday Review* (6 April 1889), 398; see also the remarks of an eleven-year-old London girl, who, being troubled by her life of poverty in the midst of plenty, expressed the wish to live elsewhere "because then I shouldn't see a lot of people having a lot of things I can't have" (Mrs. Dorothy Tennant, *London Street Arabs* [London, 1890], 11).

done."[53] The rapid communication of information and ideas in newspapers also helped to raise their consciousness of urban poverty. Readers were "able to know more of the general condition of society than did their fathers" and, thus, gain a keener appreciation of their mental and material privation.[54] The extension of the franchise and the growth of large cities were also believed to produce discontent by empowering the working classes to fight the inequality inherent in British society and its political system.[55]

Although such writers were clearly dissatisfied with the pace of national progress, they did not doubt that great strides had been made since Victoria's coronation in 1837. Although distress was not getting worse, improved material conditions made the continued existence of widespread poverty increasingly intolerable. As one contemporary succinctly stated, "in proportion as the evil decreases, the denunciation of it increases."[56] To put it another way, the social conscience of the Victorian middle and upper classes had finally outstripped working class progress.

For a far smaller number of social critics, nearly everything concerning the poorer classes—crime, immorality, insanity, poverty, and working class militancy—took on a pathological complexion during the final decades of the nineteenth century.[57] Such writers tended to deny or minimize the extent of working class progress since the 1830s and emphasize the misery and distress still to be found in most British cities. A few even argued that social conditions in Britain were worse than they had ever been in the past. Radical Liberal politician and former mayor of Birmingham Joseph Chamberlain stated in 1883 that "never before was the misery of the very poor more intense, or the conditions of their

---

[53] John R. Phillips, "London Landowners, London Improvements, and the Housing of the Poor," *MacMillan's Magazine* (November 1883), 8. See also Frederick Greenwood, "Misery in Our Cities," *Nineteenth Century* (May 1889).

[54] Henry R. Fox Bourne, *English Newspapers* (London, 1887), 2:374. See also B. L. Farjeon, *Toilers of Babylon* (London, 1888); and Susan Jeune, "Homes of the Poor," *Fortnightly Review* (January 1890).

[55] See Arnold Toynbee, *"Progress and Poverty": A Criticism of Mr. Henry George* (London, 1883); and Frederick Greenwood, "The Revolt of Labour," *New Review* (January 1891).

[56] Thomas Mackay, ed., *A Plea for Liberty* (London, 1891), 4. See also "The Debate of Tuesday on the Poor," *The Economist* (6 April 1889).

[57] Although degeneration theory first emerged in Britain in the late 1850s, there was an intensification of interest in this issue during the final decades of the century (Daniel Pick, *Faces of Degeneration: A European Disorder, c.1848-1918* [New York, 1989], 189-201). Degeneration was a particularly attractive topic within the literary community; Arthur Conan Doyle, George Gissing, Robert Louis Stevenson, Bram Stoker, H. G. Wells, Oscar Wilde, and others explored it at length in the works they published during the late Victorian era.

daily life more hopeless and more degraded."[58] Another writer exclaimed that same year that Victorian Britain was "a country of such violent contrasts as have never been witnessed since the days of Rome under the Caesars" and that it had "far more poverty . . . than the neighboring European nations."[59]

Most of these critics agreed that the squalor and depravity to be found in the slums led inevitably to the physical, mental, and moral degeneration of the British working classes.[60] Although the health of the urban working classes might be temporarily preserved by the massive influx of hardy laborers from the countryside, degeneration soon sapped their vigor and left the new migrants in a condition similar to that of the native-born population. Social investigator Hubert Llewellyn Smith noted that "muscular strength and energy, get gradually used up; the second generation . . . is of lower physique and has less power of persistent work than the first, and the third generation (where it exists) is lower than the second."[61]

Degeneration was caused by a number of different factors. Impure air and water, adulterated food, constant noise, unsanitary housing, and indoor work led, many feared, to the bodily deterioration of the urban working classes. One writer argued that the polluted atmosphere enveloping most large cities was very damaging to their health. Poisons and chemicals spewed into the air by industry made for an unhealthy environment; in addition, the "mere collection of human beings is enough, without manufactories' smoke, to render the air in such a condition that the families living in such an atmosphere dwindle and disappear."[62] It was also widely assumed that "the hurry and restless movement, the keen competition and struggle, the growth and corresponding evils of large cities"

---

[58] Joseph Chamberlain, "Laborers' and Artisans' Dwellings," *Fortnightly Review* (December 1883), 761.

[59] Samuel Smith, "Social Reform," *Nineteenth Century* (May 1883), 897. Such exaggerated claims were neither new nor original. Thomas Wright wrote in 1871 that "the present condition of the working classes shows an *absolute* decline when put in comparison with the state of things obtaining in the middle ages" (Thomas Wright, "On the Condition of the Working Classes," *Fraser's Magazine* [October 1871], 430). See also Thomas Wright, *Our New Masters* (London, 1873), 60-61.

[60] One contemporary declared that "the residuum of our population, the demoralized and incapable" were "both absolutely and relatively, on the increase" (J.A.M. MacDonald, "The Problem of the Unemployed," *New Review* [December 1893], 565). See also former Tory Home Secretary Richard A. Cross' "Housing of the Poor," *Nineteenth Century* (June 1885); and R. C. Bedford, "Urban Populations," *Fortnightly Review* (March 1893).

[61] Charles Booth, *Life and Labour of the London Poor: Poverty Series* (London, 1889-1893), 3:110. See also Richard Soloway's important article, "Counting the Degenerates: The Statistics of Race Deterioration in Edwardian England," *Journal of Contemporary History* 1982 17 (1): 137-64.

[62] James Cantlie, *Degeneration Amongst Londoners* (1885, Reprint Edition, New York, 1985), 24.

produced a substantial increase in the incidence of mental illness.[63] Workers residing in such an environment, thus, could not be expected, according to the novelist George Gissing, "to be classed with human beings, but rather with the brutes ... their degradation is actually and literally physical; that the fine organs of virtue in which *we* possess all that we have of the intellectual and refined, have absolutely perished from their frames."[64]

Furthermore, the declining British birthrate—from 36.3 live births per thousand in 1876 to 28.5 in 1901—worried many within the educated classes because, while the number of middle and upper class births fell substantially during the late Victorian period, the working classes—and especially the poorest, most demoralized workers—continued to be highly fertile. Cambridge economist Alfred Marshall postulated that "if the lower classes of Englishmen multiply more rapidly than those which are morally and physically superior ... the population of England [will eventually] deteriorate."[65] The danger to British industry was, many believed, quite serious. If the most degenerate classes were reproducing faster than any other portion of Victorian society, then they might flood the British workforce with unfit laborers. As troubling, the "residuum" was feared to be also gaining strength through the demoralization of formerly respectable workers; by infecting their industrious neighbors with their improvidence, intemperance, and laziness, the degenerate poor further undermined Britain's ability to compete. With the United States and Germany providing increasingly fierce industrial competition at home and abroad after 1870, such threats to national productivity had to be taken extremely seriously. Degeneration among the working classes, thus, not only threatened to depress Britain's standard of living, but also "insidiously nibbles away at the profits of capital, and puts the enterprises even of the ablest captains of industry increasingly at the mercy of foreign competition."[66] The remedy had been laid down by the social critic Charles Trevelyan as early as 1870. "Our only chance is to make superior efficiency compensate for superior numbers, by turning our entire proletaire class into orderly productive workers; to make them a cause of health, and strength, and credit, instead of being a burden and a disgrace."[67]

Although most commentators interested in the subject emphasized the economic dangers of degeneration during the late Victorian period, a few expressed concern over the stunted, unhealthy workers presently enlisting in the British

---

[63] Special Report of the Commissioners in Lunacy, "The Alleged Increase of Insanity" (1897 [87], xxxviii, 2). This assumption was disproved by the commissioners.

[64] George Gissing, *Workers in the Dawn* (1880, Reprint Edition, Brighton, England, 1985), 1:258.

[65] Alfred Marshall, *The Economics of Industry* (London, 1881), 31.

[66] Sidney and Beatrice Webb, *The Public Organisation of the Labour Market* (London, 1909), xi.

[67] Charles Trevelyan, *Seven Articles on London Pauperism* (London, 1870), 6. See also R. H. Patterson, *The State, the Poor, and the Country* (London, 1870); and Reginald Brabazon, "The Decay of Bodily Strength in Towns," *Nineteenth Century* (May 1887).

military. Would they have the physical stamina for honorable service overseas? As one writer stated, the "arts of peace cannot be carried out successfully by men ... feeble in body and weak in health."[68] As the vast majority of the British armed forces were now drawn from industrial towns and large cities, it was no wonder that the national military rejection rate stood at between thirty and forty percent of all enlistees.[69] One critic noted pessimistically that "while the physique of the English army is deteriorating ... the material from which foreign armies are drawn is on the whole becoming better and more vigorous."[70] Even so, fear for the health of the British military remained a secondary concern prior to the South African War of 1899-1902. After 1900, however, public consciousness of the military consequences of "degeneration" transformed it into an issue of national importance.

Finally, a handful of social critics worried that working class degeneration might have a destabilizing influence on British politics. One writer noticed that "ill-health breeds not only poverty but also impatience and discontent.... the mind being debilitated by bodily ill-health cannot reason well, but becomes essentially emotional."[71] Novelist J. A. Steuart explained that while Britain expended much effort in "wiping out frontier tribes" and "frantically extending the empire," it should realize that "all the foreign enemies in the world are not half so dangerous as the inhabitants of our own slums."[72] The outbreak of unrest in metropolitan London during the latter half of the 1880s—the "unemployed" riot of February 1886, "Bloody Sunday" in November 1887, the popular reaction to the Jack the Ripper murders in the autumn of 1888, and the dock and gas workers' strikes of 1889—seemed to support the contention that degeneration was already sapping the foundation of Britain's political stability.

Nevertheless, prior to Queen Victoria's death in 1901, a sizable majority of middle and upper class Victorians remained optimistic about the prospects for continued working class progress; most also vigorously disputed the claim that Britain's urban poor were suffering from degeneration in any real sense. They realized that there was no factual or statistical basis for the existence of degeneration within the urban working classes. The available empirical evidence,

---

[68] Reginald Brabazon, "The Decay of Bodily Strength in Towns," *Nineteenth Century* (May 1887), 676.

[69] Walter M. Gattie, "The Physique of European Armies," *Fortnightly Review* (April 1890), 583. See also Richard Soloway, "Counting the Degenerates: The Statistics of Race Deterioration in Edwardian England," *Journal of Contemporary History* 1982 17 (1): 137-64. Soloway questions whether army recruits were truly representative of the working classes as a whole and asks whether the substitution of medical officers for sergeants to carry out induction examinations after 1879 may have had something to do with the increased number of rejections.

[70] Walter M. Gattie, "The Physique of European Armies," *Fortnightly Review* (April 1890), 583.

[71] G. Rome Hall, "Public Health and Politics," *National Review* (January 1890), 613.

[72] J. A. Steuart, *Wine on the Lees* (New York, 1899), 278.

in fact, indicated the exact opposite; conditions had improved and were continuing to improve during the late Victorian period. British workers were as energetic, healthy, and robust as ever. As Robert Giffen cautioned, "discontent with the present must not make us forget that things have been so much worse" in the past.[73] Although much maligned during the late Victorian period, degeneration theory—a disconcerting new interpretation of how poverty might weaken the health, erode the international industrial competitiveness, enfeeble the armed forces, and unsettle the politics of the British Empire—raised a series of troubling questions that could not be taken lightly.

Britain emerged from the era of the "New Imperialism" with a larger and more popular colonial empire than ever before. The parliamentary electorate, while more inclusive than at any point in the past, was still limited to about sixty percent of adult males in 1900. The industrialization of the United States and Germany, while representing a serious threat to British markets at home and abroad, could be offset, many believed, by improved technical education, government promotion of domestic industry, and progressive manufacturing and selling techniques. The "Great Depression in Trade and Agriculture," while causing severe distress in certain select industries and several years of high unemployment, was recognized at the time to be more damaging to the propertied and entrepreneurial classes than to the laboring masses.

Even so, middle and upper class perceptions of progress and poverty could not help but be heavily influenced by the difficult challenges—political, imperial, and economic—of the "Great Depression" era. A number of writers pessimistically denigrated the pace of working class progress or undermined it with their theory of relative deprivation. Others insisted, in the face of all the available evidence, that the poor were worse off than their predecessors had been earlier in the century. A handful of social critics even argued that conditions in Britain's largest cities ensured the physical, mental, and moral degeneration of their inhabitants. Although the vast majority of the middle and upper classes still firmly believed in national progress and marginalized such authors as cranks and scare-mongers, a few doubts must have crept in.[74] Within this climate of crisis and controversy, the stage was set for the revival of the "Condition of England" question during the early 1880s.

---

[73] Robert Giffen, "The Progress of the Working Classes in the Last Half Century," *Journal of the Royal Statistical Society* (December 1883), 612.

[74] Daniel Pick in his highly respected *Faces of Degeneration* (New York, 1989) argues that degeneration theorists faced "formidable resistance in England" (179) from "a recalcitrant classical liberal conception of the individual" (184). Although their speculations were not accepted "as the terms of an obvious answer . . . they were continually disseminated as the question" during the late Victorian period (189).

Chapter 3

The Revival of the "Condition of England" Question, 1883–1893

On two occasions during the nineteenth century, British public opinion engaged in a sustained, informed, and contentious national debate regarding the moral and material condition of the poorer classes. First, during the 1830s and 1840s and later, for a decade following the publication of Andrew Mearns's "The Bitter Cry of Outcast London" in 1883, British social critics forced the issues of poverty and pauperism to the forefront of public consciousness. What follows is an examination of the second of these crises, the revival of the "Condition of England" question during the late Victorian period.[1]

Two important questions need to be answered. First, why, unlike the original controversy of the 1830s and 1840s—which dealt with the impact of industrialization throughout England—did interest in the Social Question during the 1880s center almost exclusively on poverty in metropolitan London? Second, did the study of the London poor really inspire, as is so often claimed by historians, a redefinition of poverty? Would the poor now be seen not as idle, intemperate wastrels but as the innocent victims of the Industrial Revolution?

The publication in October 1883 of a slim pamphlet entitled "The Bitter Cry of Outcast London: An Inquiry into the Condition of the Abject Poor" and its dissemination within the pages of the *Pall Mall Gazette* forced the British middle and upper classes to reexamine their assumptions about the condition of their cities,

---

[1] Poverty is a lack or scarcity of the ordinary means of subsistence; pauperism, which arises from a state of extreme poverty, requires one to rely on public or private charity for survival. The phrase "Condition of England" was popularized by Thomas Carlyle in a collection of his essays, *Past and Present*, published in 1843.

the pace of working class progress, and the threat posed by the poorest segment of urban society. According to Helen Dendy Bosanquet of the Charity Organisation Society, the impact of the "Bitter Cry" could be measured by the fact that "books on the poor, poverty, and social questions, slums and like subjects" began pouring "fast and furious from the press" for a decade following the autumn of 1883.[2] At first glance, Congregationalist minister Andrew Mearns's polemic on the material squalor and moral turpitude to be found in the poorer districts of south London does not seem like the kind of work that would prompt a reexamination of the "Condition of England."[3] The information contained in his pamphlet was not particularly new; indeed, Tory housing reformer Lord Shaftesbury commented at the time that as the "disclosure of the evil was made more than forty years ago" and reported on in the press periodically since that time, the shock which attended the publication of the "Bitter Cry" was hard for him to understand.[4] The popularity enjoyed by Mearns's "Bitter Cry" can be explained, however, by the sensational format of the work itself, the publicity it received in the pages of the *Pall Mall Gazette*, and also by the climate of working class discontent and middle and upper class insecurity prevailing in London during the 1880s.

Mearns's choice of a clever and memorable title certainly helped to boost the sale of his work; for the next decade, such expressions as the "Bitter Cry" and "Outcast London" were common parlance in the discussion of metropolitan poverty. Second, Mearns's decision to describe the homes of the poor, as opposed to focusing on street life, marked a dramatic departure from earlier studies of the London poor.[5] Within the filthy, overcrowded, noxious, damp, and vermin-ridden tenements of south London, Mearns discovered "a vast mass of moral corruption,

---

[2] Helen Dendy Bosanquet, *Social Work in London* (London, 1914), 74. One nascent socialist noted in her diary that "Social questions are the vital questions of today; they take the place of religion" (Beatrice Potter Webb, *My Apprenticeship* [1926, Reprint Edition, London, 1971], 164).

[3] Although historians have traditionally attributed the authorship of "The Bitter Cry of Outcast London" to Mearns, there is some debate on this point. The pamphlet was certainly either written or heavily revised by Rev. William C. Preston, with Rev. James Munro aiding in the research and composition of the work as well.

[4] Lord Shaftesbury, "Common Sense and the Dwellings of the Poor," *Nineteenth Century* (December 1883), 934. Furthermore, the respected journalist George Sims's "How the Poor Live" articles published in *Pictorial World* only a few months before, although remarkably similar to Mearns's "Bitter Cry" in tone and content, did not capture the public's imagination.

[5] Anthony S. Wohl, "The Bitter Cry of Outcast London," *International Review of Social History* 1968 13 (2): 192. The most famous of these studies was Henry Mayhew's *London Labour and the London Poor* (London, 1861). Mayhew's description of London street traders—perhaps only five percent of all Londoners—as a species of uncivilized, nomadic outcasts was very popular at the time. Many writers—such as James Greenwood, Richard Rowe, Charles Garnett, and Adolphe Smith—built upon Mayhew's study of street life in the metropolis during the next two decades. All produced anecdotal works which emphasized the eccentricities and quaintness of the London poor.

of heart-breaking misery, and absolute godlessness."[6] Mearns's lurid description of metropolitan depravity—particularly his titillating references to prostitution, fornication, and incest—inspired great concern about the demoralization of the slum poor. Nor was sexual immorality the only indictment Mearns brought against "Outcast London." Drinking and drug use, crimes against property, wife-beating, and irreligion were, according to Mearns, widespread among the London poor. Indeed, a culture of depravity pervaded slum society; as Mearns noted, if you asked if a "man and woman living together in these rookeries are married . . . your simplicity will cause a smile. Nobody knows. Nobody cares. Nobody expects they are."[7]

Third, Mearns excited interest by hinting that many of the horrors he had uncovered during his investigation of metropolitan poverty were too ghastly to be printed in "The Bitter Cry." "*So far from making the worst of our facts for the purpose of appealing to emotion, we have been compelled to tone down everything, and wholly to omit what most needs to be known, or the ears and eyes of our readers would have been insufferably outraged*" (emphasis in original).[8] Such comments are not entirely plausible. The sensational tone and content of Mearns's "Bitter Cry" was without doubt meant to stir the emotions of his readers. Furthermore, his willingness to make the shocking assertion that "Incest is common" among the slum-dwelling poor reveals a lack of both personal reticence and excessive concern for the sensibilities of his readers.[9]

Finally, Mearns tried to use his "Bitter Cry" to promote social and religious change in London. Unlike many of his contemporaries, Mearns did not merely blame the inhabitants of the slums for their moral indiscretions and poverty. He believed that organized religion had not done enough to bring the word of God to the inner city poor; deprived of the guidance of either the propertied classes—because of their migration to the suburbs since the 1820s—or the Church, the only wonder was that conditions were not worse. Mearns called for both increased State intervention in the slums and the construction of mission halls and churches to bring Christianity to the poor. At that time, London was, in his estimation, ill-provided with houses of worship; in 1884, metropolitan churches had room for only about thirty-five percent of London's population. If nothing were done, Mearns claimed, the London poor would fall deeper into poverty, misery, and immorality.[10]

Another major factor ensuring the popularity of Mearns's "Bitter Cry of Outcast London" was the enthusiastic support it received from the *Pall Mall*

---

[6] Andrew Mearns, *The Bitter Cry of Outcast London* (1883, Reprint Edition, London, 1970), 3-4.
[7] Ibid., 61.
[8] Ibid., 5.
[9] Ibid., 9.
[10] See Andrew Mearns, *London and Its Teeming Toilers* (London, 1885).

Gazette under the editorship of William T. Stead.[11] The *PMG* devoted an enormous amount of attention first, to publishing excerpts from and commenting upon the pamphlet itself and later, to the general problem of London poverty. Between mid-October and early November 1883, the *PMG* published at least an article each day on "Outcast London." Calling for a Royal Commission on working class housing and the strengthening of local sanitary boards, the *PMG*—along with the *Daily News*—kept public interest concerning the condition of the metropolitan poor at a fever pitch for the next two months.[12]

In doing so, Stead helped to create what became known as the "New Journalism" of the 1880s. Taking over from John Morley at the *Pall Mall Gazette* in August 1883, Stead immediately revealed his flair for the dramatic and sense of moral righteousness. Although occasionally accused of sensationalizing the news, Stead's reliance on interviews, pictures, large headlines, and a more readable style proved to be extremely popular.[13] Stead agreed with one of his chief competitors, T. P. O'Connor of the *Star*, that "there must be no mistake about your meaning . . . you must strike your reader right between the eyes."[14] Nor did Stead believe that the press was only supposed to convey information to the public. He saw himself as a public servant, representing "at once the eye and the ear and the tongue of the people."[15] Unfortunately, because of the lack of modern polling methods, it was often difficult for any given newspaper editor to determine public opinion during the late Victorian period. Stead realized that the present "journalistic assumption of uttering the opinion of the public is in most cases a hollow fraud. In the case of most London editors absolutely no attempt is made to ascertain what Demos really

---

[11] Stead, the son of a Congregationalist minister, made a name for himself as the editor of the *Northern Echo* by supporting Gladstone's condemnation of the "Bulgarian Horrors" during the late 1870s. His advocacy of housing reform, the sending of Charles Gordon to Khartoum, raising the age of consent, naval expansion, and his opposition to the Boer War made him a very controversial figure. En route on board the ill-fated *Titanic* to attend a peace conference in New York City in April 1912, Stead perished along with 1,500 of his fellow passengers. See Raymond L. Schults, *Crusader in Babylon: W. T. Stead and the Pall Mall Gazette* (Lincoln, Neb., 1972) for a colorful account of his life and times.

[12] In addition, between 31 January and 11 February 1884, the *PMG* conducted its own investigation of working class living conditions, concentrating on a corner of St. James' Parish, Westminster. It found the same grim, unsanitary, and dangerous tenements there that Mearns had found south of the Thames.

[13] See Evelyn Phillips, "The New Journalism," *New Review* (August 1895); and Cyril Waters, "Steadism in Politics: A National Danger," *Westminster Review* (June 1892). Both writers believed that Stead sinned against good taste by his puritanical and spirited coverage of the Social Question.

[14] T. P. O'Connor, "The New Journalism," *New Review* (October 1889), 434.

[15] William T. Stead, "Government by Journalism," *Contemporary Review* (May 1886), 656.

thinks."[16] To remedy this situation, Stead wished to set up regional offices across England in order to determine systematically what the public was thinking and what it cared about.

This is not to say that Stead thought editors had no role in the education of public opinion. He realized that an editor always had the right

> to excite interest, or allay it . . . provoke public impatience, or convince people that no one need worry themselves about the matter . . . administer either a stimulant or a narcotic to the minds of his readers . . . [and] force questions to the front which, but for his timely aid, would have lain dormant for many a year.[17]

Over the course of the next decade, Stead would prove on several occasions his ability to provoke controversy and raise public consciousness of a host of social issues. Stead's coverage of "The Bitter Cry" in 1883, of child prostitution—the so-called "Maiden Tribute of Modern Babylon"—in the summer of 1885, and of the Jack the Ripper murders in the autumn of 1888 all called attention to the problems of the London poor. Without the energetic backing of William Stead and the *Pall Mall Gazette*, the "Condition of England" might never have been taken so seriously during the 1880s.[18]

The key to the promotion of social reform was two-fold. First, according to future Conservative Prime Minister Lord Salisbury, "the public mind must be roused" because "failing this, no effectual attempt can be made to root out these centres of misery and crime which are sapping the contentment and loyalty of the working classes of the Metropolis."[19] Second, British public opinion needed to remain focused on the problems of the urban poor for a long enough period of time to effect substantive reform. In the past, this had not always been the case.

---

[16] William T. Stead, "The Future of Journalism," *Contemporary Review* (November 1886), 664. As one journalist noted, although politicians "are less often disturbed by a press-created public opinion, they are frequently moved by a press-revealed public opinion" (Frederick Greenwood, "The Newspaper Press," *Blackwood's Magazine* [May 1897], 842).

[17] William T. Stead, "Government by Journalism," *Contemporary Review* (May 1886), 662.

[18] Stead's importance to the social debates of the 1880s has been widely recognized. Indeed, one recent historian has argued that the "moral and political panics of the period were heavily orchestrated from start to finish by W. T. Stead of the Pall Mall Gazette" (Judith Walkowitz, *City of Dreadful Delight* [Chicago, 1992], 29). Surprisingly, a large number of both his Victorian contemporaries and modern historians have denied that British newspapers as a whole played much of a galvanizing role. See Henry W. Massingham, *The London Daily Press* (New York, 1892); Francis Hitchman, "The Penny Press," *MacMillan's Magazine* (March 1881); Lucy Brown, *Victorian News and Newspapers* (Oxford, 1986); Alan Lee, *The Origins of the Popular Press, 1855-1914* (London, 1976); and Joel Wiener, ed., *Papers for the Millions: The New Journalism in Britain, 1850-1914* (New York, 1988).

[19] Robert Cecil, Marquess of Salisbury, "Labourers' and Artisans' Dwellings," *National Review* (December 1883), 431.

Every now and then a sensational romance, or the sickening details of some horrible crime, arouse the respectable and the wealthy classes to the reality of the terrible state of things which exists in their close proximity; but the spasmodic thrill exhausted, like an electric shock which is spent, they sink back into their usual lethargy, and the evil which so rudely awakened their sensibility for a moment is allowed to go on festering and spreading without further disturbing their serenity.[20]

The answer why the "Condition of England" question of the 1880s proved to be so durable lies primarily in the peculiar nature of metropolitan London. By examining what made London seem both typical and, at the same time, unique to the Victorians, we will begin to understand why the social debates of the 1880s and early 1890s concentrated almost exclusively on the condition of the London poor and why, prior to the publication of Seebohm Rowntree's study of York at the turn of the century, most social commentators believed the investigation of other English cities to be superfluous.[21]

London garnered the lion's share of attention partly because of its status as the center of both English book-publishing and the national daily press.[22] In addition, London's numerous philanthropic societies were certain to take advantage of a period of heightened public awareness of urban poverty to publicize their activities and, thus, generate larger charitable donations. Finally, and perhaps most important, many within the middle and upper classes believed London to be the one place in Great Britain where the massing of immorality, criminality, and social degradation might pose a significant threat to public order. Any danger, however fleeting, to the stability or prosperity of Britain's financial, administrative, political, and cultural capital was sure to be treated extremely seriously.

Apprehensiveness among the well-to-do seemed justified by the increased militancy of the London working classes and the rise of metropolitan socialism during the 1880s. The London riot of 8 February 1886, the mass protest meetings in Trafalgar Square throughout much of 1887, "Bloody Sunday" on 13 November 1887, the popular response to the Jack the Ripper murders—particularly the organization of working class vigilante groups to protect the women of east London—in the autumn of 1888, and the London dock and gasworkers' strikes during the second half of 1889 all made the examination of the condition and character of the London poor seem especially pertinent. Taken together, the 1880s represented the most serious outbreak of working class agitation in Britain since the 1840s and the most dangerous threat to public order in the Metropolis since the

---

[20] *Charity Organisation Review*, March 1889, 101.

[21] See E. P. Hennock, "The Measurement of Urban Poverty: From the Metropolis to the Nation, 1880-1920," *Economic History Review* 1987 40 (2): 208-27.

[22] Nearly one-half of all British authors, editors, and journalists lived in London during the late Victorian era (Lucy Brown, *Victorian News and Newspapers* [Oxford, 1986], 38).

Gordon riots over a century before.[23]

On 8 February 1886, a meeting of the Fair Trade League in Trafalgar Square calling for protective tariffs and public works for the unemployed was disrupted by several thousand supporters of the Marxist Social Democratic Federation. As the Metropolitan Police had received advance warning that the SDF might cause trouble, some 563 policemen were positioned in the vicinity of the square; 66 officers—including Commissioner Edmund Henderson—were actually in Trafalgar Square. Unfortunately, although the police took great care to protect businesses along the route from the East End to Trafalgar Square, no one thought to station considerable forces either to the north or west of the square. As Commissioner Henderson explained after the fact, "experience [had] led him to believe that crowds invariably went back by the routes they had come."[24]

As a result, when between three thousand and five thousand supporters of the SDF marched off in the direction of Hyde Park—to the west—around 3:30 P.M., no substantial police forces were available to control them. After having been allegedly taunted by members of the private clubs along Pall Mall, the SDF demonstrators began to riot, first breaking windows and then looting stores along the major West End thoroughfares. Only around 4:00 P.M. did Commissioner Henderson dispatch a verbal message to Scotland Yard requesting that one hundred officers be sent to Pall Mall. Henderson's order was by this time irrelevant, as the rioters had already proceeded past Pall Mall; furthermore, because his message had been garbled in transmission, the reinforcements were directed to take up positions along the Mall. The rioters were, thus, allowed to destroy property worth some £50,000 with impunity for an hour and a half, before being dispersed at 5:00 P.M. by a small detachment of sixteen police officers.

Press, public, and parliamentary criticism of the Metropolitan Police was not long in coming. Inept command coordination, poor communications between Scotland Yard and its officers in the field, the failure to use mounted police, a lack of initiative displayed by some officers, and the general incompetence of Commissioner Henderson—who suffered the double humiliation of allowing both a riot to take place on his watch and his pocket to be picked while on duty in Trafalgar Square—were all blamed for the Metropolitan Police's temporary loss of control in the streets of London. Most agreed that the riot had been "only made

---

[23] Parliament's refusal to consider immediately a petition collected by Lord George Gordon and his Protestant Association for the repeal of the Roman Catholic Relief Act in June 1780 led to a week of rioting in the Metropolis; a large number of chapels, homes, businesses, and prisons were looted or destroyed, and over three hundred Londoners lost their lives (see George Rudé, *Paris and London in the Eighteenth Century: Studies in Popular Protest* [New York, 1971], 268-92).

[24] "Report of the Committee on the Origin and Character of the Disturbances which took place in the Metropolis on Monday, the 8th of February" (Select Committee, House of Commons, "London Riots," 1886 [c.4665], v. 34, iv).

possible by the scandalous mismanagement of the chiefs of the police."[25] Perhaps "half a dozen policemen armed with revolvers would have prevented the destruction of thousands of pounds of property."[26]

Still, a number of commentators warned that the police would have to act aggressively in the future if it was to stamp out revolutionary sentiment among the unemployed. One questioned whether it would "not [have] been better if in the recent riot a hundred of the ruffians had been shot or bayoneted, than that a hundred worthy citizens should have to suffer from their acts of wanton villainy or systematic plunder."[27] A retired British military officer agreed that the Metropolitan Police should not be afraid to use force to quell dissent: "if the actors in a disorderly drama are thought to be not merely mischievous but really vicious, then calculated, methodical, and controlled severity will prove in the long run the truest humanity."[28] Public opinion, while perhaps not supporting such extreme measures, did swing solidly in opposition to the SDF and those who had supposedly incited the riot. The Metropolitan Police arrested four individuals—John Burns, Henry Champion, Jack Williams, and Henry Hyndman—arguing that they should be held accountable for their inflammatory rhetoric prior to and on the day of the riot. In a trial shortly thereafter, however, all four defendants were acquitted for lack of evidence.[29]

A number of historians—most notably Gareth Stedman Jones—have exaggerated the alarm felt by the middle and upper classes after the London riot of 8 February. Although some metropolitan merchants and businessmen feared that police incompetence would embolden the "mob" to strike again, most recognized that the riot had been the product of a series of unfortunate mistakes that had now been rectified. The tame response of the Metropolitan Police and the Conservative government of Lord Salisbury to the gathering of large numbers of the unemployed in Trafalgar Square during the latter half of the following year indicates that the fear of revolution did not run very deep.

The new commissioner of the Metropolitan Police, Charles Warren, had long argued that Trafalgar Square be kept clear of demonstrators and the unemployed. By October 1887, due to the permissiveness of the Conservative Home Secretary, Henry Matthews, Trafalgar Square had been transformed into an encampment for the down-and-out, a place where they could congregate, hear speeches, and, most

---

[25] "The No-Police Riots," *Saturday Review* (13 February 1886), 219.

[26] (London) *Times*, 9 February 1886.

[27] "Law and Licence," *Fortnightly Review* (March 1886), 299; according to this writer, if the police had acted in a competent manner, the rioters would have been caught "like vermin in a trap" (305).

[28] W. W. Knollys, "Mobs and Revolutions," *Fortnightly Review* (December 1886), 711.

[29] See "The No-Police Riots," *Saturday Review* (13 February 1886); "The Riots and the Police," *Saturday Review* (20 February 1886); and "Prosecutions for Rioting," *The Economist* (20 February 1886).

important, receive the charitable donations of the well-to-do. Increasingly, however, delegations of bankers, merchants, hotel keepers, tradesmen, and workers pressured Matthews to forbid future meetings in the square since they disrupted business, clogged the roads of central London, and represented a public nuisance.[30] On 8 November, Commissioner Warren gave notice, for the second time since October, that no meetings or speeches were to be held in Trafalgar Square in the future; his reasoning was that as the square "belonged" to the Crown—not the public—access to it for political purposes could be restricted. Five days later, a large demonstration in support of imprisoned Irish nationalists tested the government's willingness to use force to prevent the holding of meetings in the square; on this occasion, the government called the demonstrators' bluff. Their peaceful procession was violently dispersed by several squadrons of mounted troops on "Bloody Sunday," 13 November 1887. Scores of protesters were injured, and several killed. John Burns and Cunninghame Graham were tried, convicted, and sentenced to six weeks in prison for their participation in the demonstration.

The popular response to Charles Warren's clearing of Trafalgar Square was generally positive. Most believed it to be very important to preserve London from the forces of disorder, Social Democracy, and demagoguery.[31] In Charles Warren's opinion, his actions had been both highly appropriate and historically significant: "almost for the first time during this century the mob failed in its ascendency over London and in coercing the Government."[32] This task accomplished, Warren believed that the Metropolitan Police might be able to be reduced from 12,000 to 10,000 officers in the near future.[33]

Public opinion viewed the London "mob"—even during the darkest days of the mid-1880s—not with fear, but with contempt. The rioters of 1886 and the demonstrators of 1887 were commonly believed to be young, healthy, vice-ridden trouble-makers, not members of the "real" unemployed; they were, in brief, "lazy ruffians who do not want to work."[34] One should not be surprised, another critic noted, when the demoralized poor rioted; this is what they always did when given

---

[30] On 12 November, one such delegation presented Matthews with a petition signed by some six thousand persons. See (London) *Times*, 12 November 1887; and "The Reign of the Rough," *Saturday Review* (5 November 1887).

[31] William Stead of the *Pall Mall Gazette*, a long-time proponent of free speech and opponent of the policies pursued by the Metropolitan Police, predictably, opposed the closing of Trafalgar Square.

[32] Charles Warren, "The Police of the Metropolis," *Murray's Magazine* (November 1888), 579.

[33] Ibid. Other commentators felt that the size of the Metropolitan Police should be increased—perhaps to 20,000. See "The Strength of the Police of London," *The Economist* (22 September 1888), 1187.

[34] "The Reign of the Rough," *Saturday Review* (5 November 1887), 617. See also (London) *Times* 12 February 1886 and 20 October 1887.

half a chance.[35] The Victorian middle and upper classes, however, strongly believed that honest, respectable workers were as outraged by the riots and demonstrations of the period as they were. Social disorder was not just bad for business; it reduced employment and economic opportunity for the working classes as well.

Periodic bouts of urban unrest, however destructive, are not usually dangerous to the body politic in the long term because they do not offer a positive program for the construction of a better society. London socialism, on the other hand, although made up almost entirely of middle class intellectuals disenchanted with the development of Britain's modern industrial economy and split into a host of competing organizations, commanded the talents of a handful of individuals who were fully capable of offering a theory of revolution that might, in a period of political anarchy, provide just such a comprehensive platform. Although Henry Hyndman, William Morris, George Bernard Shaw, Sidney and Beatrice Webb, and others rarely advocated the violent overthrow of bourgeois society in explicit terms, their numerous public speeches, articles, and books ensured that the socialist critique of British capitalism would continue to haunt the imaginations of the wealthy long after the social disturbances of the 1880s had dissipated.

The "Condition of England" question, therefore, revived at a moment of great stress. The crucial period between 1884 and 1887 witnessed the "Scramble for Africa" in international affairs, the further democratization of the British electorate under the Third Reform Act, the splintering of the Gladstonian Liberal Party over Home Rule for Ireland, the sharpest downturn in the national economy since the 1840s, and the most serious rioting in London in a century.[36] Each of these factors, by raising doubts about the stability of either the British economy or its political system, helped to perpetuate a culture of crisis conducive to the continuation of popular discontent and, in this case, the discussion of metropolitan poverty. One does not have to go so far as to argue, as Gareth Stedman Jones and Anthony Wohl do, that the Victorians' interest in poverty resulted largely from a fear of social disorder and revolution. It is enough to say that the economic and political climate of the 1880s made the consideration of the Social Question in London seem a reasonable thing to do.[37]

---

[35] "The No-Police Riots," *Saturday Review* (13 February 1886).

[36] Prime Minister William E. Gladstone's sponsorship of a bill to create a separate parliament and executive responsible for Irish domestic affairs split the Liberal Party in 1886. Ninety-three Liberals helped to vote down the bill in June; moreover, a number of high-profile Liberals, including the Marquess of Hartington and Joseph Chamberlain, deserted Gladstone and began their gravitation towards the Conservative Party.

[37] See Gareth Stedman Jones, *Outcast London* (Oxford, 1971); Anthony S. Wohl, "The Bitter Cry of Outcast London," *International Review of Social History* 1968 13 (2): 189-245; and H. J. Dyos, "The Slums of Victorian London," *Victorian Studies* 1967 11 (1): 5-40. A few did argue that as long as the poor "live as they have now to do there lurks a real danger which may involve society in an overwhelming overthrow," but they were rare exceptions, not the rule (John R. Phillips, "London Landowners, London Improvements, and the Housing of the Poor," *MacMillan's Magazine* [November 1883], 8).

The investigation of London poverty was attractive for another reason: its size. During the late Victorian period, London had as many inhabitants as Paris, Berlin, Vienna, and St. Petersburg combined; with seven million residents, the Greater London Area was home to nearly twenty percent of the total British population. London was also extremely cosmopolitan. By the end of the century, it housed more Scots than Aberdeen, more Irish than Dublin, more Jews than all of Palestine, and more Catholics than Rome.[38] Here in the world's largest city, one could view under the sociological microscope every species of urban poverty. According to the novelist Henry James, London was the "epitome of the round world, and just as it is a commonplace to say that there is nothing one can't 'get' there, it is equally true that there is nothing one can't study at first hand" there.[39] Not that this was always a good thing. James commented further that

It is not what London fails to do that strikes the observer, but the general fact that she does everything to excess. Excess is her highest reproach, and it is her incurable misfortune that there is really too much of her. She overwhelms you by quantity and number—she ends by making human life, by making civilization, appear cheap to you.[40]

Furthermore, while metropolitan poverty might be "a local symptom of a national problem" stretching "all over the land, drawing virulent and poisonous life from every village, town, and city of the empire," it was commonly believed to exist in its most dangerous incarnation within the poorest precincts of the British capital.[41] Although other British cities might suffer worse from economic distress or chronic overcrowding *per capita*, nowhere did the size and scope of the Social Question exceed that existing in London.[42] It was this massing of poverty which allowed, many critics feared, the demoralized poor to live in their segregated neighborhoods untouched by morality, decency, or feelings of personal responsibility. The movement of the middle and upper classes to the London suburbs from the 1820s—because of a legitimate fear that the inner city was a breeding-ground for disease—had, therefore, made matters worse by removing the beneficial moral influences of the respectable classes from contact with the poorest

---

[38] London's size and wealth made it unique among the cities of the world; judged by its total wealth, the Metropolis was exceeded by only fourteen empires and kingdoms on earth.

[39] Henry James, *Essays in London and Elsewhere* (New York, 1893), 9-10.

[40] Ibid., 42. In the same piece, James referred to London as "hideous, vicious, cruel" and as "a mighty ogress who devours human flesh."

[41] George S. Reaney, "Outcast London," *Fortnightly Review* (December 1886), 694. See also Donald Olsen, *The Growth of Victorian London* (New York, 1977), 323.

[42] See "The Slum and the Cellar," *Saturday Review* (27 October 1883); and Francis Sheppard, "London and the Nation in the Nineteenth Century," *Transactions of the Royal Historical Society* 1985 (35): 51-74.

inhabitants of the Metropolis. In addition, the increasing separation of rich from poor in London seems to have made both the wealthy more callous about those living in the slums and the indigent less interested in the moral reforms sponsored by the middle classes during the third quarter of the nineteenth century.[43]

For these reasons, London was widely assumed not only to harbor but also to nurture criminality, disease, immorality, and pauperism. "Outcast London" was, as one critic noted, "monstrous and huddled beside its stained river, pushing its sordid arms out into the green country like some invertebrate deformity against the doors of England."[44] Such descriptions were, of course, nothing new; traditional anecdotal accounts of London poverty had often spoken of the poorer districts in such "monstrous" terms; the impoverished were themselves, of course, seen as a race apart, living by their own rules of morality and decency. Writers frequently felt compelled to use disgusting images in order to get across to their readers the social and moral distance between the "outcast" poor and polite society. Poet Laureate Alfred Lord Tennyson, for example, wrote in one of his later poems:

Is it well that while we range with Science, glorying in the Time,
City children soak and blacken soul and sense in city slime?
Then among the gloomy alleys Progress halts on palsied feet,
Crime and hunger cast our maidens by the thousand on the street.
There the master scrimps his haggard sempstress of her daily bread,
There a single sordid attic holds the living and the dead.
There the smouldering fire of fever creeps across the rotted floor,
And the crowded couch of incest in the warrens of the poor.[45]

London's slums were by definition dreary, squalid, and filthy. The very atmosphere there was fetid, if not indeed poisonous. Fumes from the metropolitan chemical works and off the polluted Thames River choked the inhabitants of some poor districts. As a contemporary noted, "In such a country as this children dwindle and die, and even strong men droop and fail. It is far away from authority; there are no wealthy people to be annoyed by the smells; nobody, therefore, to check nuisances that would not be tolerated for a month in richer districts."[46] In addition, sewer gases, fog, and the smoke from thousands of coal fires caused depression, sickness, and, on occasion, death for those with delicate constitutions. Many commentators feared that the lack of pure air, clean water, and open spaces

---

[43] See Donald Olsen, "Victorian London: Specialization, Segregation, and Privacy," *Victorian Studies* 1974 17 (3): 265-78; Jean P. Hulin and Pierre Coustillas, eds., *Victorian Writers and the City* (Lille, France, 1979); and Gareth Stedman Jones, "Working Class Culture and Working Class Politics in London, 1870-1900," *Journal of Social History* 1974 7 (4): 460-508.

[44] W. J. Dawson, *London Idylls* (New York, 1895), v-vi.

[45] Alfred Lord Tennyson, *The Works of Alfred Lord Tennyson* (New York, 1894), 8:102-3.

[46] "London: About the Docks," *All the Year Round* (14-21 February 1885), 471.

in the poorest districts raised the already high death-rate, diminished the vitality, and stunted the growth of the people living there.[47] The polluted rain that often fell upon the streets of "Outcast London" turned them into a morass of blackened mud, manure, and refuse. Upon drying, according to one critic, you could watch as an "unsavoury steam rises from the down-trodden slime of the East End streets."[48]

Furthermore, the overcrowding of the poor revealed by Andrew Mearns in "The Bitter Cry of Outcast London" was fully substantiated by later writers. Most agreed with Mearns that a filthy, crowded environment did much to explain the prevalence of crime, sexual immorality, disease, and hopelessness among the slum poor. Unfortunately, overcrowding seemed to have worsened during the 1880s, especially in central London. As late as 1901, nearly thirty percent of all Londoners lived in overcrowded apartments, with two or more individuals to a room.[49]

Dysfunctional, antisocial, and criminal behavior seemed almost the norm in many slum districts. Spousal abuse occurred with frightening regularity. The novelist Margaret Harkness observed that many working class husbands believed they had a right to beat their wives if they got out of line.[50] Gangs of burglars, garroters, and pickpockets operated almost without check in many parts of the Metropolis.[51] Infanticide was thought to be common, especially among unwed mothers and among those who had taken out insurance policies on their children.[52] Poverty and a lack of decent employment opportunities in the slums induced a large number of young women to sell their sexual favors in the music halls, public

---

[47] See Francis Peek and Edwin Hall, "Unhealthiness of Cities," *Contemporary Review* (February 1892); and Reverend Samuel A. Barnett, "Twenty-five Years of East London," *Contemporary Review* (August 1898).

[48] Beatrice Potter (Webb), "East London Labour," *Nineteenth Century* (August 1888), 301. Another author wrote that the idea of "the rain that falls in East London possessing cleansing power, in however small a degree, would be enough to excite to merriment the gravest of those who know the district" (C. M. Miall, "Cyclops in London," *Cornhill Magazine* [February 1893] 170).

[49] Anthony S. Wohl, "The Housing of the Working Classes in London, 1815-1914," in *The History of Working Class Housing* (Totowa, N.J., 1971), 24-25.

[50] Margaret Harkness, *A City Girl* (London, 1887), 13.

[51] See Clarence Rook, *Hooligan Nights* (London, 1898); "Wild London," *Saturday Review* (16 October 1886); and R. Sindall, "The London Garotting Panics of 1856 and 1862," *Social History* 1987 12 (3): 351-59. The garotte was a Spanish method of execution which used a cord or metal collar tightened with a screw-like device. Garroters were those who strangled their victims into a state of insensibility before robbing them.

[52] Statistics bear out neither of these contentions; between 1860 and 1900 fewer than two hundred children under the age of seven were reported murdered each year in England and Wales—as compared to thirty to forty thousand illegitimate births. Furthermore, working class mothers cared as much about their children as did those of other classes. See Ann R. Higginbotham, " 'Sin of the Age': Infanticide and Illegitimacy in Victorian London," *Victorian Studies* 1989 32 (3): 319-37; and Edward Berdoe, "Slum Mothers and Death Clubs," *Nineteenth Century* (April 1891).

houses, or streets of the Metropolis, if only for a couple of years in their late teens or early twenties.

Several important Victorian authors, fascinated by the fact that so many working class women chose "casual" prostitution as a profession, examined the unequal conflict between morality and economics. In both instances, as was so often the case with the working classes, economics won hands down. In George Gissing's novel *The Unclassed* (1884), the heroine Ida Starr chose prostitution over laboring for pennies an hour in a sweatshop. George Bernard Shaw argued likewise in his popular play "Mrs. Warren's Profession," first staged a decade later, that it was better for a young woman to become a prostitute than to work for twelve hours per day in a white-lead factory for nine shillings a week. Gissing and Shaw, unlike Andrew Mearns, did not condemn the poor for their open-minded, pragmatic attitude towards sex. They realized that poor women did what they had to do in order to make ends meet; feeling guilty would not do anyone any good. Furthermore, as the noted social investigator and Fabian Socialist Beatrice Potter (Webb) commented in 1888, one "cannot accuse them of immorality, for they have no consciousness of Sin."[53]

The condition of London labor represented another cause for concern during the 1880s. Low wages, excessive hours, and poor sanitation in many metropolitan workshops combined to make life a misery. Sweated labor—especially in the cheap clothing, furniture, and cutlery trades—represented the worst form of industrial exploitation; as these workers, many of them women, labored either at home or in small workshops, they had few opportunities to organize in order to obtain higher wages, shorter hours, or improved working conditions. Furthermore, because of the glutted unskilled labor market in London, recalcitrant workers could be easily replaced.[54]

Late Victorian social critics were also deeply troubled by the existence of thousands of casual laborers in the Metropolis. Casuals, men who worked only a few hours each day by picking up odd-jobs here and there, were commonly thought to be improvident, intemperate, and lazy. Their low earnings prevented them from providing for their families adequately or saving for their old age. Not surprisingly, casual workers, who often relied on private charity or Poor Law out relief to make ends meet, drew funds away from more deserving individuals. Worst of all, casuals contributed to the demoralization of the respectable metropolitan working classes by their antisocial behavior. What was needed, therefore, many writers

---

[53] Beatrice Potter (Webb), "East London Labour," *Nineteenth Century* (August 1888), 311. See also Judith Walkowitz, *Prostitution and Victorian Society* (New York, 1980); George Gissing, *The Unclassed* (1884, Reprint Edition, New York, 1968); and George Bernard Shaw, "Mrs. Warren's Profession" (London, 1898).

[54] See Robert Sherard, *White Slaves of England* (London, 1897); and James A. Schmiechen, *Sweated Industries and Sweated Labor* (Urbana, Ill., 1984).

argued, was a way to transform casual labor into regular, full-time work.[55]

Even more problematic than physical decay and filthy conditions was the fact that "Outcast London" represented the leveling downward of civilization. The novelist and social commentator Walter Besant was particularly critical of the dreariness and what he saw as a lack of culture in south and east London. Besant pondered the significance of a city—South London—without civic history or patriotism; without newspapers, magazines, a university, or colleges, apart from medicine; without an intellectual, artistic, scientific, musical, or literary center; without clubs, theaters, or public buildings of note. Everywhere he looked, Besant saw the same monotonous passivity and suffering; it was no wonder that the London poor had been ignored for so long.[56] For Besant, the most troubling thing about "Outcast London" was not the danger it might hypothetically pose to Victorian society, but the cultural deprivation suffered by its inhabitants.

Many other writers took up Besant's theme that the soul-deadening uniformity of inner city life ground down humanity to its lowest common denominator; here resided a lost generation with few opportunities to escape from a life of hardship and degradation. According to the popular novelist Arthur Morrison, the slum poor were, almost as a matter of course, fatalistic, inclined to idleness, irreligious, culturally illiterate, apathetic, and ignorant. They led dull, colorless lives. In the slums, love was snuffed out at an early age; no one laughed, sang, or enjoyed the pleasures of the mind. For Morrison, "Outcast London" was an infernal prison without hope, a Dark Continent that cast its dreary shadow upon all who lived within its precincts.[57]

Such authors expected every day to revolve around the same bleak struggle for survival.[58] The novelist Joseph Hatton declared, for instance, that London was a "cruel city, a scramble for wealth and pleasure; a fight for meat and drink, millions working that the few may be happy; the East, like Dives in hell, looking up to Lazarus in the West."[59] This rather simplistic division of London—perpetrated by Hatton, Besant, and many others—between the "Outcast" East End and the wealthy West End districts was very common during the late Victorian period. Metropolitan London was commonly interpreted as a city where the extremes of great wealth and poverty lived side by side in uneasy harmony.

---

[55] See Gareth Stedman Jones, *Outcast London* (Oxford, 1971).

[56] See Walter Besant's *All Sorts and Conditions of Men* (1882, Reprint Edition, New York, 1889) and *South London* (London, 1898).

[57] See Arthur Morrison's, *Tales of Mean Streets* (London, 1894) and "A Street," *MacMillan's Magazine* (October 1891).

[58] See Samuel Smiles, *Life and Labour, or Characteristics of Men of Industry, Culture, and Genius* (London, 1887); and Henry King, *Savage London* (London, 1888).

[59] Joseph Hatton, *Cruel London* (1873, Reprint Edition, New York, 1883), 314. "There is a desperate reality about the struggle for existence going on there which is very painful and very horrible, but certainly not dull" (Hugh E. Hoare, "Homes for the Criminal Classes," *National Review* [August 1883], 238-39).

Alongside glittering theaters, art galleries, and concert auditoriums could be found brothels, public houses, and music halls. Large department stores competed side-by-side with small markets and street vendors for customers. The most fashionably expensive luxuries could be purchased within hailing distance of the most wretched slums. The parks of West London—Kensington, Hyde, and Regents most famously—hovered tantalizingly out of reach of the majority of the London poor. During periods of economic difficulty—as in the mid-1880s—a combination of "material discontent, engendered by the lack of physical well-being, and . . . sentimental discontent, excited by the spectacle of inequality" increased the frustration felt by the inhabitants of the slums.[60]

It was no wonder, therefore, that many impoverished Londoners turned to the music halls, public houses, or opium dens of the Metropolis for consolation. As one social reformer remarked, their "work is so monotonous, their surroundings so squalid and depressing, that the only moments when they are forgetful . . . are when the spirit which they have imbibed begins to rise to their brains."[61] While inducing forgetfulness, drink was also commonly regarded as a major cause of absenteeism from work, low productivity, crime, and poverty. The Tory politician Randolph Churchill believed that liquor consumption caused half of all crime and two-thirds of poverty; the Liberal reformer and later Prime Minister David Lloyd George went one better, arguing that alcohol caused ninety percent of all crime. Labour leaders—such as J. Keir Hardie, Arthur Henderson, and John Burns—agreed that the consumption of alcohol helped to retard working class progress.[62]

Some writers, however, did attempt to moderate the negative impression of "Outcast London" provided by Mearns, Besant, Morrison, and others by stressing the positive aspects of social change in the Metropolis. London's death rate at the turn of the century, for instance, was lower than that of many other large cities such as Berlin, Paris, Vienna, St. Petersburg, New York, Dublin, Glasgow, Manchester, and Liverpool. Furthermore, it had been dropping since the 1870s, largely in response to better sanitation and a rising working class standard of living. By the late Victorian period, London had cleaner, better-lit streets, improved hospitals, and more open spaces than in the past.[63] The much maligned London fog was, according to at least one author, made up essentially of water—not smoke. In his

---

[60] Alfred Austin, "Rich Men's Dwellings," *National Review* (December 1883), 464.

[61] See Earl Meath, "Work for the London County Council," *Nineteenth Century* (April 1889), 509. See also "London Opium Dens," *Good Words* (1885).

[62] See John B. Brown, "The Pig or the Stye," *International Review of Social History* 1973 18 (3): 380-95; Select Committee, House of Commons, "Habitual Drunkards" (1872 [242], ix); Select Committee, House of Lords, "Intemperance" (1878-1879 [113], x); and William Hoyle, *Our National Drink Bill* (London, 1884).

[63] See A. O'Donnell Bartholeyns, "The Sick Poor of the Metropolis," *National Review* (February 1889); Samuel A. and Henrietta Barnett, *Practicable Socialism* (1888, Reprint Edition, London, 1894); and Samuel A. Barnett, "Twenty-Five Years of East London," *Contemporary Review* (August 1898).

estimation, for so large a city, London had an exceptionally pure atmosphere; in addition, the fresh air of the Kent and Surrey countryside was within easy reach of all Londoners.[64]

The Metropolitan Police, growing in strength from 7,000 to 17,000 officers between 1860 and 1900, provided better protection against crime than during the first half of the nineteenth century. Crimes of all descriptions declined substantially after the mid-1850s. From the early 1860s to the late 1890s, trials for indictable offenses, for instance, fell by forty-three percent. The homicide rate dropped even more, by some seventy percent between the 1830s and World War I. Working class violence towards women in London decreased dramatically between 1850 and 1890 as well. Historians have ascribed the falling Victorian crime rate to a number of factors, including the growing acceptance of middle class morality, better living conditions, rising incomes, a more settled urban population, the destruction of slum rookeries, improved education, a larger number of reform schools for juvenile offenders, and better policing.[65] Whatever the reason, all could agree that "in the second half of the century, there was little in the crime figures to cause the authorities [of London] much concern."[66]

By reputation, however, the poorer districts of the Metropolis—and especially the East End—were believed to be awash in criminality. A few writers attempted to dispel such fears by arguing that all parts of London had their dangerous quarters; the East End did not have a monopoly on sin and crime. Further, the vast majority of the inhabitants of east London were well-intentioned, law-abiding, and highly ethical. The existing criminal class there was small and its haunts were well known; it was not representative of the general condition east of London's financial district, the City. The Metropolitan Police and public opinion should not, according to such writers, confuse the poor with the criminal classes; as one contemporary noted, "the greatest folly in the world is to pursue such a course as places the poorer classes and the criminal classes in the same category."[67]

More than anything else, the Jack the Ripper murders in the autumn of 1888 focused attention on the criminal depravity to be found in the East End. Although fighting a losing battle against popular opinion, a few authors countered that the murders were not the natural result of a degraded social environment, but an

---

[64] See J. Burney Yeo, "On Change of Air," *Nineteenth Century* (August 1889).

[65] See J. J. Tobias, *Urban Crime in Victorian England* (New York, 1972); V.A.C. Gatrell, "The Decline of Theft and Violence in Victorian and Edwardian England," in *Crime and the Law* (London, 1980); and Nancy Tomes, " 'A Torrent of Abuse': Crimes of Violence between Working Class Men and Women in London, 1840-1875," *Journal of Social History* 1978 11 (3): 328-45.

[66] David Jones, "Crime in London, 1831-1892," in *Crime, Protest, Community, and Police* (London, 1982), 142.

[67] James Stuart, "The Metropolitan Police," *Contemporary Review* (April 1889), 628. See also Henrietta Barnett's "East London and Crime," *National Review* (December 1888); and "The Social Problem," *National Review* (December 1888). An East London Defense Society was formed at this time to combat such negative stereotypes.

unfortunate anomaly. Conditions in east London were, in fact, steadily improving; the poor were not becoming poorer or the wicked more wicked. Because vice was more public in the poorest districts, people tended to assume that it was worse there than elsewhere in the Metropolis or in other British cities.[68] One religious leader remarked that the "vast majority of the inhabitants [of the East End] live quiet respectable lives of hard work, and deserve no more to be called vicious or degraded than the inhabitants of Mayfair."[69] Unfortunately, lurid tales of the overcrowding, drunkenness, immorality, and criminality of the East End remained popular throughout the late Victorian era, largely because "what is abnormal and exaggerated yields the readiest and most picturesque material for the writer."[70]

The London economy was also, as noted above, often believed to suffer from the worst form of industrial distress. What contemporaries and some modern historians have not taken into account is that the Metropolis—Britain's busiest seaport and one of its most important manufacturing cities—was able to cushion the impact of any single economic downturn. The predominance of casual labor and small workshops in London militated against the heavy levels of unemployment that caused great suffering in many northern cities during the late Victorian "Great Depression."[71]

Cyclical unemployment was heaviest among workers in the export and capital goods industries during the late Victorian period. The industrial cities of northern England might have as much as forty percent of their labor force working in these industries; in London, by contrast, only about twenty percent of workers filled these kinds of jobs. Furthermore, because London specialized in service and consumer goods industries which were dependent upon internally generated demand and because most of London's exports were in services such as banking and insurance, not the traditional industries of the Industrial Revolution, the Metropolis could be expected to escape from the worst periods of distress and unemployment relatively unscathed. As one historian observed, "For long-run prosperity, therefore, the service/consumer economy must be judged to be clearly superior to the industrial export-oriented economy. Thus we should interpret Victorian Britain in terms of the South-East being the most advanced region in the British economy."[72]

---

[68] Reverend Harry Jones, the author of *East and West London* (London, 1875), indeed, argued that the East End poor drank and begged less, were more independent, and had a superior physique to the West End poor.

[69] William Wakefield, "East London," *Contemporary Review* (December 1888), 797. See also W. Glenny Crory, *East London Industries* (London, 1876).

[70] "East End Parish," *All the Year Round* (10 July 1880), 212.

[71] Humphrey Southall, "The Origins of the Depressed Areas: Unemployment, Growth, and Regional Economic Structure in Britain before 1914," *Economic History Review* 1988 41 (2): 256.

[72] C. H. Lee, "Regional Growth and Structural Change in Victorian Britain," *Economic History Review* 1981 34 (3): 452.

Mary MacKinnon, a historian of the English Poor Law, provides support for this hypothesis in her analysis of Victorian pauperism returns; they reveal that southern England and London were much less affected than the north by either trade depressions or recoveries. Her study of British pauperism indicates a "more regionally diverse, and cyclically less volatile levels of unemployment" than statistics based on skilled, male, trade union workers.[73]

While it is undeniable that many London workers experienced real hardship during the late Victorian period, it is improbable that the number of those out of work—with the notable exception of the mid-1880s—at this time was any greater than during the era of mid-Victorian expansion. Perhaps for this reason, unemployment was not a particularly important element of the "Condition of England" debates of the late Victorian period; underemployment, specifically the prevalence and debilitating moral impact of casual and sweated labor in London, generated a great deal more interest and controversy.[74]

A number of social commentators also denied Walter Besant and Arthur Morrison's interpretation of "the labouring, or even the destitute population as ceaselessly groaning beneath the burden of their existence. Go along the poorest street in the East End of London, and you will hear as much laughter, witness as much gaiety, as in any thoroughfare of the West."[75] In brief, their "realism" was overdrawn, an idealization of urban squalor peopled with exaggerated stereotypes.[76] The "real" working classes—although often suffering from overwork, bad or inadequate food, and lacking the barest of consumer comforts—"did not seem unhappy. They talked and laughed as if life still mattered to them, and death were not their only chance for rest and peace."[77] Life in "Outcast London" was neither joyless nor immoral. Workers were not actively hostile to religion. East London mothers loved their children and spent as much or more time raising them than those in the West. The poor were, by and large, as moral, compassionate, and hopeful as better off people; in addition, they bore the

---

[73] Mary MacKinnon, "Poor Law Policy, Unemployment, and Pauperism," *Explorations in Economic History* 1986 23 (3): 299.

[74] During only two years of the "Great Depression"—1886 and 1887—was the discussion of the unemployed in London a big issue.

[75] George Gissing, *Demos, A Story of English Socialism* (1886, Reprint Edition, New York, 1928), 383-84. See also Jane Stuart-Wortley, "The East End as Represented by Mr. Besant," *Nineteenth Century* (September 1887).

[76] This was not entirely the authors' fault. Each new work of slum fiction had to be more sensational than the last if it was to generate popular interest and sales. See Archdeacon Farrar, "The Netherworld," *Contemporary Review* (September 1889); Frederick Dolman, "The Social Reformer in Fiction," *Westminster Review* (May 1892); and H. D. Traill, "The New Realism," *Fortnightly Review* (January 1897).

[77] Edwin Pugh, *A Street in Suburbia* (London, 1895), 107.

hardships of daily life that beset them patiently and bravely.[78]

Furthermore, there was "less drunkenness and less violence [than in the past]. The bulk of the men are more reasonable, and they have in some measure improved their tastes and sentiments."[79] The peak of working class drinking had, in fact, already passed. In 1875, a typical worker drank one and a half gallons of spirits and thirty-four gallons of beer each year; by the end of the century, the average worker consumed one gallon of spirits and between twenty-eight and thirty gallons of beer per year. Not surprisingly, expenditure on alcohol as a percentage of total consumer spending fell from fifteen to twelve percent between 1870 and 1900.[80] Thus, "In spite of all that may be adduced to the contrary, I thankfully and unhesitatingly say that physically, morally, and religiously we are better—in the East End of London, at least—than we were, and that there are signs of still further improvement."[81] By peeling away the stereotypes, one could recognize "much, very much, that is truly admirable in the lives of the lowliest."[82]

Liverpool ship-owner Charles Booth's *Life and Labour of the People in London*, a massive multivolume work published between 1889 and 1903, marked the first real attempt of the late Victorian period to move beyond superficialities to a close statistical analysis of metropolitan poverty.[83] Responding both to the industrial and political discontent of the mid-1880s and to the fact that no one seemed to know the extent of London poverty, Booth and his associates set out to quantify economic distress in the Metropolis.[84] The questions Booth posed were daunting.

Is the distress a mere temporary thing, or is it more or less permanent among a part of the population of our great towns? . . . Are the men and women who suffer from it industrious

---

[78] See William Wakefield, "The East End," *Contemporary Review* (December 1888); Margaret Harkness, *A City Girl* (London, 1887); and Thomas Wright, *The Pinch of Poverty: Suffering and Heroism of the London Poor* (London, 1892).

[79] *Charity Organisation Review*, July 1887, 275.

[80] A. E. Dingle, "Drink and Working Class Living Standards in Britain, 1870-1914," *Economic History Review* 1972 25 (4): 609-11. See also Olivia Bennet, Countess of Tankerville, *From the Depths* (London, 1885); and A. R. Neuman, "Practicable Socialism," *Westminster Review* (September 1889).

[81] R. C. Bedford, "Urban Populations," *Fortnightly Review* (March 1893), 393.

[82] J. Dodsworth Brayshaw, *Slum Silhouettes* (1898, Reprint Edition, London, 1904), v-vi.

[83] Booth's work was broken down into three series: Poverty—four volumes, 1889-1893; Industry—five volumes, 1895-1897; and Religious Influences—seven volumes, 1897-1903. His investigators included Mary Booth, Clara Collet, Stephen Fox, David Schloss, Beatrice Potter (Webb), Hubert Llewellyn Smith, and twenty-seven others (see Rosemary O'Day and David Englander, *Mr. Charles Booth's Inquiry* [London, 1993]).

[84] These two issues were closely related. On 7 September 1889 the *Illustrated London News* commented that the "liability of London to social 'scares' . . . is due partly to the want of accurate knowledge of special circumstances, particularly those of the main industrial operations carried on at 'the East End' " (295).

workpeople who could and would work if they had the chance, or are they the weaker members of their class who have been shouldered out by the stronger?[85]

Which areas of the Metropolis contained the largest concentrations of poverty? How much of a danger did the London poor represent to the health of the working classes and to the British nation as a whole? All these were serious questions that had to be answered if Booth was to understand fully the problems of and the threat posed by the London poor.

Because so much attention had already been lavished on the condition of London's East End and as "East London contains, as is generally understood, the most destitute population in England, Mr. Booth may justly claim that to state the problem here is to state it everywhere, and to solve it here is to solve it everywhere."[86] Booth's investigation of the Tower Hamlets of the East End found that sixty-five percent of moderately sized families lived on more than eighteen to twenty-one shillings per week; twenty-two percent rested upon this "poverty line," while thirteen percent fell chronically beneath it.[87] Booth had expected such figures for east London. What surprised him was that poverty south of the Thames actually exceeded that present in the East End. Southwark with sixty-eight percent, Bermondsey with fifty-six, and Horselydown with fifty-five all surpassed the amount of poverty found in the poorest East End districts—Whitechapel and Bethnal Green. Impoverished conditions in south London, indeed, threw off Booth's predictions about the total amount of London poverty. Originally, he had thought the final figure for London would hover around twenty-five percent; in reality, it was closer to thirty-one percent.[88]

To explain and describe metropolitan poverty, Booth dissected London into eight classes:

A: (Poorest Casuals, Loafers, Criminals)	1.0%
B: (Casuals, Those in Chronic Want)	7.5%
C/D: (Those with Small Earnings)	22.2%
E/F: (The Regularly Employed)	51.5%
G/H: (The Middle and Upper Classes)	17.8%

---

[85] "The Unemployed," *Saturday Review* (27 February 1886), 282.

[86] "Life and Labour in East London," *London Quarterly Review* (July 1890), 317. Historians have tended to agree that "by the mid-eighties the East End of London had become as potent a symbol of urban poverty . . . as Manchester had been of industrial conditions in the 1840s" (P. J. Keating, "Fact and Fiction in the East End," in *The Victorian City* [London, 1973], 585). See also Asa Briggs, *Victorian Cities* (London, 1963), 323.

[87] Charles Booth, "The Inhabitants of the Tower Hamlets," *Journal of the Royal Statistical Society* (June 1887), 375. Whitechapel, Mile End Old Town, Poplar, Stepney, and St. George's in the East made up the "Tower Hamlets"; along with Limehouse and Bethnal Green, they composed the infamous East End.

[88] Booth was also surprised—as many others were—by the fact that poverty in the Metropolis as a whole approached in severity that existing in the East End.

According to Booth's calculations, 69.3 percent of Londoners, classes E through H, lived in relative comfort; 22.2 percent, classes C and D, lived on the "poverty line"; while 8.5 percent, classes A and B, fell below it. The 30.7 percent of Londoners "in poverty" were not, however, according to Booth, necessarily in want or distress.[89] Only Class B was in chronic "want," and only a portion of it was in "distress" at any given time. Classes C and D were neither ill-nourished nor ill-clad; they led healthy but restricted lives defined by a lack of any surplus income.

Social critics could—and did—take comfort from Booth's *Life and Labour of the People in London*. He and his associates had proven the fabled "starving millions" to be a figment of the middle classes' imagination. He had demonstrated that roughly fifty-two percent of all Londoners were respectable members of the working classes. Furthermore, Booth was well aware that the "Condition of England" had improved substantially during his lifetime; in his estimation, a study conducted along the same lines fifty years earlier would have revealed "a greater proportion of depravity and misery than now exists" in the Metropolis.[90] As the poor were both less numerous and less poor than in the past, Booth considered them to be a disgrace, but not a danger, to British society. "This is a serious state of things, but not visibly fraught with imminent social danger, or leading straight to social revolution . . . we can afford to be calm and give to attempts at improvement the time and patience which are absolutely needed if we are to do any good at all."[91] By early 1887, therefore, Booth had recognized that any legitimate solution to the Social Question had to accomplish two goals: the relieving of the destitute and the raising of the poor. As the latter was, by far, the more difficult problem, it would necessitate drastic action on the part of the State.

For Booth, metropolitan poverty could best be reduced through the elimination of Class B. The removal of the 100,000 casual laborers of Class B—345,000 Londoners once their families had been taken into account—into a system of industrial and agricultural labor colonies would immeasurably improve the lives of those presently living on the "poverty line."[92] According to Booth, his research had demonstrated "that this helpless class [B] hangs fatally round the necks of the classes above it, and especially of those but just above it" and that "it

---

[89] They were most likely living in crowded conditions; Booth found that thirty-two percent of Londoners—a remarkably similar figure—lived two or three to a room (Charles Booth, "Life and Labour of the People of London," *Journal of the Royal Statistical Society* [December 1893], 565-66).

[90] Charles Booth, *Life and Labour of the London Poor* (London, 1889-1893), 1:174.

[91] Charles Booth, "The Inhabitants of the Tower Hamlets," *Journal of the Royal Statistical Society* (June 1887), 375.

[92] This idea was by no means new. British social critics had long advocated the establishment of colonies overseas and the direction of the underemployed of the Metropolis to the "hives of industry" in northern England. For instance, see Charles Trevelyan, *Seven Articles on London Pauperism* (London, 1870); and Countess Cowper, "Some Experiences of Work in an East End District," *Nineteenth Century* (November 1885).

is industrially valueless as well as socially pernicious."[93] In addition, Class B was not so large "as to render the expense of dealing with it in some semi-socialistic fashion, in the interest of self-supporting labour, a crushing burthen to the community."[94]

Historians have long argued whether Booth believed that Class B was to blame for its poverty, while that of Classes C and D resulted from causes beyond their control. Although there is room for debate on this point, it does not appear that the question was all that important to Booth himself. Class B might or might not be at fault for its poverty, but it was degraded just the same. In addition, as poverty among the "poor," Classes C and D, was caused in large part by their competition for employment and resources with the "very poor," whether Class B was demoralized or not made very little difference. Only after their removal would the "poor" have a realistic opportunity to better their condition.[95]

Booth's careful analysis of the London poor from 1887 marked a new phase in the "Condition of England" controversy. Improved economic conditions—at least relative to the worst years of the "Great Depression"—and the absence of unrest in the metropolis following the peaceful settlement of the London dock and gasworkers' strikes in 1889 allowed the discussion of poverty during the first half of the 1890s to evolve in a less sensational, more pragmatic direction. Monographic, journalistic, and parliamentary investigators devoted less attention to the mere description of slum conditions and expended more energy in the search for limited, practical solutions to the Social Question; proposals calling for the provision of pensions for the aged and labor colonies for the unemployed, the elimination of pauper immigration, and the regulation of sweated labor were especially popular at this time. Neither the economic recession between 1892 and 1895 nor the rise of the Independent Labour Party did much to alter the basic trajectory of the social debates of the 1890s or spur the consideration of more radical solutions to the problems of the British poor.

After the middle of the 1890s, with the national economy clearly recovering, the Independent Labour Party strongly repudiated at the polls, the socialist movement fragmented into a number of warring factions, the "New Unionism" in decline, and enthusiasm for the betterment of the poor waning rapidly in the face of fiscal and political realities, however, there was little pressure on parliament to enact even the relatively modest reforms suggested since the 1880s. The public's interest in the "Condition of England" had decreased to such an extent that parliament was able to devote most of its attention over the next decade to international affairs: specifically imperial challenges in South Africa, the Sudan,

---

[93] Charles Booth, *Life and Labour of the London Poor* (London, 1889-1893), 2:591.
[94] Ibid.
[95] See John Brown's "Charles Booth and Labour Colonies," *Economic History Review* 1968 21 (2): 349-60, and "Social Judgements and Social Policy," *Economic History Review* 1971 24 (1): 106-13; see also Trevor Lummis, "Charles Booth: Moralist or Social Scientist?" *Economic History Review* 1971 24 (1): 100-105.

and China, and also the threat posed by Imperial Germany's decision to construct a large, modern navy after 1898.[96] Although both Liberals and Conservatives in parliament continued to study the causes and consequences of urban poverty and argue the merits of various solutions after 1895, little was accomplished legislatively in the realm of social reform—outside of the Workmen's Compensation Act of 1897 and the Unemployed Workmen's Act of 1905—prior to the Liberal Party's electoral landslide of 1906.[97]

One final shift in the social debates of the late Victorian era, however, must be noted. The publication in 1901 of Seebohm Rowntree's examination of York, *Poverty: A Study of Town Life*, added a national dimension to the Social Question. As indicated above, London had dominated the investigation of the "Condition of England" prior to the turn of the century. Rowntree's contention, that even after the impressive gains of the last half century "from 25 to 30 percent of the town populations of the United Kingdom are living in poverty," ensured that the condition of all British cities would now have to be taken into account.[98] In addition, the distinction Rowntree drew between primary poverty—those with an income insufficient to maintain physical efficiency—and secondary poverty—income that would be sufficient were it not wasted—marked a significant step forward in the discussion of poverty. Although Rowntree set his "poverty line" (21s. 6d. per week for a family of five) at an artificially low level, he still determined that ten percent of York's population lived in primary and eighteen percent in secondary poverty. The similarity between Rowntree's twenty-eight percent poverty rate in York and the roughly thirty-one percent found by Charles Booth in London during the late 1880s supported his hypothesis that Britain suffered from a national poverty rate of between twenty-five and thirty percent.[99] Even more than Booth, however, Rowntree was willing to call upon the State to solve the problems of urban poverty. In 1911, Rowntree argued in favor of "wide industrial and economic reforms" including industrial training, public works, labor

---

[96] One writer commented that a "striking change has come over the public mind since this month last year . . . the unemployed seem to have disappeared beneath the surface of Society, and our attention is diverted to high politics and international relationships" (*Labour Prophet*, February 1896, 19).

[97] The Workmen's Compensation Act strengthened earlier legislation by forcing employers to pay the medical bills of those injured while on the job; the Unemployed Workmen's Act set up local committees to help men find work and facilitated the distribution of voluntary public contributions to the unemployed.

[98] B. Seebohm Rowntree, *Poverty: A Study of Town Life* (1901, Reprint Edition, New York, 1971), 356.

[99] See E. P. Hennock's "Concepts of Poverty in the British Social Surveys from Charles Booth to Arthur Bowley," in *The Social Survey in Historical Perspective* (New York, 1991) and "The Measurement of Urban Poverty: From the Metropolis to the Nation, 1880-1920," *Economic History Review* 1987 40 (2): 208-27.

exchanges, workers' insurance, and the decentralization of town populations.[100]

For many historians the works of Charles Booth and Seebohm Rowntree reveal an important shift in the definition of the Social Question. In their opinion, the late Victorian "Condition of England" was increasingly seen as having to do with poverty, not pauperism. Furthermore, the poor were no longer believed to be demoralized, incapable, or even at fault for their poverty. When Booth argued that heavy drinking was the root cause of only fourteen percent of poverty within Classes A and B and thirteen percent in Classes C and D, and when Rowntree stated that in half of all families in primary poverty the primary bread-winner was in regular employment, they, according to such historians, effectively destroyed the idea that personal or moral failings were the root cause of most poverty. As the noted social historian Gareth Stedman Jones has written: the "theory of poverty that emerged from this literature differed significantly from the literature of the 1860s and 1870s . . . drink, early marriage, improvidence, irreligion, and idleness . . . were now seen as symptoms rather than causes."[101] Finally, for the intellectual historian Gertrude Himmelfarb, Booth and Rowntree, by "remoralizing" the bulk of the working classes and distinguishing them from the "immoral" residuum, made the poor "deserving" of societal relief.[102]

All of this raises a number of questions. Was the theory that personal and moral failings were not the main cause of poverty really new? Most assuredly not. Between 1849 and 1850, Henry Mayhew, a highly respected correspondent for the *Morning Chronicle*, discussed the evils of casual labor, unregulated capitalism, and political economy in depth; before leaving the paper following a dispute with his editors over the efficacy of protection and the regulation of sweated labor, Mayhew argued that the true cause of poverty was low wages, not morality; with higher wages, the poor would consume more—thus spurring economic growth—and be saved from the choice of either the workhouse, a life of crime, or emigration overseas. Mayhew's later writings about the poor, which tended to be sentimental, anecdotal, and superficial, made people forget the cutting edge social analysis he had produced during the London cholera epidemic of the late 1840s.[103]

Furthermore, it is worth asking whether Charles Booth and Seebohm Rowntree really believed that poverty was primarily caused by a combination of

---

[100] B. Seebohm Rowntree and Bruno Lasker, *Unemployment: A Social Study* (1911, Reprint Edition, New York, 1980), 305.

[101] Gareth Stedman Jones, *Outcast London* (Oxford, 1971), 286. See also James Treble, *Urban Poverty in Britain, 1830-1914* (London, 1979); Derek Fraser, *The Evolution of the British Welfare State* (London, 1973); and E. P. Hennock, "Poverty and Social Theory in England: The Experience of the Eighteen-Eighties," *Social History* 1976 (1): 67-91.

[102] Gertrude Himmelfarb, *Poverty and Compassion: The Moral Imagination of the Late Victorians* (New York, 1991), 312.

[103] Edward P. Thompson, "The Political Education of Henry Mayhew," *Victorian Studies* 1967 11 (1): 41-62; for a contrary view, see Gertrude Himmelfarb's "The Culture of Poverty," in *The Victorian City* (London, 1973) and "Mayhew's Poor: A Problem of Identity," *Victorian Studies* 1971 14 (3): 307-20.

impersonal economic forces and a deprived social environment. If so, how can one account for Charles Booth's comment in 1895 that between "these two great causes of domestic poverty—irregularity of earnings and irregularity of conduct . . . it is not possible to divide very exactly the responsibility for impoverished homes"?[104] Furthermore, why would Rowntree in 1911 argue that setting aside the "work-shy"—some eight percent of the unemployed in York in that year—half of the remainder were morally or technically disqualified for work? Rowntree seems to be saying that over half of those out of work in York in 1911 were not in regular employment because of their shiftlessness, intemperance, or lack of industrial skills.[105] Neither Booth nor Rowntree appear to have been strongly convinced that most poverty resulted from the workings of the industrial economy; the moral failings of the poor still had a lot to say about whether one made it or not.

Even if a handful of British social theorists began to conceive of poverty differently during the late Victorian period—a debatable point—did it really matter? Were their theories widely disseminated in the public forum? Were they supported by large numbers of people? If such theorists *were* influential or represented a wider Victorian consensus, how are we to explain the lack of significant parliamentary social reform during the late Victorian and early Edwardian periods? Why, on the contrary, was it private philanthropy that was energized at the expense of the State during the revival of the "Condition of England" question? Finally, why were attacks on this "new" interpretation of poverty so popular at this time? Helen Dendy Bosanquet, the wife of one of the founders of the Charity Organisation Society, for example, denied that "structural" poverty existed in York independent of "moral" influences; commented that Mayhew, Booth, and Rowntree had missed the main point about poverty, that the vast majority of it was due to unwise behavior, not insufficient income; and claimed that all poverty was preventable through the moral reformation of the poorer classes. Nor was she alone. Arguments such as these resonated widely through British society and constituted the standard view throughout the Victorian period.[106]

---

[104] Charles Booth, *Life and Labour of the People in London* (London, 1903), 5:25-26.

[105] B. Seebohm Rowntree and Bruno Lasker, *Unemployment: A Social Study* (1911, Reprint Edition, New York, 1980), 301.

[106] See Helen Dendy Bosanquet's *The Poverty Line* (London, 1902), her letters to the (London) *Times* of 16 September and 4 October 1902, and her essay "Wages and Housekeeping" in *Methods of Social Advance* (London, 1904).

Chapter 4

The Purification of Philanthropy and the Reform of the Poor Law

Although there are some similarities between the original "Condition of England" debates of the 1830s and 1840s and the revival of interest in the Social Question during the 1880s, there is one profound difference. During the early Victorian period, a heightened awareness of British poverty within the middle and upper classes prompted the passage of a series of significant social reforms; the discourse of the 1880s and early 1890s, on the other hand, spurred the attempt to reform and expand private philanthropy and to limit the charitable functions of the Poor Law. As the historian Gertrude Himmelfarb notes "One might have expected the reverse, that with the relaxation of *laissez-faire* and the growth of the administrative agencies of the state, later generations would have been inclined to look to Parliament and the State for the solution of social problems."[1] Himmelfarb's explanation of why this was not the case is simply inadequate. The "intensity," "zeal," and "sacrifice" of Victorian charity does not account for the absence of parliamentary social reform. Neither does her argument that "Parliament had to wait until the 'new' social problem was defined in such a way as to make it amenable to legislative action"—a common enough claim among modern historians—appear sufficient.[2] If Charles Booth provided a "new" definition of the Social Question, how are we to explain the time-lag between his exposure of the extent of London poverty in the late 1880s and the onset of substantive legislative reform, specifically the establishment of Old Age Pensions, in 1908? It seems that Victorian public opinion had more to do with the slow pace of parliamentary social

---

[1] Gertrude Himmelfarb, "The Idea of Poverty," *History Today* 1984 34 (April), 28.
[2] Ibid.

reform than many historians have thought. Common beliefs about working class morality, the efficacy of private philanthropy and self-help, and the general perception that State attempts to alleviate poverty often made matters worse help to explain Victorian resistance to the expansion of the State during the last decades of the nineteenth century.

The Victorian middle and upper classes had always been suspicious of working-class morality; and the poorer the worker under consideration was, the more suspicious they became. The poorest classes were, not surprisingly, commonly thought to be untouched by respectable middle class virtues and, therefore, "morally different in a fundamentally inferior way."[3] When the very poor were forced to rely upon private charity or poor law relief, the well-to-do found it easy to blame them for their distress; if they had led morally upright lives, most believed, they would have been able to maintain themselves without having to ask for charity. Contemporary examples of such thinking are not difficult to find. The influential proponent of colonial emigration for the poor, Earl Meath, argued that the "vast majority of paupers and of the 'unemployed' owe their condition to" their own moral disabilities.[4] Professor Leone Levi explained in 1887 that "poverty proper . . . was more frequently produced by vice, extravagance and waste, or by unfitness for work, the result in many cases of immoral habits, than by real want of employment or low wages."[5] The poorest class of workers were most often characterized as being drunken, improvident, irreligious, and lazy.

Drink was believed by many to be a prime cause of pauperism—between seventy-five and ninety-nine percent of it according to one social critic.[6] Another lamented that "the inevitable companionship of drunkenness with sanitary and social degradation is strongly confirmed by the fact that the alcoholic god sways his sceptre most potently in the more pestilential quarters."[7] The excessive consumption of alcohol made workers less efficient on the job and more willing to absent themselves from work. It caused a great deal of working class violence and

---

[3] Paul Johnson, "Class Law in Victorian England," *Past and Present* 1993 (141): 168. One journalist argued that "the working classes are quite unlike the middle classes. They are more swayed by sentiment and less by interest; they have little self-reliance; they are accustomed to act in flocks; and they like to be led" (*The Graphic*, 31 January 1891, 114).

[4] Reginald Brabazon, Earl Meath, "A Thousand More Mouths Everyday," *Nineteenth Century* (January 1889), 69.

[5] See Charles Booth, "The Inhabitants of the Tower Hamlets," *Journal of the Royal Statistical Society* (June 1887), 394. See also "The Condition of the Poor in the East End of London," *Church Quarterly* (October 1889); Alfred Austin, "Rich Man's Dwellings," *National Review* (December 1883); and Hugh Hoare, "Homes of the Criminal Classes," *National Review* (August 1883).

[6] See Louise Twining, "Some Facts on the Working of the Poor Law," *National Review* (June 1888). William Booth, the founder of the Salvation Army, agreed that alcohol was the primary cause of most poverty and crime ("General Booth's Darkest England," *London Quarterly Review* [January 1891]).

[7] E.H. Bramley, "London Haunts," *Good Words* (1883), 379.

reduced inhibitions to various immoral sexual practices. Furthermore, drink destroyed working class families by sapping their financial resources and sabotaging their ability to provide for themselves.

Drunkenness also increased working class discontent by driving down their standard of living. "If temperance were as much the rule among the lower as it is among the upper and middle classes," one writer moralized, "the people . . . would soon find their pay increased without the trouble of resorting to such a wasteful and barbarous expedient as a strike."[8] Finally, the widespread abuse of alcohol among the pregnant mothers of the poor caused "a considerable portion" of working class children to be "born with the drink craving, which to them is the root of all evil."[9] Until the very poor could be weaned away from their reliance on alcohol, little real progress would be made in the struggle against urban poverty.[10]

Although the well-to-do considered money spent on alcohol to be the greatest drain on working class income, it was by no means the only wasteful activity of which the poor were accused. Any form of conspicuous consumption might be deemed imprudent if it made it impossible for a family to set aside funds for the future. Those who were unable to limit their expenditures to a level below that of their income were commonly thought to be improvident. Naturally, many observers believed that "Imprudence and the insufficient exercise of self-control are doubtless the chief sources of the great social ills at present endured"; one critic argued, indeed, that improvidence was the cause of roughly ninety percent of human suffering.[11]

In addition, the urban working classes appear to have been increasingly indifferent—if not actively hostile—to organized Christianity during the latter half of the nineteenth century.[12]

---

[8] *The Graphic*, 31 August 1889, 254. See also Cardinal Manning, "A Pleading for the Worthless," *Nineteenth Century* (March 1888); and Joseph Hocking, *All Men Are Liars* (Boston, 1895).

[9] Charles Garnett, "London Haunts—A Rookery District," *Good Words* (1883), 544.

[10] "No laws, no reform, no franchise, no revolution, can do any good to this enormous class of Englishmen who live to drink" ("Nostrums for the Poor," *Saturday Review* [17 November 1883], 618). Still, a few individuals, like Edwin Chadwick, argued that drink was the product, not the cause, of unhealthy homes ([London] *Times*, 7 December 1883).

[11] "Poverty," *Westminster Review* (October 1888), 433. See also George C. T. Bartley, *The Work of Charity in Promoting Provident Habits* (London, 1879).

[12] See Edward Salmon, "The Working Classes and Religion," *National Review* (May 1888); Mrs. Humphrey Ward, *Robert Elsmere* (Leipzig, Germany, 1888); Hugh McLeod, *Class and Religion in the Late Victorian City* (Hamden, Conn., 1974); and R. Mudie-Smith, *The Religious Life of London* (London, 1904). The following chart is based upon two religious surveys, one conducted by the *British Weekly* in 1886-1887 and the other by the *Daily News* in 1902-1903.

Church Attendance in London (as a percentage of population)

	1886-1887	1902-1903
Elite Areas	36.3%	26.3%
White Collar	33.3%	24.1%
Other Suburbs	25.6%	19.1%
Inner Ring	20.2%	18.5%
All London	28.5%	22.0%

For most impoverished workers, the Church was simply irrelevant to their lives. As one fictional laborer exclaimed, "Christianity is a failure. . . . If there is a devil, he is the individual to pray to. He seems to have all the power."[13] Declining faith that one would be rewarded in Heaven for leading a righteous life on earth helped the Victorians to explain the existence of widespread sexual immorality among the working poor. With their moral base eroded almost beyond repair, was it any wonder that "working-class morality" seemed to be an oxymoron to large segments of the middle and upper classes?[14]

Alongside moral corruption was crime. Indeed, the movement from a loss of religious faith to defiance of the laws of God and man was clearly recognized as "the natural course of progression in iniquity as everyone knows."[15] Whereas immorality merely destroyed lives among the poor, crime represented a direct danger to the physical well-being of the propertied classes. "Roughs"—young men of small means whose antagonism towards polite society induced them not just to rob, but also to assault the well-to-do—were considered to be particularly dangerous. According to one reporter, "their idea of active amusement is to maltreat and, if possible, to murder anybody who happens to come in their way who has a look of respectability."[16] Although such attacks were relatively infrequent in London during the late Victorian period, those that did occur caused great concern within the wealthy classes.

The problem of the "unemployed" was also generally thought to have a large moral dimension. One social critic warned that of those out of work "probably not two percent . . . are persons of good character as well as average ability in their trades."[17] Another explained that much of the "distress of which we hear so much may be very unreal, for there is undoubtedly a considerable class of men and

---

[13] Joseph Hatton, *Cruel London* (1873, Reprint Edition, New York, 1883), 315-16.

[14] See Françoise Barret-Ducrocq's *Love in the Time of Victoria* (New York, 1992) for a full discussion of Victorian attitudes about the sexual immorality of the very poor.

[15] S. R. Crockett, *Cleg Kelly: Arab of the City* (New York, 1896), 5.

[16] "Street Ruffianism," *Saturday Review* (22 April 1882), 488. See also "Garotting," *Saturday Review* (29 Sept. 1883); and R. Sindall, "The London Garotting Panics of 1856 and 1862," *Social History* 1987 12 (3): 351-59.

[17] Francis Peek, "The Workless, the Thriftless, and the Worthless," *Contemporary Review* (January 1888), 41-43. See also W. J. Gordon, *How London Lives* (London, 1890), 224.

women who would not work if they had the chance."[18] A writer for the *Saturday Review* agreed that "a very large percentage of the unemployed, and the most noisy part too, belong to that considerable body of Englishmen who have the vagabondizing spirit very strong in them, and who prefer occasional starvation, with odd jobs now and then, to regular and monotonous work."[19] Still, the fact that "their misery is in many cases due to faults of their own makes them none the less discontented, and all the more dangerous."[20]

Finally, a large number, perhaps the majority, of the very poor were believed to have been thoroughly demoralized by their surroundings and lifestyle. Many writers commented that the impoverished could not conceive of, or even wish for, a better life. One observer noted that "the people whom you find in the slums like the slums, and moreover will soon make into a slum any place they live in."[21] An editorialist for the London *Times* in 1883 reflected that

there are in London very many families, comprising thousands of persons, who do not care for a decent home in the least; persons to whom dirt is in no way disagreeable, who do not object to vermin, whose nostrils are not offended by stench, who have no vestige of anything which can be called self-respect.[22]

Most social reformers believed that even if they provided the demoralized poor with new, clean, well-ventilated homes, within a fortnight they would be in much the same condition as the slums they had replaced. Until the moral atmosphere in the slums had been improved substantially, there was little hope that material conditions could be ameliorated. Reformers had first to remedy the "inherited indifference to the duties and responsibilities of life" that flourished in the slums.[23]

It was not enough to point out the "road to wealth and happiness" as had so

---

[18] *The Graphic*, 19 November 1892, 602.

[19] "The Unemployed," *Saturday Review* (27 February 1886), 282. It was only in the 1880s that the term "unemployed" came to mean those out of work. The morally neutral concept—"unemployment"—only emerged after the turn of the century; prior to that time "middle-class reformers had trouble in putting a word on it" largely because "they steadily denied that the free market could lead to any recurrent disequilibrium" (Christian Topalov, "Understanding Unemployment: Scientific Vocabulary and Social Reform in Britain, France, and the United States, 1880-1910," a paper read at the University of Virginia on 27 January 1995).

[20] *The Graphic*, 12 November 1887, 518. See also the *Charity Organisation Review*, June 1888, 266.

[21] Countess Cowper, "Some Experiences of Work in an East End District," *Nineteenth Century* (November 1885), 787.

[22] (London) *Times*, 30 November 1883. See also "Charity, Pauperism, and Self-Help," *Westminster Review* (January 1875).

[23] Harold Thomis, "Poverty and Crime," *Westminster Review* (January 1896), 75. See also "London Lodging Houses," *The Month* (January 1887); William Glazier, "Common Sense and the Dwellings of the Poor," *Nineteenth Century* (December 1883); and Bernard Bosanquet, ed., *Aspects of the Social Problem* (1895, Reprint Edition, New York, 1968).

often been done by various "magazine philosophers" in the past; the moral reformation of the poor would only be possible if the respectable middle and upper classes organized themselves, committed large amounts of their time and energy to personal interaction with the impoverished, and did not become discouraged if their efforts failed to bear fruit immediately.[24] However difficult, the work was worth the cost. Moral reform would make the poor more worthy and better able to benefit from societal relief. It would also open the hearts and pocketbooks of the well-to-do; after all, few would wish to give if they thought the recipient of their charity to be "an idle, drunken, thieving scoundrel."[25]

The Charity Organisation Society, founded in April 1869 in response to growing pauperism in London and other large cities during the 1860s, served as the cornerstone of late Victorian efforts to raise the moral condition of the urban poor.[26] From its inception, the COS found many sympathizers within the British governing class. With Queen Victoria as its patron, the Archbishop of Canterbury as honorary president, and vice presidents including Princess Louise, two dukes, four earls, six bishops, two marquesses, and four other peers, the COS possessed a strong base of support within the hereditary aristocracy; a number of notable political figures also associated themselves with the COS—Tories like Lords Derby, Salisbury, and Shaftesbury, and Liberals such as William E. Gladstone, George J. Goschen, and William E. Forster. Among the twenty-odd commoners present at the christening of the COS were such veteran social reformers as Charles Bosanquet, Reverend Samuel Barnett, Octavia Hill, Henry Cardinal Manning, and John Ruskin.[27]

According to the Charity Organisation Society, the present administration of British philanthropy was terribly flawed. Charity, they held, was most often distributed without any discrimination between the applicants for relief. Specifically, far too many able-bodied paupers were presently allowed to take advantage of the generosity of the well-to-do. COS founder Octavia Hill, who was appalled by the resulting pauperization of the London poor, stated that "men who should hold up their heads as self-respecting fathers of families [are] learning to sing like beggars in the street—all because we give pennies."[28] By sapping the independence of the poor, indiscriminate charity actually made matters worse. "Is

---

[24] *The Labour Standard*, 9 June 1883, 5.

[25] *Illustrated London News*, 20 February 1886, 178. See also William Gilbert, "An Unappreciated Charity," *Good Words* (1879).

[26] The full title of the COS was The Society for Organising Charitable Relief and Repressing Mendicancy.

[27] See *The Charity Organisation Society: Its Objects and Mode of Operation*, 3rd Edition (London, 1875).

[28] Octavia Hill, "A Paper Read at Fulham Palace," *COS Occasional Paper, no. 15* (1 February 1889), 25. See also William Chance, *Our Treatment of the Poor* (London, 1879); and Francis Peek, "The Workless, the Thriftless, and the Worthless," *Contemporary Review* (January 1888).

there hunger? Let us have a *cheap* soup-house, and more hunger. Are there homeless? Let us erect *cheap* refuges, and make more homeless. Are there unemployed? Let us have *sham* work, and multiply the number."[29]

The COS recognized two important points. First, a man who "could get... [food and shelter] without working would be a fool to work."[30] Second, a large number of formerly independent workers were quite "willing to swallow their independence with the soup."[31] The remedy was, according to Charles Stewart Loch—general secretary of the COS between 1875 and 1913—to replace "bad" charity with "good": "Bad charity tends to tempt [the poor] into the indigent classes; good charity... prevents their falling into that class... good charity with adequate help raises them to self-support; bad charity with intermittent, purposeless help degrades them to ever lower degradation."[32] The rich had a responsibility both to oversee the distribution of their own wealth for the public good and to aid those of good character; charity should be organized for the promotion of virtue, not—as was so often the case—the rewarding of vice.[33]

As a result, the COS established a general council and thirty-five district committees, one in each of London's Poor Law unions or parishes. Their task was to examine those applying for relief, coordinate a host of private relief agencies, and provide a link between private charity and the Poor Law. Rigorous investigations at the district level would allow the COS to separate the "deserving"—those entitled to private charity—from the "undeserving" poor —those who were to be remanded to the Poor Law workhouse. As Charles B. P. Bosanquet, the first general secretary of the COS, argued,

charity should direct its efforts primarily to assisting those whose character and circumstances render it probable that their position can be effectually and permanently improved, and should for the most part leave those whose distress, either from their own habits or from the nature of the case, does not admit of cure, to the relief provided for them by [the Poor] law.[34]

For the "deserving," therefore, the COS would provide loans, an employment

---

[29] *Charity Organisation Review*, December 1887, 455. See also F. M. Foster, "Women as Social Reformers," *National Review* (April 1889); and Edward Reeves, "Poverty in London," *Westminster Review* (September 1892).

[30] Arthur Morrison, *To London Town* (London, 1899), 200.

[31] Israel Zangwill, *Children of the Ghetto* (1892, Reprint Edition, Philadelphia, 1938), 6.

[32] Charles S. Loch, *How to Help Cases of Distress* (London, 1883), 6.

[33] See Andrew Carnegie, "The Gospel of Wealth," *National Review* (June 1889).

[34] Charles B. P. Bosanquet, *The Organisation of Charity* (London, 1874), 6. Charles S. Loch, the second general secretary of the COS, agreed that charity should seek not just to relieve pauperism, but to prevent it. See Charles S. Loch, *Charity Organisation* (London, 1890); and Bishop Charles Bromby, "The Social Problem," *National Review* (December 1888).

service, letters of recommendation, monetary grants, and, in a few cases, pensions.[35]

	Cases Investigated	Assisted	% Assisted[36]
1887	25,533	14,289	56.0
1893	24,472	10,501	42.9
1897	17,814	7,524	42.2

The Charity Organisation Society also attempted to reform or suppress charities that did not properly distinguish between the "deserving" and the "undeserving" poor. The COS particularly opposed soup kitchens, night refuges, those who gave money to street beggars, respondents to begging letters, and voting charities, which received letters from supplicants and then "voted" on who was to receive aid without having even met the applicants for relief. Such indiscriminate alms-giving was often in response to the perception of economic hard times, particularly during the cold winter months. Octavia Hill commented in 1893 that during such periods,

Great are the temptations to politicians, to newspaper-writers, to philanthropists, to the indolent whose uneasy consciences are aroused, to rush into hasty action which ever more degrades, and induces a gambling recklessness in the miserable receivers of gifts suddenly lavished, and again withheld.[37]

Occasionally indiscriminate charity resulted neither from the onset of commercial depression nor from a severe winter, but from fear. The example of the Mansion House Relief Fund of 1886—established in direct response to social unrest in London's poorer districts—was often cited, and criticized, by the supporters of the COS. The relief granted by the Mansion House was inadequate, and—as there was no attempt made to discriminate between the applicants—demoralizing as well. This was not charity, but ransom "thrown, not brought, from the West to the East."[38]

---

[35] The COS only approved of pensions if the candidates were thoroughly investigated. For example, see those proposed for aged teachers and governesses by Frances Low, "How Poor Ladies Live," *Nineteenth Century* (March 1897).

[36] Charles Loch Mowat, *The Charity Organisation Society, 1869-1913* (London, 1961), 96.

[37] Octavia Hill, "Signs of the Times: Trained Workers for the Poor," *Nineteenth Century* (January 1893), 42. See also *Charity Organisation Review*, June 1888, 266.

[38] Samuel A. Barnett, "Distress in East London," *Nineteenth Century* (November 1886), 687. A few years earlier a journalist had noted that "Nothing can be weaker than to go about confessing that we are benevolent because we are in fright" ("The Slum and the Cellar," *Saturday Review* [27 October 1883], 522). One noted historian has commented that if the Mansion House Relief Fund was "ransom" to disarm "Outcast London," then the payment necessary was pitifully small—some £60,000 in all (Victor Bailey, "The Metropolitan Police, the Home Office, and the Threat of Outcast London," in *Policing and Punishment* [London, 1981], 99-104).

Philanthropy and the Reform of the Poor Law

The well-to-do West-enders, unwilling to dedicate persistent thought and feeling to their fellow citizens, suffer from periodical panic, and under the influence of a somewhat contemptible combination of fear and stricken conscience fling huge sums of money into the yawning gulf of hopeless destitution.[39]

In addition, according to the COS, much of the "starvation" and "distress" witnessed in the streets of London was in fact a fraud. Beggars and imposters "look forward with pleasure to that season of the year when, as the weather gets colder, hearts become warmer, and hard frosts open purses that remain closed to the calls of charity during the summer months."[40] By referring the street-beggar to the relieving officer and the begging-letter to the COS, one would limit fraud and enhance the effectiveness of private charity. The elimination of indiscriminate charity would also reduce the influx of mendicants into—and thus overcrowding in—London and other large cities and provide the indigent with an opportunity to recapture their self-respect and independence.[41] Sometimes, according to one critic of Victorian philanthropy,

the less [that] is done for the poor, the more they will do for themselves. A refusal to give is often the truest form of charity. The most lavish giver is he who appears to give nothing, but who, by influence on character and encouragement of self-reliance, so awakens the latent capabilities of the man he seeks to help as to save him from the painful necessity of asking for any material gift at all.[42]

Although the central and district committees of the Charity Organisation Society were important in setting general policy and investigating large-scale abuses, they were in reality too detached from the poor to deliver relief effectively. Aid distributed through a large charitable organization like the COS did little to moralize the poor. Long-time philanthropist Charles Trevelyan warned that "By passing through official hands the gift loses the redeeming influence of personal kindness, and the recipient regards it, not as charity, but as a largess to which he

---

[39] Beatrice Potter (Webb), "Dock Life of East London," *Nineteenth Century* (October 1887), 498.

[40] *Charity Organisation Reporter*, 11 December 1879, 268. See also J. Hornsby Wright, *Beggars and Imposters* (London, 1883); Samuel A. and Henrietta Barnett, *Practicable Socialism* (1888, Reprint Edition, London, 1894); Henry Tregarthen, "Pauperism, Distress, and the Coming Winter," *National Review* (November 1887); and Charles Loch Mowat, *The Charity Organisation Society, 1869-1913* (London, 1961).

[41] See Helen Dendy Bosanquet, *Social Work in London* (London, 1914). One writer commented that "the ordinary seduction of great cities, aggravated by the corrupting influence of indiscriminate voluntary and legal charity, have made our Metropolis and other principal towns gigantic engines for depraving and degrading our population" (Charles Trevelyan, *Seven Articles on London Pauperism* [London, 1870], 17).

[42] H. V. Toynbee, "A More Excellent Way," *Longman's Magazine* (February 1893), 418.

has a right."[43] The noted housing reformer Octavia Hill agreed in 1872 that the COS "can never be a vital, loving, living force; it can never wake up enthusiasm, nor gently lead wanderers, nor stir by unexpected mercy, nor strengthen by repeated words of guidance."[44] What was needed was "to bring the rich and poor, the educated and uneducated, more and more into direct communication . . . to enlist the thought, knowledge, sympathy, foresight, and gentleness of the educated in the service of the poor."[45]

Without the personal interaction of rich and poor, the aid granted by private philanthropy might do more harm than good. Compassion properly administered, however, would both reduce the danger of class conflict and strengthen Victorian society by giving the "deserving" poor an opportunity to become respectable, independent, and productive citizens.[46] As the poor could best be dealt with as individuals by individuals, hundreds of district visitors were needed to begin the remoralization of the poor. The COS advised visitors to call upon the poor on a regular basis in order to gather information, give advice, and form friendships. The COS hoped that the close interaction of rich and poor would promote morality, decency, and cleanliness among the poor while teaching them to abhor violence, political agitation, strikes, and socialism.[47]

The danger that district visitors would hinder the moral reformation of the poor by being disrespectful, intrusive, or domineering was, however, very serious. The author of an influential manual on the visitation of the poor explained that visitors should never enter a working class dwelling without knocking, take a seat without being asked, arrive at the dinner hour, or force their company upon the poor. If visitors were to have any chance to moralize the poor, they must first be welcome in their homes. Visitors needed to have open, honest, and pleasant manners; they should not demand information in a dictatorial tone of voice. They should also guard against showing either favoritism or impatience should some of those under their care progress faster than others. Above all, visitors must never dispense relief directly; however tempting it might be to aid those one knew well, visitors should in all cases refer the "deserving" either to the local committee of the

---

[43] Charles Trevelyan, *Three Letters to "The Times" on London Pauperism* (London, 1870), 30.

[44] Octavia Hill, "Work of Volunteers in the Organisation of Charity," *MacMillan's Magazine* (October 1872), 449.

[45] Ibid., 441-42.

[46] But for such charity, according to the Tory housing reformer Lord Shaftesbury, "East and South London would long since have marched to the sack of the West" (Earl Meath, "A Thousand More Mouths Everyday," *Nineteenth Century* [January 1889], 61).

[47] See Charles B.P. Bosanquet, *A Handy-Book for Visitors of the Poor in London* (London, 1874); "Enlightenment for Artisans," *The Economist* (16 March 1878); Henrietta O. Barnett, " 'At Home' to the Poor," *Cornhill Magazine* (May 1881); Octavia Hill, "Our Dealings with the Poor," *Nineteenth Century* (August 1891); and Helen Dendy Bosanquet, *Rich and Poor* (London, 1896).

COS or to a more-experienced supervisor.[48]

Upon gaining the trust of the poor, visitors were to encourage cleanliness, literacy, good manners, morality, temperance, thrift, and hard work. They might also oversee the management of the household budget, because a "great number of the ills and trials of life come,—not so much from the want of money, as from the wrong use of it."[49] As large families led to much poverty, visitors were to instruct the poor to postpone marriage until they could raise a family in a modicum of comfort and decency. In all of these ways, the poor were to be shown that they could have some control over their lives; they were not wholly in the hands of fate. By planning ahead, the poor could lead more prosperous and secure lives.[50]

The number of district visitors at work during the late Victorian period was impressive. In 1905, London-based churches, missions, and charities supported some 7,500 volunteers and almost 1,000 paid visitors, the vast majority of them being middle or upper class women. Perhaps this should not be surprising since during the Victorian era women were commonly believed to be uniquely skilled in caring for the young, the sick, the elderly, and the disadvantaged; in addition, charity work was one of the few respectable occupations open to the wives and daughters of the well-to-do.[51] Although in most organizations men provided the leadership and strategic planning, women, as district visitors, performed the practical task of attempting to transplant the values and ideals of middle class domesticity into the homes of the poor.[52]

Many examples may be cited. District nurses from the more than fifty

---

[48] See Reverend William E. Littlewood, *The Visitation of the Poor: A Practical Manual* (London, 1876); and Thomas Canning, "The Labour Problem," *Dublin Review* (October 1890).

[49] H. L. Hamilton, *Household Management for the Labouring Classes* (London, 1882), 25. See also George Bartley, *The Work of Charity in Promoting Provident Habits* (London, 1879); Octavia Hill, "Signs of the Times: Trained Workers for the Poor," *Nineteenth Century* (January 1893); Samuel A. Barnett, "University Teaching: East and West," *New Review* (June 1893); and Clementia Black, "Life and Labour in London," *Contemporary Review* (August 1891).

[50] See Helen Dendy, "Marriage in East London," *Contemporary Review* (March 1894); Henry Cardinal Manning, "A Pleading for the Worthless," *Nineteenth Century* (March 1888); and Samuel A. Barnett, "The Failure of Philanthropy," *MacMillan's Magazine* (March 1896).

[51] George Gissing, *The Unclassed* (1884, Reprint Edition, New York, 1968), 211. An even more cynical view is provided by some historians; one commented that "Philanthropy helped to validate existing social institutions by highlighting the generosity of the rich and the inadequacies of the poor" (Brian Harrison, "Philanthropy and the Victorians," *Victorian Studies* 1966 9 [4]: 368). Harrison also noted the role of charity as a means of advancing one's social status.

[52] See *Sketches from Life, or Work Among the Poor of London* (London, 1879); Frank Prochaska, *Women and Philanthropy in Nineteenth Century England* (Oxford, 1980); and Anne Summers, "A Home from Home—Women's Philanthropic Work in the Nineteenth Century," in *Fit Work for Women* (New York, 1979).

metropolitan hospitals, while visiting recovering patients, tried to teach the poor about the causes of disease and the importance of proper sanitation. Ellen Ranyard's "Bible Nurses" and Florence Nightingale's Metropolitan and National Nursing Association also provided the poor with information about nutrition, cleanliness, medical care, and Christianity. Because it was important for them to make a good first impression, such nurses were expected to be modest, compassionate, moral, patient, religious, and gentle. By winning their patients' trust, they could hope to have a positive moral impact on those under their care.[53]

Although district visitors hoped that by raising the moral level of working class parents—and thus assuring better parenting—they would be able to break the cycle of poverty in the poorer districts of the Metropolis, many came to realize that mere visiting was not enough. Victorian philanthropists increasingly recognized that if "the citadel of poverty and ignorance and vice is to be taken at all, it must be besieged from every point on the compass."[54] Any project which promised to teach the poor economy, sobriety, or personal morality was worthy of support.

Several reformers, for instance, believed that the bringing of cheap, hot meals into working class neighborhoods and selling them at a reasonable price would greatly benefit the slum poor. According to Henrietta Barnett, "while wages are at the present rate the large mass of our nation cannot get enough food to maintain them in robust health."[55] As a result, private philanthropy should explore the idea of "People's Kitchens" such as were already in operation on the Continent in Berlin, Prague, Vienna, and elsewhere, and in the British Isles in Glasgow, Scotland. Healthy meals of beef, potatoes, and pudding could be provided for as little as six pence if bought in bulk. One reformer, indeed, argued that he could provide three meals a day for as little as one shilling, nearly fifty percent less than what many poor citizens were presently spending for food.[56] As these meals would be sold just over cost, they would not demoralize the poor; they would get what they paid for. Another idea was that as workers needed meat in their diet for good health and as butcher's prices in London were often too high for them to afford, philanthropists should buy meat directly from farmers and sell it at cost to the poor.[57]

Other reformers proposed a number of disparate projects. One recommended

---

[53] See Frank Prochaska, "Body and Soul: Bible Nurses and the Poor in Victorian London," *Historical Research* 1987 60 (143): 336-48; and Florence Craven, "Servants of the Sick Poor," *Nineteenth Century* (April 1883).

[54] W. Stanley Jevons, "Methods of Social Reform," *Contemporary Review* (October 1878), 499.

[55] Henrietta Barnett, "National Enemies and National Defenses," *National Review* (July 1886), 664.

[56] See Frederick Greenwood, "Misery in Great Cities," *Nineteenth Century* (May 1889); Mary Mallocks, "Restaurants for the Labouring Classes," *National Review* (March 1893); and Edith Sellers, "The People's Kitchen in Vienna," *Nineteenth Century* (November 1894).

[57] See Freeman Wills, "Meat for the People," *Contemporary Review* (July 1886).

that local charitable organizations should collect small sums each week from parents to ensure that they could afford new clothes and primary school fees for their children. It was sometimes necessary, the author of this proposal remarked, to take money out of the family economy before the parents wasted it upon themselves. Another heralded the establishment of a London shelter in 1887 which cross-examined applicants prior to entry, required references, and turned the "worthless" away from their door. A third writer hoped to aid "fallen women" by establishing a system of refuges. Through close supervision, training, and help finding jobs, charity workers would gradually instill order, obedience, regularity, good habits, and, finally, a rudimentary knowledge of religion into these women. In time, the refuges would be able to restore the "fallen" to a respectable position within the working class community.[58]

Education—in the broadest sense—was commonly believed to be exceptionally important to the moral reformation of the poorer classes. As the study of art, music, literature, history, and other subjects would make for a more enlightened urban population, many philanthropists called for the construction of night schools. By teaching both poor children and underemployed workers a trade, charity would help to reduce the number of unskilled workers glutting the labor market. Middle and upper class philanthropists also believed that increased working class access to the theater, open-air concerts, public libraries, clubs, and museums would aid in the moralization of the poor.[59]

Moral reformers also promoted the establishment of missions in the slums as a way to reach the poor. By living amongst the poor, charity workers would be in direct, daily contact with those they wished to elevate. Many of these early missions were established by various evangelical sects in order to bring religion into the slums. Even the church missions were, however, not exclusively devoted to the spreading of Christianity among the poor. The women's ministry in Bethnal Green, established in 1866, provided a night school, medical services, and home visiting to extend both moral and practical advice.[60] According to one religious reformer, in order to make the poor virtuous, honest, and industrious, church missions needed to provide social services, wholesome entertainment, and schools,

---

[58] See Laura Oldfield, "Children of the Poor," *MacMillan's Magazine* (February 1873); Susan Jeune, "Helping the Fallen," *Fortnightly Review* (November 1885); and Harold Boulton, "A London House of Shelter," *Fortnightly Review* (February 1894).

[59] See J. H. Bridges, "The Moral and Social Aspects of Health," *Fortnightly Review* (November 1877).

[60] See Olivia Bennet, Countess of Tankerville, *A Bright Spot in Outcast London* (London, 1884); Francis E. Smiley, *The Evangelization of a Great City* (1885, Reprint Edition, Philadelphia, 1890); Henry Walker, *East London: Sketches of Christian Work and Workers* (1896, Reprint Edition, Bucks, England, 1987); and "The Church in East London," *Church Quarterly* (January 1885).

in addition to charity.[61]

The secular missions established in the poorer districts of metropolitan London during the 1880s had many of the same goals. Reverend Samuel A. Barnett's Toynbee Hall, founded in 1884 in the East End district of Whitechapel, was intended to build a sense of community, bridge class differences, teach the virtues of self-help, and promote an appreciation for higher things.[62] By no means was this Barnett's first sojourn into the field of social reform. Since his arrival in the East End in 1873, Barnett had sponsored night classes, art exhibitions, a literary society, a penny bank, and a pension scheme for the poor of Whitechapel. Toynbee Hall—his masterpiece—would provide expanded services for those who wished to take advantage of them. Between 1884 and 1900, the roughly one hundred residents of Toynbee Hall—most of them students from Oxford or Cambridge who were in residence for a couple of years—provided lectures, discussion groups, clubs, and entertainment to the poor.[63] As the poor were, according to Barnett, essentially children without a culture of their own, they needed to be taught to appreciate music, history, art, and, eventually, religion.[64] Furthermore, by exposing the working classes of his district to higher education and constructive leisure activities, Barnett hoped to instill in them a respect for authority, tradition, and public order. By gaining the confidence of the masses, the personnel of such institutions would be able to guide and mold their ideas; as wise councillors working in the interest of the poor, Barnett expected his middle and upper class residents to take the place of street agitators and other assorted East End troublemakers.[65]

One of the early supporters of the settlement house movement, Walter Besant, hoped that Toynbee Hall would be the first of some fifty London missions—housing perhaps 1,500 volunteers—to raise the culture, civic pride, and

---

[61] See Reverend J. Edmond Long, *The Hopeful Cry of Outcast London* (London, 1884); and Reverend David Rice Jones, *In the Slums* (London, 1884).

[62] Barnett named Toynbee Hall after his friend, the London-born, Oxford-educated historian and social reformer Arnold Toynbee, who had died at the young age of thirty-one in 1883.

[63] Among the lecturers invited to speak at Toynbee Hall were Charles Booth, Albert V. Dicey, Herbert Asquith, Richard Haldane, Tom Mann, Oscar Wilde, and Leslie Stephen.

[64] See Samuel A. Barnett, "Universities and the Poor," *Nineteenth Century* (February 1884); Henrietta Barnett, "Passionless Reformers," *Fortnightly Review* (August 1882); Richard Whiteing, *No. 5 John Street* (1899, Reprint Edition, London, 1902); and Standish Meacham, *Toynbee Hall and Social Reform, 1880-1914* (New Haven, Conn., 1987). Interestingly, several of the architects of the modern British Welfare State served as residents at Toynbee Hall. William Beveridge was subwarden of Toynbee Hall during the early 1900s; Clement Attlee, the leader of the British Labour Party from 1935 to 1955, became secretary of Toynbee Hall in 1910.

[65] See John M. Knapp, ed., *The Universities and the Social Problem* (1895, Reprint Edition, New York, 1985).

piety of the London poor and to cement friendships across class lines.[66] Not surprisingly, therefore, the People's Palace of east London—founded under Besant's watchful eye in 1887—provided many of the same services as did Toynbee Hall. For a small fee, one could enroll in music, art, and history classes; attend concerts and dance recitals; receive technical education; use the library and gymnasium; join the debating society; and participate in swimming, cricket, chess, and soccer matches. Besant's goal, like Barnett's, was to elevate and ennoble the working classes by giving them an alternative to the demoralizing theaters, music halls, and public houses of the East End. In essence, the People's Palace would, Besant hoped, give the poor an opportunity to better their own lives.[67]

In addition to the good they might do adults, the missions were also intended to provide an outlet for young people away from the pubs and music halls of the Metropolis. Young working class men needed clubs, recreation rooms, music concerts, evening classes, supervised dances, and athletic games to remove them from their usually degraded surroundings. Many writers strongly believed that the more money that was spent on recreation and education for the poor while they were young, the less would have to be spent later on crime and pauperism. British youth could be taught to be good citizens and good Christians by instructing them in the arts of self-respect, self-control, honesty, and independence.[68] Nor should young working class women be neglected; after all, the temptations of the music halls, pubs, and theaters had a deleterious impact on the morality of both sexes. Both men and women wished to escape from their crowded apartments, particularly in the evenings after a long day at work. Clubs for young women, therefore, performed a dual function. They taught manners, polite conversation, and refinement and, as important, gave young women somewhere "safe" to go in the evening. Once ennobled by club membership, supporters hoped, they would have a positive moral impact on their friends and siblings, and, in time, on their husbands and children as well.[69] In addition to the clubs, Besant was also interested in the establishment of industrial schools. By teaching the unskilled a marketable trade, British industry would become more competitive in international markets; crime and drinking would be reduced; and the poor would lead more dignified and

---

[66] See Walter Besant, *South London* (London, 1898).

[67] See Brooke Lambert, "Jacob's Answer to Esau's Cry," *Contemporary Review* (September 1884); Walter Besant, "The People's Palace," *Contemporary Review* (February 1887); and Edmund Currie, "The Working of the People's Palace," *Nineteenth Century* (February 1890).

[68] See Violet Greville, "Social Reforms for the London Poor," *Fortnightly Review* (January 1884); Mary A. Lewis, "Our Future Masters," *Fortnightly Review* (October 1885); and Edward Salmon, "The Democracy and the Drama," *National Review* (November 1888).

[69] See Maude Stanley, "Clubs for Working Girls," *Nineteenth Century* (January 1889); and Susan Jeune, "Amusements of the Poor," *National Review* (May 1893).

upright lives.[70] Although obviously deeply interested in moral reform, Besant was careful not to stress it openly. As he said, if young workers "think the palace is a trap to catch them, and make them sober, good, religious and temperate, there will be an end."[71]

In addition to the mission house movement, many reformers believed that the poor needed to have easier access to metropolitan parks, gardens, and playgrounds. Because so many of the poorest inhabitants of Britain's largest cities lived in small, crowded apartments, they needed open spaces more than anyone else. As Octavia Hill, one of the founders of the Charity Organisation Society, noted, "these are the people who stay in town most, if not all, of the year, whose rooms are most crowded, and whose facilities for getting about are least."[72] The problem was that although west London, dividing the Metropolis at Charing Cross Road, had one acre of parks for every 682 residents, the East End possessed only one acre for every 7,481 inhabitants. As one critic remarked, the ancient city of "Babylon, with a little more than a fourth of the population of London, consisted of nine-tenths of fields, parks, and gardens."[73] London, the capital of an even greater empire, could afford to do better.

It was up to private philanthropy, according to Hill, to purchase recreation areas where they were scarce, as in London's East End.[74] Paralleling Octavia Hill's efforts, the Metropolitan Public Gardens Association, which was supported by such noted reformers as Reginald Brabazon, Henry Cardinal Manning, and Walter Besant, funded some eighty projects in east London between its founding in 1882 and 1900. In addition, two pieces of legislation—the Metropolitan Open Spaces Act of 1881 and the Disused Burial Grounds Act of 1884—simplified the transfer of gardens and cemeteries into the public domain. Working together, reformers in both the public and private sectors expected the provision of open spaces to bring substantial physical and moral benefits to the poor. They would now have places to exercise or relax with their families away from the temptations of the local public house or music hall.[75] Well-kept parks also gave the middle and upper classes of London a reassuring sign of public order and allowed for the closer surveillance of the poor's leisure activities.[76]

Housing reform provided another forum for the moralization of the working

---

[70] See Walter Besant, "St. Katherine's by the Tower," *Contemporary Review* (December 1887).

[71] Walter Besant, "Amusements of the People," *Contemporary Review* (March 1884), 353.

[72] Octavia Hill, "More Air for London," *Nineteenth Century* (February 1888), 182-83.

[73] "The Progress of the Metropolitan Open Space Movement," *The Lancet* (12 November 1887), 977.

[74] Ibid.

[75] See Octavia Hill's "Space for the People," *MacMillan's Magazine* (August 1875) and "Colour, Space, and Music for the People," *Nineteenth Century* (May 1884).

[76] See Howard L. Malchow, "Public Gardens and Social Action in Late Victorian London," *Victorian Studies* 1985 29 (1): 97-124.

classes. Without a decent home, many feared, the poor could hardly be expected to live a life of virtue. According to the most famous Victorian proponent of "self-help," Samuel Smiles, it "is mainly in the home that the heart is opened, the habits are formed, the intellect is awakened, the character molded for good or evil."[77] Overcrowding in the slums, unfortunately, tended to have a pernicious influence on working class ethics and made the task of moral reform even more difficult. As one contemporary questioned, "how can we expect genuine progress among classes that have to herd together in vile abodes?"[78]

Private philanthropy was, unfortunately, ill-suited to provide decent homes to the poorest class of metropolitan workers. Indeed, it did not even try.[79] Housing reformers concerned themselves with the construction and management of model dwellings for the most respectable and affluent class of workers—those, in fact, least in need of their aid. The rents they charged, in an attempt to make a modest profit, ensured that only workers in regular employment could afford to live there. Even so, reformers assumed that their efforts were having a positive impact on the housing market; as respectable workers found better accommodations, their less fortunate neighbors would benefit by being able to move into their vacated dwellings.[80]

In 1862 George Peabody, an American from Philadelphia who moved to London in 1837, founded the most famous society providing homes for the skilled artisan classes. With £150,000 of initial capital at his disposal, Peabody had several buildings constructed in the inner-city Spitalfields district of London by early 1864; in later years, Peabody built dwellings in Bermondsey, Chelsea, Islington, and Shadwell. His goal was to house the working poor in healthy dwellings as long as they were of good character, conducted themselves responsibly, and paid their rent on time.[81] The Peabody fund had its greatest impact on the London housing market during the first fifteen years after its

---

[77] Samuel Smiles, *Character* (London, 1871), 31.

[78] *The Graphic*, 26 April 1879, 403. It "may be questioned whether the attempt to educate men who cannot be decently housed . . . [is] something like erecting a pyramid on its apex" (ibid., 423).

[79] There were a large number of housing associations active in the Metropolis during the late Victorian period: the Peabody and Guinness trusts, the East End Dwellings Company, the Improved Industrial Dwellings Company, the Metropolitan Association for Improving the Dwellings of the Industrious Classes, and the Society for Improving the Condition of the Labouring Classes to name just a few.

[80] See Harry Jones, "The Homes of the Town Poor," *Cornhill Magazine* (October 1880); and Octavia Hill, *Homes of the London Poor* (1875, Reprint Edition, London, 1970).

[81] The relative healthfulness of Peabody's buildings is beyond dispute; the death-rate therein was two per thousand less than in the rest of London, and their inhabitants suffered less from infantile mortality and infectious disease than those living elsewhere in the Metropolis (Arthur Newsholme, "The Vital Statistics of Peabody Buildings and other Artisans' and Labourers' Block Dwellings," *Journal of the Royal Statistical Society* [March 1891], 93).

founder's death in 1869; unfortunately, no major projects were undertaken between 1885 and 1900, the worst years of the housing crisis, as the Peabody Trust had at that time to pay down the huge loans taken out during the first twenty years of its existence.[82]

Octavia Hill, like Peabody, believed that without first ensuring that her tenants were of good character, an improved environment would do no good. If, as Hill hoped, the rich and the educated could be persuaded to act as landlords in poor neighborhoods, their supervision would have a very beneficial impact on the poor. Hill expected her superintendents to collect rents regularly, make all needed repairs, and evict unwanted lodgers—drunkards, prostitutes, troublemakers, and criminals in particular; she also instructed her managers to cultivate regular habits in the poor, inspire them to pay their rent on time, and keep their apartments clean and in proper order. By replacing the demoralizing influences of damp, filthy, crowded, and poorly ventilated tenements and degraded companions with a clean, airy apartment supervised by a member of the respectable middle or upper classes, Hill hoped to bring about the gradual moral reformation of the slum poor.[83]

By the 1880s, Hill and her associates had housed nearly 4,000 workers and owned an estimated £70,000 worth of London real estate, all run on sound commercial principles; boarders had, in other words, to pay the full cost of their lodgings. Hill, like Peabody, believed that

> It is far better to prove that you can provide a tolerable tenement which will pay, than a perfect one that will not.... Give him by all means as much as you can for his money, but do not house him by charity, or you will house few but him, and discourage instead of stimulating others to build for the poor.[84]

Although her rooms were a little on the expensive side, her tenants could still afford them. Plus, Hill argued that the "shilling added to the rent will be more than saved by that greater ability to work and to refrain from drink which will come with better health and better habits."[85]

Even so, the Victorians' reliance on private housing associations did have a number of drawbacks. Most societies learned to avoid the poorest neighborhoods of London and other large cities because investment there simply did not pay. Overcrowded conditions in east and south London, for instance, attracted little

---

[82] See John N. Tarn, "The Peabody Donation Fund," *Victorian Studies* 1966 10 (1): 7-38.

[83] For Hill, reformers should "purify the courts in the deepest, most spiritual way . . . . rule a little kingdom in righteousness, and help to eradicate evil by slow but thorough ways" (Octavia Hill, "A Few Words to Fresh Workers," *Nineteenth Century* [September 1889], 459). See also Octavia Hill, "Blank Court," *MacMillan's Magazine* (October 1871); Charles Gatliffe, "On Improved Dwellings and their Beneficial Effect," *Journal of the Royal Statistical Society* (March 1875); and Evelyn M. Phillips, "The Working Lady in London," *Fortnightly Review* (August 1892).

[84] Octavia Hill, *Homes of the London Poor* (1875, Reprint Edition, London, 1970), 88.

[85] "Houses of the Poor in Towns," *Cornhill Magazine* (July 1874), 83.

attention from the major metropolitan housing societies. In west London, where reformers could take advantage of subsidies from local landlords and from the Metropolitan Board of Works, there was, however, a considerable amount of building activity. The model dwellings movement, therefore, tended to reinforce, not alleviate, the existing segregation between rich and poor and between the various strata of the working classes in London.[86]

In addition, as noted above, the provision of model dwellings for the artisan classes did little for those of lesser means; while the "labor aristocracy" was, in effect, rewarded for possessing a modicum of respectability, those most in need of assistance continued to be neglected. Finally, the various metropolitan housing associations of the late Victorian era did little to reduce overcrowding in London. One of the largest, the Metropolitan Association for Improving the Dwellings of the Industrious Classes, for example, housed only 26,000 individuals between 1870 and 1900; this figure was slightly less than the annual natural rate of increase in the Metropolis. As early as 1874, Octavia Hill recognized "the enormous magnitude of the problem which must be dealt with and the small progress which up to that time had been made in solving it."[87]

While the pace of reform might be slow, the Charity Organisation Society would never condemn the model dwellings movement for providing homes to those who had already proven themselves to be respectable and, thus, deserving of aid. What the COS was extremely concerned about from the late 1870s was the existence in London of a large organization that habitually distributed charity without making the slightest attempt to determine whether the applicants for its relief were "deserving" or not: the Salvation Army. The Salvation Army, founded by Methodist minister William Booth and his wife Catherine in 1878, indeed, appeared to use indiscriminate charity—along with music, marches, open-air preaching, and public conversions—as a way to attract a following among the metropolitan poor. While the Booths were definitely most interested in the spiritual salvation of the London poor, both recognized the importance of Christian charity and the strong connection between physical and moral well-being.[88] By 1890, the Salvation Army provided a substantial amount of charitable relief through its

---

[86] See Richard Dennis's seminal article, "The Geography of Victorian Values: Philanthropic Housing in London, 1840-1900," *Journal of Historical Geography* 1989 15 (1): 40-54. This fact was recognized at the time by some critics. See, for example, "The Death-rate in London Tenements," *The Lancet* (28 April 1884); and Harold Boulton, "Housing of the Poor," *Fortnightly Review* (February 1888).

[87] Octavia Hill, "The Homes of the London Poor," *MacMillan's Magazine* (June 1874), 131.

[88] William Booth (1829-1912) was born in Nottingham, trained as a Methodist minister, and began his evangelical work in London in 1865; in 1878, he named his London organization the Salvation Army. The Salvation Army was very much a family affair. Eldest son William Bramwell Booth was "Chief-of-Staff" from 1880 and "General" of the Salvation Army from 1912 until 1929; Booth's other sons commanded the Salvation Army in Canada, the United States, India, and Australia during his lifetime.

twelve food depots, sixteen night shelters, thirteen refuges for women, and numerous soup kitchens. The Salvation Army also held annual clothing and blanket drives, sold life insurance, and owned a savings bank during the 1880s.[89]

In the fall of 1890 the Salvation Army was just another religious organization practicing indiscriminate charity and, in the opinion of the COS, demoralizing the poor. With the publication of William Booth's *Darkest England* in October of that year, however, the Salvation Army placed itself upon the cutting edge of national social reform. Booth drew attention to the Salvation Army by advocating a rather simple proposal. If private donors agreed to contribute £100,000, he would establish a number of city workshops and farm colonies to elevate the moral and material condition of the London poor. Within the workshops and colonies, the poor would be required to submit to strict discipline and moral supervision. They were also expected to take their work seriously. Those who graduated from one of the city workshops would be transferred to a farm colony in England; later, after they had proven themselves as farm laborers, they would be allowed to migrate overseas, either to a Salvation Army farm colony in Canada or Australia or to a homestead of their own.[90] Pursuant to these goals, the Salvation Army purchased a one-thousand-acre estate in Essex for mixed farming and brick manufacture in 1891. By 1893, the Salvation Army had organized five city colonies in London providing work for 2,700 people—a match factory, a creche-knitting factory, a book-binding factory, a laundry, and a text-making and needlework factory; the Salvation Army also sponsored eighteen labor bureaux and a registry office for unemployed domestic servants.[91] Although seemingly quite expensive, many people believed that Booth's program would be cost effective over time, particularly in comparison with the Poor Law.

General [Booth]: "I'll provide him [the poor] with food, shelter, work, and good and honest influences for 3s. 6d. per week."

Prison [Poor Law] authorities: "For 12s. 6d. a week I'll give him jail, shelter, food, take away his character, and turn him out worse than he was before."[92]

---

[89] See the *Darkest England Gazette* (July 1893). The number helped by the Salvation Army was immense. In 1896, the Salvation Army distributed 3.2 million meals, provided lodgings for 1.3 million, and found employment for 12,000 men (See *War Cry*, 26 December 1896).

[90] Booth's *Darkest England* was heavily influenced by a number of important social theorists of the day, including Arnold White, Reverend Herbert Mills, Frank Smith, W. L. Rees, and William T. Stead; indeed, rumor has it that Stead had a hand in the composition of *Darkest England*.

[91] See William Booth, *In Darkest England, and the Way Out* (New York, 1890); *Darkest England Gazette*, July 1893; and Victor Bailey, "In Darkest England: The Salvation Army, Social Reform, and the Labour Movement," *International Review of Social History* 1984 29 (2): 133-71.

[92] *Darkest England Gazette*, 6 February 1897.

Furthermore, if Booth's plan were successful, Britain would emerge with a stronger empire, an enhanced ability to feed itself, and a much more productive and moral working class.[93]

Not surprisingly given these inducements, Booth's *Darkest England* was a great popular success, selling roughly 115,000 copies within the first few months after its publication. In addition, Booth received strong support in the British press—particularly from *The Times, Reynold's Newspaper*, and *The Star*—and also from a number of important London labor leaders, Tom Mann, and Ben Tillet.[94] The Salvation Army enjoyed, at least in some quarters, great popularity. One commentator asserted that the Salvation Army's scheme should be supported because their past "success in reclaiming the outcasts and turning multitudes from a life of degradation to one of virtue is little short of miraculous."[95] Because of his long involvement in the alleviation of London poverty, a large number of writers assumed that Booth could be trusted to act in the public interest.

Even so, Booth's program did not go unchallenged. A large part of the Labour and all of the Socialist press condemned Booth's proposals. The *People's Press*, for example, commented that "The favourable reception given this extraordinary scheme by the capitalist Press only shews how eagerly the well-to-do classes will embrace any philanthropic proposal that does not interfere with their right to continue to enslave and plunder the people."[96] Having failed to gain the support of the Socialist press, Booth lost credibility among conservatives when several of his strongest supporters—T. H. Huxley, Ben Tillet, and the editors of *Reynold's Newspaper*—argued that his system of colonies and workshops actually promoted socialism in Britain.[97] The Charity Organisation Society, of course, also strongly objected to Booth's scheme, arguing that Booth's method of indiscriminate charity had been tried, and had failed, many times in the past.[98] Every large scale charitable experiment of this kind inevitably led to greater poverty and improvidence. Booth could offer no proof that his attempt to moralize and elevate the poor would end any differently. Even if his "colonies" were

---

[93] These hopes proved to be far too sanguine. While the city workshops and farm colony in Essex expanded somewhat during the 1890s, the Salvation Army was unable to found an overseas colony prior to the turn of the century (Victor Bailey, "In Darkest England: The Salvation Army, Social Reform, and the Labour Movement," *International Review of Social History* 1984 29 (2): 162-64).

[94] (London) *Times*, 20 December 1890.

[95] Francis Peek, "In Darkest England and a Way Out," *Contemporary Review* (December 1890), 796. See also Margaret Harkness, *In Darkest London: Captain Lobe, A Story of the Salvation Army* (London, 1891), i.

[96] *People's Press*, 1 November 1890, 3.

[97] (London) *Times*, 29 December 1890.

[98] (London) *Times*, 20 December 1890.

successful in the short term, the COS reasoned, they would most likely eventually have to be taken over by the national government—a dangerous expansion of State power.[99]

Booth's critics also worried that the establishment of city and farm colonies by the Salvation Army would draw thousands of paupers to London in search of relief. Would not labor performed in Salvation Army workshops and colonies have to be given a penal character, one commentator asked, so as not to attract either the scum of Europe or honest British workingmen?[100] Moreover, as large numbers of people were already unemployed because of the glut of unskilled workers clogging the labor market, would not Salvation Army workshops throw British workers out of work? If food and shelter had to be worked for every day in the Salvation Army colonies and workshops, how was Booth's scheme different from that of the Poor Law?[101] Either his system of colonies would be a complete and costly failure, or it would only reach those who were willing both to work and to take orders from the Salvation Army.[102]

Finally, a number of critics cast doubt on the efficiency of the Salvation Army and on Booth's abilities as a social reformer. One writer stated that "apart from eccentric show, noise, and buffoonery, we know of nothing that entitles the [Salvation] Army to take precedence over all other philanthropic institutions."[103] An editorialist for the London *Times* agreed and stated further that the Salvation Army's reputation for social reform was inflated, partly through its own publications.[104] The noted social reformer Mary Jeune dismissed Booth in 1891 as "a man whose modes of religion and leading have only created amusement and scorn."[105] To entrust large amounts of money to an untried organization headed by an unconventional autocrat might spell disaster, if not for the Salvation Army, then for other more worthy philanthropic enterprises.[106]

Nor were the activities of the Salvation Army the only source of indiscriminate charity of concern to the Charity Organisation Society; the abuse of medical charities was a major problem during the late Victorian period. Excluding paupers, roughly thirty percent of all Londoners received some form of medical charity in 1870. As most were not deserving of such relief in the eyes of the COS

---

[99] See " 'In Darkest England': Suggestions," *National Review* (February 1891); Susan Jeune, "General Booth's Scheme," *National Review* (January 1891); and D. M. Stevenson, "Darkest England," *Westminster Review* (April 1891).

[100] See " 'General' Booth's Scheme," *The Economist* (22 November 1890).

[101] See Francis Peek's "In Darkest England and a Way Out," *Contemporary Review* (December 1890) and "General Booth's Social Work," *Contemporary Review* (July 1892).

[102] "General Booth's *Darkest England*," *London Quarterly Review* (January 1891).

[103] "Still in the Dark," *Saturday Review* (6 December 1890), 642.

[104] (London) *Times*, 27 November 1890.

[105] Susan Jeune, "General Booth's Scheme," *National Review* (January 1891), 697.

[106] The £100,000 donation was only the down-payment on a £1 million total. Booth would require £30,000 per year for the next thirty years to keep his system of colonies operational.

and as the flood of applicants for free medical services prevented a high quality of care for those truly in need, the COS proposed a number of reforms. Paupers should only be treated in the workhouse infirmary or in a public hospital; all those of independent means applying for in-patient care were to be treated in authorized provident hospitals for a fee. District dispensaries were to care for those who could be treated quickly and then released. As the metropolitan medical charities needed to be both reorganized and forced to discriminate between the applicants for relief so that they would no longer overlap with the medical services provided by the Poor Law, the COS proposed that a board be established to audit, inspect, and report upon their policies and finances.[107]

Another source of great concern to the Charity Organisation Society was the misapplication of the City of London Parochial Charity Fund, the largest single concentration of endowments in the United Kingdom at the time. These monies had originally been intended to be used to ameliorate the condition of the poor living within the City, London's financial district and the area formerly enclosed within the medieval town walls. As the population of the City had declined sharply over the previous thirty years—from 130,000 in 1850 to 50,000 in 1881—few paupers remained in residence to benefit from these endowed charities. In consequence, large sums of money were being either misspent on the renovation of church properties or left unspent. With an annual income of over £100,000 drawn from capital assets worth nearly £2.5 million, the Parochial Charity Fund could no longer be left in its present state. Charles Trevelyan and the COS argued that the City funds should be used to provide for the poor living in surrounding parishes. A Royal Commission investigation in the early 1880s led to James Bryce's Parochial Charities Act of 1883 which broadened the geographic area covered by these endowments. Although the revenues of the five largest City parishes were left untouched, Bryce's Act turned over those of more than one hundred moribund parishes to the Charity Commissioners; in the future, these monies were to be used for the provision of educational facilities and materials, libraries, museums, and open spaces for the metropolitan poor.[108]

The Charity Organisation Society, in addition to its attempts to curtail indiscriminate alms-giving by private charities and individuals, also tried to reform the administration of the Poor Law. Unfortunately, from the perspective of

---

[107] See "Medical Charity: Methods of Administering It," *Westminster Review* (April 1874); Charles Trevelyan, *Metropolitan Medical Relief*, 2nd Edition (London, 1879); A. O'Donnel Bartholeyns, "The Sick Poor of the Metropolis," *National Review* (February 1889); and Charles S. Loch, "The Confusion in Medical Charities," *Nineteenth Century* (August 1892).

[108] See "City Parochial Charities," *Good Words* (1879); Robert Hunter, "The Future of the City Charities," *Nineteenth Century* (January 1890); and David Owen, "The City Parochial Charities," *Journal of British Studies* 1962 1 (2): 115-35. In 1889 the Charity Commissioners made a serious commitment to the financing of trade schools for the poor at the expense of other types of reform.

the COS, during the forty years since the passage of the Poor Law Amendment Act of 1834, the worst aspects of the old Poor Law—specifically the distribution of outdoor relief to the able-bodied in aid of wages—had continued to be practiced.[109] Indeed, according to social reformer Henry Fawcett in 1871, "much of the evil influence exerted by the old Poor Law upon the general social condition of the country still continues in operation."[110] The increasing amount of metropolitan pauperism—reaching as high as 5.6 percent of all Londoners in 1867—and a number of legal changes helped to spur a reexamination of the Poor Law during the late 1860s. The Poor Law Union Rateability Act of 1865, by ending inequalities between the poor-rates within unions, ensured that wealthier parishes now had to pay a larger portion of the total cost; the Metropolitan Poor Act of 1867, which set up a common poor fund into which all unions and parishes had to contribute, had much the same impact on London. Both acts encouraged a rethinking of the Poor Law among the well-to-do.[111]

In response, George J. Goschen—a member of parliament, president of the Poor Law Board under Liberal Prime Minister William Gladstone between 1868 and 1871, and staunch supporter of the Charity Organisation Society—wrote in 1869 a *minute* on the disastrous influence the indiscriminate distribution of Poor Law relief was having on the metropolitan poor. Goschen complained that

One of the most recognized principles in our Poor Law is, that relief should be given only to the actually destitute, and not in aid of wages. In the case of widows with families . . . the rule is frequently departed from, but, as a general principle, it lies at the root of the present system of relief. . . relief is given, not as a matter of charity but of legal obligation, and to extend this legal obligation beyond the class to which it now applies, namely, the actually destitute, to a further and much larger class, namely, those in receipt of insufficient wages, would be not only to increase to an unlimited extent the present enormous expenditure, but to allow the belief in a legal claim to public money in every emergency to supplant, in a further portion of the population, the full recognition of the necessity for self-reliance and thrift.[112]

As only about fifteen percent of those in receipt of Poor Law relief in England and Wales were forced to enter the workhouse, it was no wonder, Goschen thought, that London pauperism was such a serious problem; his solution was for the Guardians

---

[109] Outdoor relief, or out relief as it was sometimes called, was state aid distributed by the Poor Law Guardians without forcing the applicant to enter the workhouse.

[110] Henry Fawcett, *Pauperism: Its Causes and Remedies* (London, 1871), 26.

[111] See Mary MacKinnon, "English Poor Law Policy and the Crusade Against Out Relief," *Journal of Economic History* 1987 47 (3): 603-25.

[112] Cited in Michael E. Rose, compiler, *The English Poor Law, 1780-1930* (New York, 1971), 226-27.

to return to the spirit of the Poor Law of 1834.[113] "Had the Poor Law been administered, since 1834, strictly on these principles" in the first place, one critic lamented, "pauperism would probably have been reduced to a negligible quantity" by this time.[114]

For the Charity Organisation Society, indiscriminate outdoor Poor Law relief was just as demoralizing as any Salvation Army soup kitchen. Providing such aid to the "undeserving" poor lowered their self-esteem, destroyed their independence, encouraged indolence, and lessened the consequences of immoral or intemperate behavior; if the State would, in the final analysis, take care of them, why should the poor provide for themselves? Even the thrifty were encouraged to act as if they had saved nothing; if their savings became known to the relieving officer, they might be refused outdoor relief.[115] Furthermore, easy access to outdoor relief promoted fraud and imposture within the poorer classes. Oftentimes, the "noisy complainer who stands at the out-relief door of the workhouse is . . . much better off than many of the quiet people in well-worn clothes who are to be met at every turn" in the poorest parts of London.[116]

Not surprisingly, the late Victorian "Crusade against Out-relief" brought some remarkable changes in the administration of the Poor Law. The total amount spent on Poor Law relief fell by nearly twelve percent during the 1870s; outdoor relief declined even more, by nearly fifty percent, while the percentage of paupers incarcerated in British workhouses doubled to nearly thirty percent by the early 1900s.

Paupers Per Thousand[117]

	Indoor	Outdoor	Total
1852	6.2	44.7	50.9
1862	6.6	39.0	45.6
1872	6.6	36.3	42.9
1882	7.1	23.2	30.3
1892	6.4	19.2	25.6

Because many of those denied out relief after 1870 were unwilling to enter the workhouse, Poor Law expenditures and the percentage of British paupers continued

---

[113] The ratio of those receiving outdoor relief to those incarcerated in the workhouse was over five to one in England and Wales as a whole. London's rate, however, was only half the national average in the early 1870s. The agricultural districts of southwestern England and Wales were the worst offenders with regard to outdoor relief.

[114] William Chance, *The Better Administration of the Poor Law* (London, 1895), v.

[115] See J. R. Pretyman, *Dispauperization* (London, 1876); "The Present Misapplication of Poor Law Relief," *The Economist* (27 June 1874); and "Out-door Relief," *Westminster Review* (April 1874).

[116] Edmund Currie, "The Working of the People's Palace," *Nineteenth Century* (February 1890), 350.

[117] Royal Commission *On the Aged Poor* (1895 [cd. 7684-84ii]), ix-x.

to decline throughout the era of the "Great Depression." By 1881, the number of British citizens in receipt of State aid had been cut almost in half.[118] In the estimation of one strong supporter of Poor Law reform, all of these changes were for the better. As "indoor relief is far superior to outdoor relief in reducing pauperism and expenditure, and if it reduces pauperism it almost follows that its moral effect must be good, for every pauper lost implies a good citizen gained."[119]

Few poor people protested against the tightened administration of the Poor Law during the 1870s—perhaps because it was already an unimportant part of their lives. Such reforms induced the poor to provide for themselves or to rely upon friends, family, and private charity to a greater extent than before. The Poor Law workhouse of the late Victorian period increasingly served as a refuge of last resort for the sick, the disabled, orphans, destitute widows, and the elderly. Outdoor relief was limited to the aged, the infirm, and widows who could prove that misfortune had befallen them in spite of their providence and respectability.[120] The limitations placed on the distribution of outdoor relief after 1870 were not entirely cost-free, however. The elderly, in particular, according to one historian, lost around eight percent of their yearly income as a result of the new restrictions on out relief.[121]

Placing limitations on the distribution of outdoor relief was not enough for some critics; a few called for its elimination altogether. One reformer argued that if outdoor relief were phased out over a ten-year period and provision were made for whole districts to be declared "destitute" during periods of exceptionally severe economic distress, popular discontent could be kept to a minimum.[122] An even smaller number of reformers believed that the dismantling of the Poor Law itself would be beneficial to Victorian society; they expected that the moral character of the poor would be enhanced and that the various classes would become more

---

[118] "The Metropolitan Common Poor Fund," *The Economist* (November 1882), 1430. The percentage of English citizens receiving outdoor relief fell from three and a half percent in the early 1870s to two percent during the 1890s (Roderick Floud and Donald McCloskey, *The Economic History of Britain since 1700* [New York, 1994], 288).

[119] William Chance, "Indoor versus Outdoor Relief," *National Review* (July 1895), 689.

[120] See Mary MacKinnon, "English Poor Law Policy and the Crusade Against Out-Relief," *Journal of Economic History* 1987 47 (3): 603-25; Jose Harris, *Private Lives, Public Spirit: A Social History of Britain, 1870-1914* (New York, 1993); Michael Rose, ed., *The Poor and the City* (Leicester, England, 1985); and Pat Thane, "Women and the Poor Law in Victorian and Edwardian England," *History Workshop* 1978 (6): 29-51.

[121] See Mary MacKinnon, "Poverty and Policy: The English Poor Law, 1860-1910," *Journal of Economic History* 1986 46 (2): 500-502.

[122] See "Mr. Smith's Proposal for Improving the Poor Law Administration," *The Economist* (13 May 1871); George C. T. Bartley, *The Poor Law and Its Effects on Thrift*, 2nd Edition (London, 1873); "Out-door Relief," *Westminster Review* (April 1874); T. W. Fowle, "A Plea for the Abolition of Outdoor Relief," *Fortnightly Review* (June 1880); Thomas Mackay, "The Unpopularity of the Poor Law," *National Review* (August 1892); and William Chance, *The Better Administration of the Poor Law* (London, 1895).

dependent upon each other once this demoralizing prop had been removed. Reverend J. R. Pretyman argued that "In the absence of legal relief, the more prosperous would be obliged to give increased attention to the conditions of the less prosperous; whereas, at present, they were encouraged to throw all this trouble on the parochial authorities."[123] Pretyman believed that in view of Britain's advanced civilization, internal peace, abundant and well-paid labor, and the strength of Victorian charity, there was no reason why the provident should be forced by law to support the improvident.[124] The Poor Law, in addition to being an unnatural infringement on British liberty, was not an effective instrument for the moral reformation of the poor. The impoverished accepted Poor Law relief as a right, while many members of the middle and upper classes believed that they had met all of their social obligations by paying the poor-rate.[125]

The vast majority of the Victorian middle and upper classes—who knew that neither the Poor Law nor the practice of outdoor relief would be discontinued in the foreseeable future—nevertheless believed that the administration of the workhouses could be improved. Of special interest was the treatment of children under the Poor Law. As most believed that a large proportion of present-day paupers had themselves been pauperized by their exposure to the workhouse as children, this was a crucial issue. The idea that pauper children ought to be boarded-out in "cottage homes" gained a number of adherents; by removing them from the tainted environment and immoral companions of the workhouse, they would have a chance to learn to be thrifty, honest, industrious, and moral citizens.[126] As a variant of the boarding-out system, pauper children might be allowed to migrate to the colonies. One reformer argued that a child could be transported overseas and placed with a respectable family in Canada, Australia, or New Zealand for as little as £15.[127]

More might also be done to educate pauper children properly. Pauper girls, whether boarded with families or placed in "cottage schools," would benefit most from intensive training in the domestic arts—as opposed to mere book learning. As working class women were often responsible for overseeing their families' weekly budget, preparing a nutritious and varied diet, and raising their children,

---

[123] J. R. Pretyman, *Voluntary Versus Legal Relief* (London, 1879), 6.

[124] Ibid., 7.

[125] See Charles Trevelyan, *Address on the Systematic Visitation of the Poor* (London, 1870); and "Christian Charity and Political Economy," *Dublin Review* (October 1877). More than one critic stressed "the absolute harmfulness of the collectivist principle which lies at the root of our English poor law system" (Thomas Mackay, *Methods of Social Reform* [London, 1896], 2).

[126] See Thomas Archer, *The Terrible Sights of London* (London, 1870); Joanna Hill, "Homes for the Homeless," *MacMillan's Magazine* (June 1875); Francis Peek, "Hereditary Pauperism and Pauper Education," *Contemporary Review* (December 1877); and Gathorne Gathorne-Hardy, Viscount Cranbrook, "Hereditary Pauperism and Boarding Out," *National Review* (December 1883).

[127] See Ellice Hopkins, "Social Wreckage," *Contemporary Review* (July 1883).

society had an obligation to ensure that pauper girls received suitable training in these areas. Beyond this, young girls were to be taught practical skills, such as sewing and dress-making, that might come in handy later on at home or in the workplace.[128] Pauper boys were also, of course, to be required to learn a trade while under State tutelage. The passage of such reforms would ensure that pauper children would grow up to be healthy, well-adjusted, ethical, and employable.[129]

Aside from reforming the treatment of pauper children, an increasing number of social critics called for a more compassionate attitude towards the aged poor under the Poor Law. Workhouse relief was widely believed to be degrading, insulting, and demoralizing to the aged. Elderly workhouse inmates often complained about bad food, cold rooms, inattentive or inhumane Guardians, and, most important, their association with the "undeserving" poor. Unless aged paupers were removed from the humiliating atmosphere of the workhouse and placed into separate domiciles, they would run the risk of being morally contaminated by a combination of degrading surroundings and demoralized companions.[130]

In "cottage homes" housing from three to ten inmates, however, the aged would have more privacy, better health care, a more nutritious diet, and more individual freedom than in the workhouse. Such homes would eliminate the stigma of pauperism from those who had been industrious throughout their lives; no longer would the "deserving" fear the onset of old age. Nor would the establishment of a system of "cottage homes" for the elderly be excessively expensive. According to one reformer, three-quarters of the cost could be paid by the county and parish councils; parliament would contribute the final quarter.[131]

Nor were such ideas exactly new during the era of the "Great Depression." There was already a precedent for the separation of the "deserving" from the "undeserving" poor under the Victorian Poor Law. In 1865, the Poor Law Board issued a circular insisting upon the separation of sick wards from the rest of the workhouse; two years later, the Metropolitan Poor Act required separate asylums for the sick, insane, and infirm within London. Cambridge economist Alfred Marshall went even further in 1890 by arguing for the establishment of separate

---

[128] See Ellice Hopkins, "The Industrial Training of Pauper and Neglected Girls," *Contemporary Review* (July 1882); and Amelia Lewis, "Benevolence and Pauperism," *Dark Blue* (October 1871).

[129] See the Special Report of the Departmental Committee of the Local Government Board, "Maintenance and Education of Pauper Children" (1896 [c.8027], xliii).

[130] See James Pitt, "Convivial Pauperism," *St. Pauls* (February 1871); and H. Shaen Solly, "Poor Law Relief and Private Charity," *Modern Review* (April 1882).

[131] See John Hutton's "Cottage Homes for the Aged Poor," *Nineteenth Century* (April 1898); "The Aged Poor," *National Review* (March 1899); and Geoffrey Drage, "The Problem of the Aged Poor," *Fortnightly Review* (October 1899).

workhouses for worthy and unworthy paupers.[132] Such a program, Reverend Samuel Barnett of Toynbee Hall argued, would allow for the industrial training of the "deserving" and the disciplining of the idle and the incorrigible.[133] As a variant of William Booth's proposal, a number of reformers contended that the Poor Law should prepare "deserving," able-bodied paupers for migration overseas by giving them training in modern agricultural techniques.[134]

Most of these ideas about Poor Law reform had already been incorporated into the Viennese Poor Law. Public relief in the capital of the Austro-Hungarian empire served three classes of citizens—the young, the elderly, and the able-bodied. Viennese pauper children were boarded out with selected families; those older than sixty received a small pension. Among the able-bodied, "deserving" paupers were provided with technical training, advice, and, in many cases, public assistance to allow them to regain their independence; the "undeserving," however, were incarcerated in a nearby labor camp and placed under a rigorous "form of disciplinary supervision."[135]

An analysis of the similarities and differences between the Viennese Poor Law and the ideology of the Charity Organisation Society is highly instructive. Both favored the separation of the "deserving" from the "undeserving" poor, as the latter would otherwise demoralize the former. Both understood that pauperism was often the result of bad character. The COS, however, sharply disagreed with several aspects of the Viennese—and for that matter the Victorian—Poor Law. The distribution of old age pensions and outdoor relief to the unemployed, however respectable they might be, was a mistake. Private charity, not the State, should, ultimately, provide pensions and aid to the "deserving" poor; the Poor Law workhouse, once shorn of its charitable function, could then be transformed into a refuge of last resort for the most demoralized, idle, and intemperate segment of society.

Nor was the brand of liberalism expounded by the Charity Organisation Society far outside of the Victorian mainstream; indeed, whatever difficulties it had in eliminating indiscriminate charity and Poor Law outdoor relief after 1870, the

---

[132] Marshall was roundly criticized on the grounds that no workhouse should be made attractive to the poor and that he was confusing the role of the Poor Law with that of private charity ("Deserving Paupers," *The Economist* [13 September 1890], 1167).

[133] See Samuel A. Barnett's "Philanthropy and the Poor Law," *MacMillan's Magazine* (November 1891) and "Poor Law Reform," *Contemporary Review* (March 1893).

[134] See (London) *Times*, 22 September 1887; Harold Moore, "The Unemployed and the Land," *Contemporary Review* (March 1893); and W. R. Bousfield, "The Unemployed," *Contemporary Review* (December 1896).

[135] (London) *Times*, 5 December 1883. See also Louise Twining, "Some Facts on the Working of the Poor Law," *National Review* (June 1888); Earl Meath, "The Brabazon Pauper Employment Scheme," *Leisure Hour* (1889); Edith Sellers, "A Humane Poor Law," *MacMillan's Magazine* (February 1893); and Lara Marks, "Medical Care for Pauper Mothers and their Infants: Poor Law Provision and Local Demand in East London, 1870-1929," *Economic History Review* 1993 46 (3): 518-42.

COS in many ways set the ideological parameters for the discussion of poverty, pauperism, philanthropy, and the State during the late Victorian period.[136] At the heart of the COS's social philosophy was the firm belief that the solution to the Social Question had to be left to the private sector. Their faith in national progress and in the efficacy of individual self-help remained unimpaired during the final decades of the nineteenth century. In addition, the COS assumed that only the private sector could, or would be willing to, undertake the personal investigations necessary to distinguish the "deserving" poor from their idle companions. In this context, the Poor Law—the most important form of Victorian State welfare—had proven to be a monumental failure; for the COS, the Poor Law, particularly through its continued practice of outdoor relief, demoralized the poor and, thus, made their moral reformation that much more difficult. The COS did not believe that other State welfare initiatives would fare any better. Although legislation might do something, much even, towards putting down abuses in the industrial system, parliament should leave the moral and material elevation of the poorer classes to private philanthropy.

For a small, but growing, number of critics—both socialists and Radical Liberals—the policies advocated by the Charity Organisation Society seemed hardhearted. In their estimation, the COS refused to recognize that poverty resulted from a combination of social, economic, and moral factors. This being the case, it was logical for such reformers to press for legislation that would provide a more level playing field for all segments of British society. Turning COS social philosophy on its head, the economist John A. Hobson commented in 1896 that

Only upon the supposition that environment affords equal opportunities for all can we possess a test of personal fitness. Then only should we be justified, after due allowance for accidental causes, in attributing the evil plight of the poor or the unemployed to personal defects of character.[137]

An examination of the extent to which the Victorians were willing to discard liberal individualism and adopt the principles which underlie the twentieth-century Welfare State follows in the next three chapters.

---

[136] See Robert Humphreys' *Sin, Organized Charity, and the Poor Law in Victorian England* (New York, 1995) for a detailed description of the problems the COS had in convincing the Victorians to adopt their brand of charitable reform prior to 1890.

[137] John A. Hobson, "The Social Philosophy of the Charity Organisation Society," *Contemporary Review* (November 1896), 726.

Chapter 5

Socialist Theory, the Labour Movement, and Social Reform

Whereas the parameters and goals of private charity were relatively well-defined, the same could not be said of the socialist movement. The term "socialism," indeed, seems to have been extraordinarily difficult for the Victorians to define precisely. Often it was confused with mere social reform. The Charity Organisation Society's comment in 1885 that "Socialism is the hobby of the day" and Liberal politician William Harcourt's alleged exclamation three years later that "We are all Socialists now" should both be understood in this context.[1] Fabian Socialist Sidney Webb muddied the waters further by arguing in 1891 that England was already a socialist country. In his estimation, democracy and industrialization had forced the passage of a great deal of collectivist legislation: factory, sanitary, local government, housing, and education acts; public ownership of gas and water services and public works; and heightened taxes on rent, interest, and real estate to name just a few. For most Britons, the progress of socialism had been entirely unconscious; according to Webb, "the great majority of citizens are still quite unaware of the extent to which Individualist principles have been abandoned."[2] Although *laissez-faire* might be dead, the "Individualist Town Councillor" still remarked with assurance: "Socialism, sir... don't waste the time of a practical

---

[1] *Charity Organisation Review*, October 1885, 417. See also A. G. Gardiner, *Life of Sir William Harcourt* (London, 1923), 1:90. Although Gardiner does not provide a date or a source for this famous utterance, the phrase had been attributed to Harcourt as early as 1889 in Hubert Bland's essay in *Fabian Essays in Socialism*. For another example of the way socialism was misconstrued at the time, see W. Rhys Cole, "Should Capitalists Advocate State Socialism?" *Westminster Review* (March 1895).

[2] Sidney Webb, *Socialism in England* (1891, Reprint Edition, London, 1987), 2.

man by your fantastic absurdities. Self-help, sir, individual self-help, that's what's made our city what it is."[3] The very imprecision with which the term "socialism" was used has confused historians of late Victorian social reform. As long as it could be "made to mean anything from the Gospel of Dynamite to a proposal to act upon certain principles which everybody has been pretending to accept for eighteen hundred years and more," socialism would continue to perplex those seeking to understand it.[4]

Perhaps partially for this reason, the most popular book advocating socialism to the late Victorians, Robert Blatchford's *Merrie England* published in 1893, sharply distinguishes between social reform and socialism. For Blatchford, the "Condition of England" was such that only radical reforms could save British society from self-destruction. Blatchford advocated a typical socialist program: universal suffrage, payment of members of parliament and their election expenses, an eight-hour day for workers, public works, pensions for the elderly, municipal housing, free schools, the taxation of ground values, a progressive income tax, and the nationalization of land, mines, railroads, and the drink traffic.[5] These reforms would, in Blatchford's estimation, represent a long first step towards socialism.

Even so, the supposed evils of capitalism—brutal competition, uncertain and scanty wages, and social inequality—would not be overcome by such inadequate measures. Capitalism would still be upheld by the greedy tyrants, robbers, libertines, and sweaters who had always profited from it. Blatchford realized that to shore up capitalism by social reform was counterproductive. The famed playwright Oscar Wilde agreed that not only would modest reform fail to cure the disease, it would prolong it; those reformers who seemed, therefore, to be doing the most good, were, according to Wilde, in fact doing the most harm. Socialists could no longer be satisfied merely to raise the material condition of the poor; their goal should be "to try and reconstruct society on such a basis that poverty will be impossible."[6] By casting off "industrial anarchy," Britain would be able to avoid the economic panics, depressions, and famines of the past; urban congestion, the unhealthy and demeaning factory system, and poverty would be eliminated forever. Once factories and farms were owned and managed by British workers for their own benefit, the "Juggernaut of our industry" would no longer advance "over the prostrate bodies of honest men, delicate women, and helpless children."[7] The lives of the working classes would, consequently, be immensely improved. They would finally be able to afford better education, food, and leisure with the advent of

---

[3] Ibid., 117.

[4] *Charity Organisation Reporter*, 5 April 1883, 105.

[5] *The Clarion*, December 1898.

[6] Oscar Wilde, *The Soul of Man under Socialism* (1891, Reprint Edition, London, 1912), 3. Karl Marx and Friedrich Engels also complained about "petty bourgeois socialism," which valued reform over revolution, in *The Communist Manifesto* of 1848.

[7] Alfred Hake, *Suffering London* (London, 1892), 159.

socialism.[8]

The rights of property would no longer be allowed to smother the rights of man. Workers would no longer be corrupted by vicious companions and a degraded environment. Old age—far more the cause of pauperism than laziness according to Blatchford—would no longer be considered a crime. Socialism, like Christianity in its purest form, would spread compassion, charity, humility, and social justice throughout British society. It would also bring about a state of true individualism, the freedom to develop one's soul, personality, and abilities to the fullest. Government would be reduced to a voluntary association meant to organize labor, manufacturing, and the distribution of necessities. The evolution of mankind—from slave to serf to wage-slave to freeman—would be complete with the establishment of socialism.[9]

Whether socialism would arise as the result of violence and revolution or through the peaceful process of gradual legislative change remained to be seen. What all socialists agreed upon was that it was coming, and sooner rather than later. England seemed to many observers to be ripe for socialism. The precarious position of its laboring poor, the expansion of political democracy, the great inequality of wealth in British society, and the rise of a revolutionary spirit within the proletariat all foretold a period of increasing class strife.[10] Although the urban poor were presently suffering in silence, they might not always do so.[11] An increasing number of workers wondered, according to the novelist George Gissing, at the disparity between the "rich and poor, the one . . . a class of brute beasts—of ignorant, besotted, starving, toil-worn creatures . . . the other . . . a class of lords and princes."[12] In the future, dissatisfaction with the *status quo* might turn to anger and passivity to revolution.

Although few workers were interested in the idea of violent revolution during the late Victorian period, many more were attracted by the quasi-religious elements of socialism. As much as a platform for political and economic change, socialism was, at root, a system of ethics. By moralizing political economy, socialism would uplift mankind. Viewed from this perspective, the rhetoric of "conversions," the "gospel of socialism," and the association of the coming revolution with the second coming of Christ becomes more intelligible. Simply put, one's soul had to be

---

[8] See Robert Blatchford's *Merrie England* (London, 1893) and *Dismal England* (London, 1899).

[9] See Oscar Wilde, *The Soul of Man under Socialism* (1891, Reprint Edition, London, 1912); William Clarke, "The Limits of Collectivism," *Contemporary Review* (February 1893); and R. Didden, "Individualism and Collectivism," *Westminster Review* (June 1898). None of the ideas in the works of Blatchford or Wilde were all that new. Karl Marx and Friedrich Engels had laid down the tenets of modern socialism—class conflict, consciousness, and revolution—as early as 1848 in *The Communist Manifesto*.

[10] See John R. Rae, *Contemporary Socialism* (New York, 1884).

[11] See A. S. Krausse, *Starving London* (London, 1886).

[12] George Gissing, *Workers in the Dawn* (London, 1880), 2:15.

prepared for socialism in much the same way as for Heaven.[13]

Not surprisingly, the Christian Socialist movement made the closest connection between the ideology of the Christian Church and that of socialism. This association did not, in their estimation, begin with Christ. According to the *Jewish Standard*, "Judaism preaches Socialism in its best sense, and, long before the phrase was invented, taught the truth itself, that 'the greatest happiness of the greatest number is the foundation of morals and legislation.' Never have there been such Socialists as the Hebrew prophets."[14] As Christianity built upon the Jewish model, it followed that "if you want to be a good Christian, you must be something very much like a good Socialist."[15] By stressing peace, forgiveness, compassion, charity, and equality, Christianity strengthened the moral fiber of the people and made possible the union of all social classes.[16]

The problem lay in the fact that so many Victorians disregarded the "one great unfailing remedy for all the ills of this poor suffering world—Christ's Gospel."[17] Modern industrialists and entrepreneurs were, according to some critics, anti-Christian. A quick perusal of Christian theology should convince them that the "owners" of land and capital in fact owned nothing; they were mere trustees during their own lifetimes. The question they ought to ask themselves, therefore, was not how much wealth they ought to retain for their own personal use, but how much they should give to charity in order to insure themselves a place in Heaven after death.[18] Furthermore, if capitalists espoused Christian doctrine, the British economy would finally become accountable to a higher, more moral law than the "survival of the fittest." Until that time, the poor would continue to suffer from the selfishness, greed, inhumanity, and sinfulness which permeated the industrial middle and upper classes.[19]

The Christian Socialist movement, unlike many of its counterparts during the late Victorian period, was not highly political. Personal moral reformation would create a better world, not revolutionary violence or expensive social programs. Indeed, its leaders—F. D. Maurice, Charles Kingsley, John Ruskin, Stewart Headlam, and Hugh Price Hughes—believed that "applied" Christianity would reduce the threat of both revolution and State expansion by creating a brotherhood of man. Christian Socialism would represent the best of, and temper the excesses

---

[13] See Stephen Yeo's seminal article, "A New Life: The Religion of Socialism in Britain," *History Workshop* 1977 (4): 5-56.

[14] *Jewish Standard*, 20 December 1889, 8.

[15] Stewart Headlam, "Christian Socialism," *Fabian Tract*, no. 42 (London, 1899), 472.

[16] See Moritz Kaufmann, "The Theory of Christian Socialism," *British Quarterly Review* (October 1884).

[17] Olivia Bennet, Countess of Tankerville, *From the Depths* (London, 1885), 21.

[18] See Rabbi Hermann Adler, Henry Cardinal Manning, and Hugh Price Hughes, "Irresponsible Wealth," *Nineteenth Century* (December 1890).

[19] See Reverend Christopher Carruthers, *The Root of the Matter, or the Only Cure for the Bitter Cry of Outcast London* (London, 1884).

of, both individualism and socialism.[20]

A few individual Christian Socialists supported "gas and water socialism" or other mild welfare measures. Many more—like Stewart Headlam, the head of the oldest socialist organization in Britain, the Guild of St. Matthew founded in 1877—although having little sympathy for organized labor, supported the land reform proposals of Henry George.[21] Overall, however, the Christian Socialist movement represented the least revolutionary, most innocuous form of Victorian socialism. While calling for the moralization of the British economy and society, it provided no machinery for the enforcement of its desires. Its role was more that of a gadfly than a real threat to the British *status quo*. In one way, the Christian Socialists did have a significant impact; by tethering socialism to Christianity, they made it seem a bit more respectable.[22]

Whereas the Christian Socialist movement had little impact on the course and direction of British socialism, the writings of an American born in Philadelphia, Henry George, certainly did. One commentator remarked in 1884 that George had "done more than any other single person to stir and deepen in this country an agitation which, if not socialistic, at least promises to be a mother of socialism."[23] Twelve years later, the Liberal reformer John A. Hobson stated that "Henry George may be considered to have exercised a more directly powerful formative and educative influence over English radicalism of the last fifteen years than any other man."[24] What George did was to dispel the idea that the State could do little to eliminate poverty; as all poverty, in George's estimation, was caused by the maldistribution of economic resources, not by the working of some vague natural law, it could be cured by a simple piece of legislation—the "single tax."

In his most important work, *Progress and Poverty*, which was published in 1879, George explained the reasoning behind the "single tax." His study of the causes of modern industrial depressions concluded that distress rose along with wealth for one simple reason—as production and wealth increased, so too did the cost of renting land. This was why the productive advances of the nineteenth century had failed to end poverty. Rent increases forced down real wages to the starvation level, reduced industrial profits, and made it extremely difficult for many workers to afford decent housing.[25] George's solution was to confiscate rent

---

[20] See E. H. Plumptre, "Christianity and Socialism," *Contemporary Review* (November 1889); John Clifford, "Socialism and the Teaching of Christ," *Fabian Tract*, no. 78 (London, 1897); and the best recent book on the subject, E. Norman's *Victorian Christian Socialists* (New York, 1987).

[21] See Stewart Headlam, "Christian Socialism," *Fabian Tract*, no. 42 (London, 1899).

[22] See Peter d'A. Jones, *The Christian Socialist Revival* (Princeton, N.J., 1968).

[23] John Rae, *Contemporary Socialism* (New York, 1884), vi.

[24] John A. Hobson, "The Influence of Henry George on England," *Fortnightly Review* (December 1897), 844.

[25] The connection George made between land and poverty was not exactly new; in 1796, Tom Paine, in his work *Agrarian Justice*, had cited the accumulation of landed property into a few hands as a major cause of poverty in Europe.

through the "single tax." Landlords would no longer be able to live off of the so-called "unearned increment"; workers would receive increased purchasing power because they would no longer have to pay exorbitant rent or taxes. At the same time, their employers' increased profits could be devoted to expanding industrial productivity.[26] With the "single tax," society would be more just and prosperous; without it, George feared for the future. "Civilization, as it progresses, *requires* a higher conscience, a keener sense of justice, a warmer brotherhood, a wider, loftier, truer public spirit. Failing these, civilization must pass into destruction. It cannot be maintained on the ethics of savagery."[27]

Many social critics, although impressed by George's ideas, saw them as only a hesitant first step. The real goal should not be the confiscation of rent, but land nationalization.[28] Some favored immediate nationalization, while others argued that it should be accomplished over a long period of time; some supported the paying of compensation to dispossessed landlords, while others did not. However land was to be nationalized, most believed that increased revenue from land-rent would allow the State to provide a host of social reforms—pensions for the elderly and better education for British children in particular—without having to raise consumer taxes unduly.[29] Land reform might also help alleviate unemployment. Local government authorities could buy land and distribute it as small holdings to the unemployed or underemployed at a reasonable rent. Over time, these small farmers might be allowed to buy their own land, an action which promoted political and economic stability, and also fostered a sense of responsibility, duty, and virtue.[30]

Whether one can justifiably consider Henry George a socialist is debatable. He did not intend to reduce inequalities of wealth due to genius, thrift, or industry. He was no revolutionary; indeed, George viewed the fact that the "single tax" could be implemented without bloodshed as a major point in its favor. He did not doubt, however, that the enactment of the "single tax" would bring about an enormous improvement in the "Condition of England" without recourse to the vast expansion

---

[26] See Henry George, *Progress and Poverty* (New York, 1879).

[27] Henry George, *Social Problems* (New York, 1883), 241.

[28] See A. J. Wilson, "Reciprocity: The Best Remedy for the Present Industrial Distress," *MacMillan's Magazine* (April 1879). For an earlier view, see William Volckman, *The Prevention of Poverty* (London, 1873). Volckman thought land ought to be gradually nationalized over sixty years.

[29] See Joseph Hyder, *The Curse of Landlordism and How to Remove It* (London, 1895). Hyder believed that rising revenues from increased land-values would allow the State to buy land without having to resort to higher taxes. See also Spencer Jackson, *Landlord Abuses and a Plan for the Extinction of Landlordism* (London, 1885).

[30] See J. T. Emmet, "Town Holdings," *Quarterly Review* (January 1893). Several newspapers, *Land and Labour* and *The Democrat* of the Land Restoration League in particular, argued strongly that as the land monopoly robbed—through its collection of rent—both capital and labor of its resources, it should be destroyed.

of the State. At the same time, George remained agnostic about the potentialities of State socialism. In 1885, he commented that if, following the passage of the "single tax," it were "found expedient to go further on the lines of Socialism, we could do so."[31] What is obvious is the enormous impact his work had on the discussion of the Social Question during the late Victorian period. Liberals Joseph Chamberlain and John A. Hobson, Fabian Socialists Sidney Webb and George Bernard Shaw, novelists William Morris and H. G. Wells, and Labour leaders John Burns and Tom Mann all attested to the power and persuasiveness of George's "single tax" idea. For more than one historian, indeed, Henry George almost single-handedly set off the socialist revival of the early 1880s.[32]

One Victorian socialist who was initially quite taken with Henry George's land reform program was Henry M. Hyndman. In 1881, Hyndman founded the Democratic Federation to promote land reform in England. Within two years, however, Hyndman had decided that Henry George's "single tax" did not go far enough; from 1883, the Social Democratic Federation adhered to the socialism of Karl Marx. Even so, many elements of the SDF platform sounded very much like traditional Victorian radicalism: universal adult suffrage, annual parliaments, proportional representation, payment of members' parliamentary election expenses, the making of corrupt practices at elections a felony, and the elimination of the national debt. Other proposals were a bit more controversial: the abolition of the House of Lords and all hereditary authorities, the disestablishment of all State churches, the establishment of national and federal parliaments, and legislative independence for Ireland.

By no means did Hyndman stop at mere radical reform. He called for the nationalization of large portions of the British economy: all land, railroads, shipping, money and credit, mines, workshops, and factories. Hyndman also argued in favor of an eight-hour workday, free compulsory education with one free meal per day at Board Schools, the construction of municipal artisans' dwellings to be let at cost, cumulative taxation on all annual incomes over £300, public works for the unemployed, pensions for the aged, and the reform of the Poor Law so as to make it more educational and less penal.[33]

Hyndman justified his program of State socialism by resorting to a host of

---

[31] Henry George, "Socialism and Rent-Appropriation," *Nineteenth Century* (February 1885), 377-78. See also George Sarson, "Progress and Poverty," *Modern Review* (January 1883).

[32] See J. Plowright, "Political Economy and Christian Polity," *Victorian Studies* 1987 30 (2): 235-52; and Peter d'A. Jones, "Henry George and British Socialism," *American Journal of Economics and Sociology* 1988 47 (4): 473-91.

[33] See *Socialism Made Plain* (London, 1883); and Henry M. Hyndman, "Wealth and Ability: A Rejoinder," *Fortnightly Review* (November 1887).

traditional Marxist arguments.[34] As labor alone created wealth, any form of capital gains or rent was robbery. Why should the producers of wealth be poor, while idle, nonproducers lived in luxury? Why should British workers continue to be enslaved by capitalism, poverty, and economic uncertainty? Why should they tolerate being overworked, badly fed, ill-clothed, and indecently housed? As capitalism seemed indifferent to the public good, the State had to intervene on behalf of the working classes. The nationalization of land and industry was not theft, but a form of restitution for all the wealth that had been drained away from the working classes in the past.

By substituting organized cooperation for industrial anarchy, "every worker would get at least four times his present wages for half his present work."[35] British workers would live and work in a safer, more secure, and healthier environment. To this end, according to Hyndman, "the greater part of our modern cities will have to be completely destroyed" as "fresh air is a necessity for healthy existence."[36] Workers would also experience a burst of freedom and enlightenment of which they had previously only dreamed. "Imagine the glorious freedom which would be the lot of each when, the task of social work complete, and done under healthy and pleasant conditions, the worker turned to science, literature, art, gymnastics, to what he would, for the joyous hours of leisure."[37]

Like Marx, Hyndman had no patience for those who merely wished to reform capitalism. The Social Democratic Federation, thus, opposed the trade union movement. Hyndman was astounded by their political apathy and by their preoccupation with wages, hours, and working conditions. They did not seem to understand that "Wage-slaves under better conditions" remained "wage-slaves still; and the causes of the economic and class antagonism remain untouched by any half-measures."[38] Hyndman regarded Labourism to be, in short, "a sorry attempt to 'dish' Socialism."[39] Nor, for Hyndman, did the Radical Liberals or Fabian Socialists provide a better alternative. The notion that the "bourgeois socialism" of Joseph Chamberlain meant real reform was, for Hyndman, simply laughable. In addition, "To speak of municipal Socialism," a favorite topic of the Fabians, "as

---

[34] See Kirk Willis, "The Introduction and Critical Reception of Marxist Thought," *Historical Journal* 1977 20 (2): 417-59.

[35] *Justice*, 30 August 1884, 1.

[36] Henry Hyndman, *The Economics of Socialism* (London, 1896), 252.

[37] Annie Besant, *Modern Socialism* (London, 1890), 50. See also Henry Hyndman's *The Social Reconstruction of England* (London, 1884) and "Socialism and Rent-Appropriation," *Nineteenth Century* (February 1885); and Henry Hyndman and Charles Bradlaugh, *Will Socialism Benefit the English People?* (London, 1884).

[38] Henry Hyndman, *The Commercial Crises of the Nineteenth Century* (1892, Reprint Edition, London, 1902), 173. See also Mark Bevir, "The British Social Democratic Federation, 1880-1885," *International Review of Social History* 1992 37 (2): 207-29.

[39] *Justice*, 28 July 1894, 4.

a solution of the social question, even temporarily," was "the baldest twaddle."[40]

How Socialism would come to pass in England was a matter of some debate, even within the ranks of the Social Democratic Federation. Political democratization might allow the working classes to bring about socialism through peaceful legislative change.[41] Socialism might arise in response to a serious political crisis or during a period of social anarchy. Hyndman believed that a "serious foreign war would very soon bring the whole to a head; for assuredly the mass of Englishmen would never again submit to heavy sacrifices which would only benefit the governing classes."[42] If the "governing classes" resisted, Britain might have "to face . . . another such period of rioting and suppressed civil war" as during the Chartist period.[43] Inciting the British working classes to revolt was not, except for a brief moment during the mid-1880s, considered a realistic policy by the SDF. Hyndman realized that the State was far too strong to be toppled by a handful of Social Democratic revolutionaries.

Indeed, during the 1880s, the Social Democratic Federation could only count on about one thousand dues-paying members; like the rest of the London socialist movement of the late Victorian era, the SDF was essentially a "stage army"; it had many leaders, but few followers. Furthermore, in 1884, several of the founders of the SDF left the organization, citing Hyndman's dictatorial personality and revolutionary rhetoric. From that year, therefore, Hyndman headed an organization that was smaller, more ideologically pure, and highly hierarchical, but also, for all of these reasons, less influential. William Morris—who, along with Karl Marx's daughter Eleanor and her lover, Edward Aveling, left the SDF in 1884—soon established the Socialist League in London.

Unfortunately for Morris and his colleagues, the Socialist League was even less successful than the SDF in attracting a mass following. Although his goal was to "make" socialists, only about five hundred people joined the League during the latter half of the 1880s. The Socialist League was most important, therefore, as a forum for William Morris's literary talents. During the next few years, Morris described his vision of a socialist utopia. After a bloody civil war between the classes, Morris argued, capitalism would finally be overthrown. His ideal society would be free of polluted factories, towns, private property, poverty, vice, crime, parliaments, and even nations. In an atmosphere of peace, fraternity, and fellowship, each individual would be allowed to pursue his own happiness and enlightenment. All could fulfill their potential because none would be overworked, undereducated, or forced to live in an inhumane social environment. All would

---

[40] *Justice*, 26 September 1891, 1. See also *Justice*, 29 September 1888, 1.

[41] See Henry Hyndman, *The Historical Basis of Socialism in England* (1883, Reprint Edition, New York, 1984); and *Justice*, 6 July 1895.

[42] Henry Hyndman, *The Coming Revolution in England* (London, 1884), 31. See also Hyndman's *England for All* (London, 1881).

[43] Henry Hyndman, "English Workers as They Are," *Contemporary Review* (July 1887), 135.

benefit from increased freedom and leisure, clean air, and open spaces. Well-being and morality would go hand-in-hand as it was in everyone's interest to see that all were happy and productive.[44]

Morris's attitude towards social reform and State socialism followed from his belief in rural communism. Like Marx and Hyndman, Morris decried those who attempted to uphold capitalism by tinkering with reform. Unlike Hyndman, however, Morris looked beyond State socialism; for Morris, as for Marx and Engels, State control of the means of production, distribution, and exchange was only a transitional stage along the road to communism. Still, Morris recognized that it might take generations for the people to shake free of the capitalist mind-set; only when the masses had been educated to think in terms of the good of the community would communism become practicable. At that point, according to Morris, the State would wither away.[45]

In 1890, the Socialist League was taken over by a group of anarchists, prompting Morris's immediate resignation. Within a couple of months, the League and its newspaper, *The Commonweal*, had gone bankrupt. Nor was the anarchist movement any more successful in most of its other initiatives during the late Victorian period. Like Morris, the anarchists—a small, uninfluential wing of Victorian socialism—rejected capitalism, the State, and the social hierarchy. Unlike Morris's League or any other portion of the Socialist movement save, perhaps, Hyndman's Social Democratic Federation, the anarchists were portrayed in the popular press in an extraordinarily negative light. Being continually pictured as lunatics, beasts at war with society, and terrorists willing to resort to murder to attain their ends, it is no wonder that mainstream socialists wished to have nothing to do with them.[46] The danger of assassination at the hands of the anarchists was, however, greatly exaggerated. As Robert Blatchford commented in 1892, the anarchists "are not very dangerous, and seldom murder anybody or anything—except the English language. They speak dynamite, but use none."[47]

Perhaps this was part of the problem. Already suffering from an extremely bad reputation, the anarchists did not help their cause by issuing comments like: "we are fully convinced that workers will never better their condition without the

---

[44] See William Morris's *News from Nowhere, or an Epoch of Rest* (Hammersmith, England, 1892), and "True and False Society" (1888) and "Useful Work" (1885) in *The Political Writings of William Morris* (London, 1984). Morris's title was obviously derived from Sir Thomas More's *Utopia* (1516); the Greek phrase "ou topos" could be translated as "nowhere" or "no place."

[45] See William Morris, *Signs of Change* (London, 1888).

[46] See Haia Shpayer-Markov, "Anarchism in British Public Opinion, 1880-1914," *Victorian Studies* 1988 31 (4): 487-516. Several British novelists picked up on the theme of anarchism as a danger to society. See Robert Louis Stevenson's *The Dynamiter* (London, 1885); and Joseph Conrad's *Secret Agent* (London, 1907).

[47] *The Clarion*, 14 May 1892, 1.

use of [violence], or without showing that they are in a position to use it."[48] Advocating the use of violence to preserve and protect human freedom—while insisting that capitalist society represented a never-ending war on the working classes—adopting the "Torch of Anarchy" as the title of one of their most popular journals, and exclaiming that "of all political parties we are the *only* real Revolutionaries" did little to improve their image.[49]

As far as their political program was concerned, the anarchists were no more radical than many other socialist organizations. Like William Morris, they envisioned a system of independent, self-supporting communes with labor organized on the principle of equality and land, factories, and dwellings held in common. Such a system would ensure, they believed, individual freedom, equality, and the brotherhood of man. Anything less would be wholly unacceptable.[50] The anarchists, therefore, agreed whole-heartedly with Hyndman, Morris, and others that "Reform, parliamentary and diplomatic law-making is not Socialism, not even a step towards it."[51] They were contemptuous of both Liberals and Tories and their

> stale old twaddle and outworn cant,
> The trumpery tinsel of warlike glory,
> The 'Peace, Reform, Retrenchment' rant.[52]

While capitalism survived, the "Condition of England" would not improve very much. Charity and social reform at most tinkered around the edges of the problem; they did not touch the true causes of poverty. Similarly, State socialism was not an end in and of itself; political anarchy and communism took socialism to its proper conclusion.

One last socialist organization worthy of consideration is the Fabian Society, which was founded in London in 1884.[53] For a number of reasons, historians have given the Fabians an unjustifiable prominence within the social debates of late Victorian era. The presence of George Bernard Shaw and Sidney and Beatrice Potter Webb among their ranks ensured that their scholarship would be taken seriously. Their policy of gradual reform placated those troubled by the specter of violent revolution. In addition, the Fabians' idea that they could "permeate" the existing Victorian political structure reassured their contemporaries, and later historians, that this, at least, was not a radical form of socialism. Not surprisingly,

---

[48] *Liberty: A Journal of Anarchist Communism*, January 1894, 2.
[49] See *The Torch of Anarchy*, 18 November 1894; to most Victorians the "Torch" was meant to burn down, not to enlighten, capitalist society.
[50] See *Party Politics and the Social Question: A Word to the Workers* (London, 1885).
[51] *Freedom*, August 1889, 35.
[52] *Freedom*, July 1888, 87.
[53] The Fabian Society took its name from the Roman general Quintus Fabius Maximus, who foiled Hannibal for a time during the Second Punic War by refusing to engage the Carthaginians in open battle.

historians have often associated Fabian Socialism with "Tory Democracy," Radical Liberalism, and the ideology of the Independent Labour Party. More than this, historians have argued that the Fabian Society was central to the supposed ideological shift of the late Victorian era. Nothing could be farther from the truth.

The Fabian Society proposed a host of reforms, none of them all that original. Many dealt with the political system: adult suffrage, an end to plural voting, and the payment of members of parliament and their election expenses. Others concerned taxation: lower customs and excise taxes, a higher land tax, the establishment of a tax on "unearned" income, heavy death duties, and a progressive income tax. The Fabians also favored free education and meals for school children; the enforcement of the factory, workshop, and sanitary acts; public works; increased aid for the aged, children, the sick, and the temporarily unemployed under the Poor Law; and technical training for the chronically unemployed. Workers would also be given the opportunity to decide whether or not they wanted an eight hour workday. Most important, the Fabians supported the municipalization or nationalization of land and many industries: canals, railroads, water and gas companies, tramways, hospitals, docks, baths, markets, libraries, and common lodging houses. Parish councils should be granted the power to buy land, build houses, run charities, and administer cooperative farms.[54] By the early 1900s, Sidney Webb was calling for a national labor exchange to provide information on shortages and surpluses of labor, the elimination of employment for children under fifteen, the limitation of employment for those under eighteen to at most thirty hours a week, and a forty-eight-hour workweek for rail, tram, and omnibus workers. Mothers with young children should receive enough governmental assistance to support themselves without having to work. Even the "residuum" were to be maintained, as long as they submitted to industrial or agricultural training; the remainder were to be consigned to detention colonies administered by the State.[55]

Although the Fabian Society showed little theoretical originality in the realm of economics or social philosophy and few of their reforms went beyond the parameters imposed by the Radical Liberal tradition, they were markedly different from their Liberal counterparts in one vital area. Simply stated, the Fabians wished to overturn capitalist society, eliminate private property, and establish a socialist system of government. George Bernard Shaw argued in 1890 that society must be organized so as to minimize man's wicked tendencies: selfishness, greed, and the exploitation of others. By intervening aggressively in the economy, the State would be able to provide increased freedom, equality, and economic opportunity

---

[54] See George Bernard Shaw, Sidney Webb, et al. *Fabian Essays in Socialism* (London, 1889); and Sidney Webb's "Facts for Londoners," *Fabian Tract*, no. 8 (London, 1889) and *The London Programme* (London, 1891).

[55] See Sidney and Beatrice Webb, *The Public Organisation of the Labour Market* (London, 1909).

to the working classes.[56]

The State that began by appropriating the "unearned increment" for public use, so that all of London's poor could be well-housed and all of her children be educated and fed free of charge, would some day, Shaw and Sidney Webb hoped, nationalize the means of production, industry, and capital.[57] At that time, even "ability" would be nationalized; the State, according to Shaw, could employ entrepreneurs and inventors as well as any private company, and for a more reasonable salary.[58] Like William Morris of the Socialist League, the Fabians wished to "make" socialists; unlike Morris, they intended to preach socialism not to the workers, but to the press, educated public opinion, and parliament.

The connection between the Fabian Society and individual members of both the Liberal and Conservative parties was quite close. Sidney Webb, a former first division clerk at the Colonial Office, counted among his friends the Radical Liberal Richard B. Haldane and, through him, the future Prime Minister Herbert Asquith and the future Foreign Secretary Sir Edward Grey as well. Webb also ingratiated himself with Arthur J. Balfour, the nephew of Conservative Prime Minister Lord Salisbury and himself a future prime minister. Sidney Webb's wife, Beatrice, had, in addition to serving as one of Charles Booth's investigators, for a time been an object of matrimonial interest to the Radical former mayor of Birmingham Joseph Chamberlain; within a few years of rejecting his offer of marriage, Beatrice had married Sidney Webb, thus beginning a partnership of nearly fifty years.

During the 1890s, the Webbs sought to "permeate" the Conservative Party. It was in power much of the time; its ideology was less wedded to individualism than the Gladstonian Liberal Party, and a number of Radical politicians—including Joseph Chamberlain—had joined Lord Salisbury following the Home Rule crisis of 1886.[59] The Fabians were, however, willing to take support wherever they found it. In February 1887, the Fabian Society founded a parliamentary league to help socialistic candidates win election to the House of Commons; until Britain had a truly socialist party, it would, according to George Bernard Shaw, be necessary for the Fabians to work within the existing political system.[60]

Somewhat surprisingly, the Fabians kept their distance from both the Labour movement—taking no part in the trade union revivals of 1889 or 1911—and

---

[56] See George Bernard Shaw's *The Road to Equality: Ten Unpublished Lectures and Essays* (Boston, 1971), particularly the essays which he wrote between 1887 and 1890.

[57] See Sidney Webb, "Figures for Londoners," *Fabian Tract* no. 10 (London, 1889).

[58] See George Bernard Shaw, "Mr. Mallock's Proposed Trumphet Performance," *Fortnightly Review* (April 1894).

[59] The Fabians often attacked the right wing of the Liberal Party—Whigs, diehards, and Manchester liberals—accusing them of thwarting the efforts of their more progressive colleagues (see, for instance, Sidney Webb and George Bernard Shaw, "To Your Tents, O Israel," *Fortnightly Review* [November 1893]).

[60] See George Bernard Shaw, *The Fabian Society: Its Early History* (1892, Reprint Edition, London, 1899).

the Independent Labour Party following its establishment in 1893. Indeed, unlike Marx and most other socialists, the Fabians did not even pretend to have faith in the wisdom of the proletariat or in their willingness to support the expansion of the State.[61] Their brand of nonproletarian, non-Marxist, middle-class socialism expected that capitalism would be overthrown as a result of administrative and legislative reform, not through revolution in the streets. Having only between one and two hundred active members during the late Victorian period, the Fabian Society could not have organized or led the working classes to power even had it been so inclined. "Permeation," however, would allow the Fabians to have an impact by spreading socialist ideas throughout the British political class.[62]

The Fabians recognized, as had Hyndman and the rest of the Victorian socialists, the difficulty of rousing the British working classes. As one critic noted, "it is most improbable that there will ever be a revolution in Britain. The majority of the lower classes have, if it be little, still sufficient to lose, to be ready to risk it in any untried methods of Government."[63] Workers did not believe property, rent, or capital to be "theft"; they were not at war with capitalist society. They did not even look to the State for answers to the Social Question.[64] In consequence, few among the laboring masses had a fondness for socialism. "Workmen of spirit," one commentator noted, "regard State Socialism as the small-pox of servility."[65] Those who did on occasion attend socialist meetings often did so for reasons other than real enthusiasm for the overthrow of capitalism. For the novelist William Pett Ridge, workers "come in a bit when it's wet, but they don't come then out of any love for the cause."[66] As the labor leader Henry Hyde Champion remarked in 1889, the British working classes were largely content to progress along traditional lines. They had "seen that the slow and steady methods of trade union and

---

[61] Beatrice Webb, according to one of her critics, had contempt both for the "so-called Socialist movement" and traditional trade unionists (Geoffrey Drage, "Mrs. Sidney Webb's Attack on the Labour Commission," *Nineteenth Century* [September 1894], 455).

[62] See Alan MacBriar, *Fabian Socialism and English Politics, 1884-1918* (Cambridge, England, 1962); Eric Hobsbawm's *Labouring Men* (New York, 1964) and *Worlds of Labour* (London, 1984); and W. Wolfe, *From Radicalism to Socialism* (New Haven, Conn., 1975).

[63] G. Rome Hall, "The Present Feeling of the Working Classes," *National Review* (July 1889), 672.

[64] See J. E. Thorold-Rodgers, "Contemporary Socialism," *Contemporary Review* (January 1885). Thorold-Rodgers doubted the wisdom of the working classes only with regard to the land question. See also Percy Greg, "The Conservative Instincts of the English People: Working Classes," *National Review* (July 1883). Greg argued that property, order, individualism, and imperialism all appealed to workers much more than either Radicalism or socialism.

[65] George Holyoake, "State Socialism," *Nineteenth Century* (June 1879), 1119. Contrary to popular opinion, education had awakened the independence and individualism of the working classes. What they, therefore, most objected to was "the attempt to capture Trade Unionism for State Socialism" (*The Trade Unionist*, October 1899, 1).

[66] William Pett Ridge, *Mord Em'ly* (London, 1898), 138.

constitutional action have secured for him solid material advantages, while the fine theories and violent declamations of Continental Socialists have left them in a state of comparative impotence and disorganization."[67]

Consequently, the most widely recognized remedy for economic uncertainty among the working classes was the expansion of the trade union movement. Unions gave workers an opportunity to agitate for higher wages, better conditions, and fewer hours on the job. Trade unions also served as benefit societies by providing aid to sick, injured, and unemployed members. In addition, many unions kept registries that helped distribute work among its members.[68] Trade unions empowered workers to look to themselves for the betterment of their condition; in doing so, they served as a strong barrier to the growth of revolutionary sentiment within the working classes.[69]

Although some employers argued that trade unions reduced profits, drove up unemployment, and made their workers lazy and irresponsible, public opinion generally supported the idea of unionism by the late Victorian era.[70] With the "wage-fund" theory—which argued that higher wages inevitably led to increased unemployment—finally popularly discredited by the late 1870s, workers could press for better pay and a shorter workday with a clear conscience. Nor was this all; for a growing number of economists and reformers, increased wages and shorter hours for the working classes would have a beneficial impact on the economy as a whole. Higher wages would increase demand in the home market for consumer goods. The rising cost of labor, by spurring industrial concentration and innovation, would raise British productivity. Furthermore, well-paid, well-rested laborers tended to be more productive than their "sweated" counterparts. In essence, "association raises the 'morale' of the employed, disciplines and educates them, and by rendering their work more intelligent, increases its value."[71] Furthermore, many believed that a shortened workday would absorb the unemployed and underemployed and thus eliminate the cause of much distress. Neither profits, production, nor Britain's industrial competitiveness would be affected by higher wages; neither prices nor unemployment would rise as a result

---

[67] Henry H. Champion, "An Eight Hour Law," *Nineteenth Century* (September 1889), 511.

[68] Sixty-two percent of unions provided unemployment benefits and thirty percent had sickness coverage or pensions in 1908. The latter figure was so much lower largely because many union workers also belonged to Friendly Societies (George Boyer, "What Did Unions Do in Nineteenth Century Britain?" *Journal of Economic History* 1988 48 [2]: 320-21).

[69] James Oliphant, compiler, *The Claims of Labour* (Edinburgh, Scotland, 1886), 36.

[70] For example, see Guilford Molesworth, "Political Economy and Its Relation to Strikes," *National Review* (February 1890).

[71] The Fifth Report of the Royal Commission *On Labour* (1894, xxxv), 33-34. See also Eugenio Biagini, "British Trade Unions and Popular Political Economy, 1860-1880," *Historical Journal* 1987 34 (4): 811-40; James Hutchinson, "Progress and Wages," *Nineteenth Century* (October 1884); and William H. Mallock, "Conservatism and the Diffusion of Property," *National Review* (May 1888).

of aggressive trade union activity.[72]

The one problem remaining was that the vast majority of British workers did not belong to a trade union. Fewer than 400,000 men did in 1872. Although this number had grown five-fold to two million by 1900, even at this late date only between ten and fifteen percent of male workers were members of a union. Furthermore, most unionists were skilled laborers concentrated in the mines and factories of England's industrial north and midlands; a few industries were heavily represented: mining, engineering, metal working, building, textiles, cloth and leather manufacture, printing, and transportation. Metropolitan London, the center of working class agitation during the late Victorian period, was surprisingly free of large-scale trade union activity prior to the late 1880s; even at the turn of the century, fewer than four percent of male workers in the Metropolis belonged to a trade union.[73] The reasons behind this startling lack of working class organization in Britain's largest labor market bear looking into.

Political apathy had been a staple of London working class life since the decline of the Chartist movement in the 1840s. Most metropolitan workers tended to immerse themselves in the pursuit of pleasure, not in agitation for new political rights or better conditions in the workplace. All too often, the public house and the music hall meant more to them than trade union membership.[74] As Friedrich Engels noted in 1888, "nowhere in the civilized world are the working people less actively resistant, more passively submitting to fate" than in London.[75] Metropolitan "passivity" was, however, nothing new. Francis Place had written to his friend and fellow reformer Richard Cobden as early as March 1840 about the difficulties of generating a working class following in the Metropolis. Place argued that London's size, diversity, and overstocked unskilled labor market made

---

[72] See Clementia Black, "What High Wages Mean," *Longman's Magazine* (July 1889); Henry H. Champion, "An Eight-Hour Law," *Nineteenth Century* (September 1889); John Rae's "State Socialism and Popular Right," *Contemporary Review* (December 1890) and "Eight Hours Day and the Unemployed," *Contemporary Review* (June 1893); B. W. Richardson, "Working Hours and Working Men," *Longman's Magazine* (October 1890); David Schloss's "Road to Social Peace," *Fortnightly Review* (February 1891) and "The 'Dearness' of Cheap Labour," *Fortnightly Review* (January 1893); and John A. Hobson, "The Economy of High Wages," *Contemporary Review* (December 1893).

[73] See Sidney and Beatrice Webb, *The History of Trade Unionism* (London, 1894); Herman Ausubel, *The Late Victorians* (New York, 1955); and Eric Hobsbawm, *Worlds of Labour* (London, 1984).

[74] See Gareth Stedman Jones, "Working Class Culture and Working Class Politics in London, 1870-1900," *Journal of Social History* 1974 7 (4): 460-508; Eric Hobsbawm, *Worlds of Labour* (London, 1984); and Neville Kirk, " 'Traditional' Working Class Culture and 'The Rise of Labour,' " *Social History* 1991 16 (2): 203-16.

[75] Margaret Harkness, *Out of Work* (London, 1888), vii.

effective trade union or political organization almost impossible.[76]

In addition, high overhead—for rent, taxes, gas, and coal—ensured that London would be dominated by thousands of small workshops, not by factories as was the case elsewhere. By relying upon the subdivision of labor, low intensity technologies, and low capital investment, the "sweated trades"—clothing, footwear, furniture, vehicle-making, brewing, and printing in particular—were able to prosper within London's inner industrial perimeter.[77] London also supported a large population of casual laborers, particularly among transport workers, dockers, builders, bakers, millers, chimney-sweeps, hawkers, waiters, coopers, and leather-workers. The percentage of Londoners in casual occupations remained high throughout the nineteenth century.

Casual workers	1861	1891[78]
10-15 years old	59%	42%
15-65 years old	25%	22%

Unskilled, casual laborers were typically believed to be the least respectable, dependable, and moral portion of the Victorian workforce. Not everyone agreed, however. The novelist Henry Nevison wittily described a casual as "one o' the Aristocracy o' Labor . . . same as the other Aristocracy, only for doin' labor now and again."[79]

Nevertheless, no one was surprised to find most London poverty concentrated within the "sweated" and "casual" trades; according to Charles Booth, dock-workers, tailors, boot-makers, and furniture manufacturers were the most likely to suffer from extreme want during the late Victorian period. The fierce competition of thousands of unskilled workers—particularly boys, emigrants from the countryside, married women, and foreign immigrants—drove down wages and decreased job security in the Metropolis. These workers, who made up some seventy-five percent of the British labor force between 1850 and 1930, were, in fact, caught in a vicious circle. To escape poverty, they had to organize themselves into unions; all too often, however, the unskilled were too poor, demoralized, disconnected, and easily replaceable to form trade unions.[80]

---

[76] Cited in D. J. Rowe, "The Failure of London Chartism," *Historical Journal* 1968 11 (3): 482.

[77] See Eric Hobsbawm, *Worlds of Labour* (London, 1984); Pat Kirkham, R. Mace, and J. Porter, *Furnishing the World: the East London Furniture Trade, 1830-1980* (London, 1987); Patrick Joyce, *Visions of the People* (New York, 1991); Raphael Samuel, "Workshop of the World: Steam Power and Hand Technology in Mid-Victorian Britain," *History Workshop* 1977 (3): 6-72; and Gareth Stedman Jones, *Outcast London* (Oxford, 1971).

[78] Gareth Stedman Jones, *Outcast London* (Oxford, 1971), 385-86.

[79] Henry Nevison, *Slum Stories of London* (New York, 1895), 23.

[80] See John Benson, *The Working Class in Britain, 1850-1939* (New York, 1989); Samuel A. Barnett's letter to the (London) *Times*, 22 October 1887; Charles Booth, *Life and Labour of the London Poor: Poverty Series* (London, 1889-1893); John A. Hobson, *The Problems of Poverty* (London, 1891); and A. Streeter, "The East End," *The Month* (February 1895).

Not surprisingly, the organization of the unskilled during the "New Unionism" of the 1880s has always been treated as a major turning point in British labor history. In particular, the momentous London Dock Strike of August 1889 has justifiably been viewed as a major success for the labor movement. One should be careful not to overstate the case. The victories won by the "New Unionism" at this time were modest and, in some cases, fleeting. Membership in the "New Unions," after rising impressively to twenty percent of all unionized workers in 1890, dropped to a mere ten percent by 1900. Even as late as 1900, fewer than twenty percent of adult male workers belonged to a union. Furthermore, the "New Unionism" did not represent the growth of socialist thought among the working classes, but a continued adherence to the traditional aims of union organization: better pay, fewer hours, job security, and more healthful conditions.

Nor did the strikes of 1888 and 1889 reflect a new attitude towards working class militancy. Union members knew that strikes could easily drain their funds and inspire employers to hire "blackleg" workers. Even when successful, strikes were often counterproductive; they damaged industry and many times led to increased class conflict between employers and their workers. The strikes of the late 1880s in London occurred under special circumstances that would prove difficult to replicate in later years. Relative economic prosperity, low unemployment, rising real wages, an increased demand for unskilled labor, and a dwindling supply of rural emigrants combined to stack the odds in favor of the "New Unionism." In the late 1880s, employers would find it difficult—for the first time in recent memory—to break strikes through the importation of "scab" laborers.[81]

Even so, of the three most important strikes in London of the late 1880s, only two were successful: the match girls' strike of July 1888 and the dock workers' of August 1889. In the case of the match girls, Fabian Socialist agitator Annie Besant provided the spearhead for reform; her article, "White Slavery in London" published in *The Link* on 23 June 1888, drew public attention to the disgraceful conditions under which these young women labored.[82] Owner Theodore Bryant's

---

[81] See Derek Matthews's seminal article, "1889 and All That: New Views on the New Unionism," *International Review of Social History* 1991 36 (1): 2-58; and, for a contemporary view, see Guilford Molesworth, "Political Economy and Its Relation to Strikes," *National Review* (February 1890).

[82] Annie Besant's use of the phrase "white slavery" clearly hearkened back to William Stead's articles on child prostitution published in the *Pall Mall Gazette* in the summer of 1885. In addition, Besant's interpretation of the "New Unionism" ran directly counter to that of her clients, the match girls. Besant, the Fabian Socialist, wished to alter society, not just to raise wages, shorten the workday, and better conditions; the match girls, it seems, were satisfied with what small gains they could make in the short term. See Annie Besant, *The Trades Union Movement* (London, 1890).

decision to fire three employees who had provided information to Besant for her article inspired first demonstrations and then a strike among the roughly three thousand female workers at the Bryant and May match factory in the Whitechapel district of east London. After a work stoppage of about three weeks in July 1888 and the formation of a match girls' union under the guidance of Annie Besant, the employers gave way; the match girls won a small wage increase, greater job security, and other minor concessions. Despite these comparatively small gains, the Bryant and May match girls' strike did have far-reaching consequences. As the first strike of unorganized workers to gain national publicity, public support—particularly from the *Pall Mall Gazette* and other liberal newspapers—and to be victorious, the match girls set an important precedent for the future.[83]

All was not well, however, at the Bryant and May match factory after the strike of July 1888. Working conditions in the factory, although criticized in Besant's article, had not really been addressed during the strike. Specifically, the dangers inherent in the production of "Lucifer" strike-anywhere, white phosphorous matches had not been remedied. The publication in *The Star* in January 1892 of stories about the existence of "phossy jaw" among some Bryant and May workers and about the hush money that had been paid to these workers to keep them quiet about their condition outraged public opinion. "Phossy jaw"—the result of frequent exposure to white phosphorous in an unventilated environment—caused facial pain and swelling, the loss of teeth and the decay of the jaw bone, disfiguration, and, in some cases, death. After documenting seven cases, *The Star* called in October 1892 for better ventilation and isolated dipping rooms at the Bryant and May factory. Unfortunately, little was done to rectify unhealthy conditions at the factory. *The Star*, indeed, discovered six more cases of "phossy jaw" in 1898 and recorded five deaths since 1892. In response, the government fined Bryant and May £25, the maximum amount that could be imposed. Only in 1910 did an international agreement ban the manufacture and sale of white phosphorous matches.[84]

Although the 1888 match girls' strike was an important precursor, the Great Dock Strike of August 1889 is commonly viewed as the decisive moment in the birth of the "New Unionism." Employment along the docks of east London during the late 1880s was difficult, poorly paid, and highly uncertain for the twenty-two hundred regular and four thousand casual laborers who worked there. Low wages among the regularly employed and irregular labor among casual dockers could not

---

[83] See Terry McCarthy, ed., *The Great Dock Strike, 1889* (London, 1988) for a brief description of the match girls' strike.

[84] See Lowell Satre, "After the Matchgirls' Strike," *Victorian Studies* 1982 26 (1): 7-31, for an examination of working conditions at the Bryant and May factory during the 1890s.

help but have a strongly negative impact on their morality and well-being. With regard to casual dock laborers, Beatrice Potter (Webb) noted in 1887 that "a large wage one week and none the next . . . are not favourable conditions to thrift, temperance, and good management."[85] Consequently, the best way for dockers to better their working conditions, Potter argued, was for them to form a union and then to agitate for higher wages and more regular work.

In this endeavor, the dockers were extraordinarily successful. By the first week in August 1889, Ben Tillet was heavily involved in the establishment of a General Dockers' Union in London and had already, on 7 August, sent a list of demands to the dock owners. One week later, the increasingly disgruntled dockers dispatched a further set of demands: in the future, no man was to be employed for fewer than four hours at a time, contract and piecework were to be abolished, and wages were to be raised to 6d. an hour and 8d. an hour for overtime. Although technically giving the dock owners until noon on the fourteenth to respond, in fact, the strike had already begun by that time. No one came in to work on the West India Docks on 14 August; by 21 August, the strike had extended to include all of the major dock complexes along the Thames.[86]

The strikers, under the able leadership of Ben Tillet, Tom Mann, Henry Champion, and John Burns, had two main objectives. First, they had to prevent the employment of "blackleg" labor; second, they needed to win the battle for public opinion. To achieve the first objective, the dockers posted over forty miles of pickets and pasted placards throughout the East End to warn away "scab" laborers. Although the dockers used intimidation and, occasionally, violence to keep "blacklegs" away from the docks, the police did not actively intervene.[87] To woo public opinion, the dockers staged mass demonstrations—some including as many as 80,000 participants—in the streets of London. The sight of large numbers of workers assembling peacefully—particularly in contrast to the riots and violence of the mid-1880s—reassured the metropolitan middle and upper classes that the dockers were worthy of their support. The London political and literary elite, convinced of the justice of the dock workers' case against their employers, gave both moral and material support to the strikers. Poor Law loans and charitable grants to the strikers and their families were a common occurrence. The Salvation Army provided a substantial amount of strike relief: money, food, and free shelter. In addition, the Dock Strike Relief fund and the Australian Relief fund together raised over £30,000 for the striking dock workers. Finally, dock employer Henry LaFone, who sympathized with the plight of his employees, continued to pay three

---

[85] Beatrice Potter, "Dock Life of East London," *Nineteenth Century* (October 1887), 493.

[86] See Terry McCarthy, ed., *The Great Dock Strike, 1889* (London, 1988).

[87] (London) *Times*, 27 August 1889.

hundred of his workers seven shillings a week for the duration of the strike.[88]

By early September, it was obvious to the dock owners that they would be unable to force their will upon the striking workers. The strikers had won the sympathy of the press, many politicians, and the Church. The Bishop of Westminster and Henry Cardinal Manning had both come out in support of the dockers. The dockers had been very well served both by their union and by the leaders of the movement—Burns, Tillet, Mann, and Champion. Good weather and industrial prosperity had reduced the dock owners' ability to import "blackleg" labor to break the strike; widespread public sympathy for the strikers had helped to convince the dock owners to resist the temptation to import foreign laborers. The sympathy strikes of lightermen along the Thames, and over 10,000 East End tailors further strengthened the dockers' position.[89] Lastly, the month-long strike had been extremely expensive. Once the opportunity for victory had passed, the dock owners quickly realized that it was in their best interest to give in to the union's demands.[90] Once again, as had been the case during the match girls' strike the previous year, socialist participation—even leadership—had not led to a marked rise in socialist ideology among the metropolitan working classes.[91]

Nevertheless, the consequences of the Great Dock Strike were many. For some, public support for the dock workers heralded an era of declining class conflict. For once, "the gulf between the rich and the poor, between capital and labour, has been spanned with the golden bridge of far-reaching human sympathy."[92] Others recognized that the dockers' hard-won gains would cost some of their fellow workers dearly. One critic noted that "the increased competition induced by higher pay will probably far outweigh the advantages accruing from the

---

[88] See Terry McCarthy, ed., *The Great Dock Strike, 1889* (London, 1988); Gareth Stedman Jones, *Outcast London* (Oxford, 1971); "The Dock Strikes," *The Economist* (31 August 1889); and "Strikes and Poor Relief," *The Economist* (22 March 1890).

[89] On 27 August 1889, 10,000 East End tailors, machinists, and pressers struck in favor of a twelve-hour workday, an hour and a half for meals, and appropriate overtime pay. Although the conservative Jewish Board of Guardians refused to relieve the striking workers, they were able to win acceptance of all of their demands by early October (Robert Wechsler, "The Jewish Garment Trade in East London, 1875-1914," Ph.D Dissertation [Columbia University, 1979], 192, 246-47).

[90] See Ellen Clarke and C. S. Devas, "The Dock Labourers Strike," *Dublin Review* (October 1889); Henry H. Champion, *The Great Dock Strike in London, August 1889* (London, 1890); and Henry Cardinal Manning and John Burns, "The Great Strike," *New Review* (October 1889). For a realistic fictional view of the struggle, see Emma Leslie, *The Seed She Sowed: A Tale of the Great Dock Strike* (London, 1891).

[91] Burns, Mann, Champion, and William Thorne of the Gasworkers Union were all members of Hyndman's Social Democratic Federation.

[92] David Schloss, "The Labour Problem," *Fortnightly Review* (October 1889), 437. See also Frederic Harrison, "The New Trades-Unionism," *Nineteenth Century* (October 1889).

latter."[93] As the best workers would now be sifted out of the casual crowd for full-time employment, distress within the "residuum" would, in fact, increase. As the *Times* remarked in mid-September 1889, "It is dawning upon the public mind, indeed, that, whatever may be the issue of the strike, the casual dock labourer will be a loser."[94]

Setting the continuing plight of casual labor aside, however, one can recognize the extent of the dockers' accomplishment. They had proven that the organization of unskilled workers on a large scale was practicable. They had won widespread public sympathy and support for their efforts. The only remaining challenge was to prove their durability. As the leaders of the union realized, holding the movement together now that the struggle was over would be an extremely difficult task. Nevertheless, the dockers and their supporters remained confident that their strike marked the beginning of a new era. Henry Cardinal Manning gave voice to a common sentiment when he stated that "What we may hope will come from this strike is a registration of labourers and an organization of labour."[95]

The disaster which befell the London gas workers barely four months after the dock workers' triumph brought the supporters of the "New Unionism" quickly back to reality. The defeat of the gas workers union in December 1889 was, in fact, all the more surprising because it had, even prior to the Great Dock Strike, proven their strength *vis à vis* their employers. In March 1889, the newly formed National Union of Gas Workers and General Labourers under the direction of its general secretary, William Thorne, won the eight-hour day with no reduction in pay—a fifty percent increase per hour—without having to go out on strike. Thorne's attempt in December to derail the South Metropolitan Gas Company's "bonus scheme"—a voluntary profit-sharing plan which promised benefits as long as workers did not join the union or go out on strike—however, proved disastrous. The company quickly replaced the two thousand striking gas workers by offering "blacklegs" 5s. 4d. for an eight-hour day.[96] As these replacement workers were

---

[93] Ellen Clarke and C. S. Devas, "The Dock Labourers Strike," *Dublin Review* (October 1889), 405.

[94] (London) *Times*, 12 September 1889. See also "The Dock Strikes," *The Economist* (31 August 1889), 1112.

[95] Henry Cardinal Manning, "The Great Strike," *New Review* (October 1889), 411. See also Hubert Llewellyn Smith and Vaughan Nash, *The Story of the Dockers' Strike* (London, 1889); R. S. Watson, "The Organization of Unskilled Labour," *Contemporary Review* (August 1890); and Sidney and Beatrice Potter Webb, *Industrial Democracy* (London, 1898).

[96] This was a decent wage considering that ten percent of British gasworkers still earned less than 20s. each week (Special Report by Robert Giffen, "Return of Rates of Wages," 1892 [c.6715], v. lxviii, xxxiv). According to one author, a weekly wage of 32s. was enough to allow a workman, his wife, and five children a simple, but comfortable existence (Miranda Hill, "Life on Thirty Shillings a Week," *Nineteenth Century* [March 1888], 462-63).

allowed to live on the company premises, the Gas Workers' Union picketers were largely ineffective. Furthermore, unlike the case of the dock workers' strike, the police prevented aggressive picketing outside the company gates. In addition, the public—perhaps fearful that darkened streets and businesses would lead to an upsurge in crime and worried about a lack of heat during the winter months—sided overwhelmingly with the gas company owners. By 19 December, a deputation of striking workers had appeared, hat in hand, before their former employers to see if they could get their old jobs back. They were told that they could not, but that striking workers could apply to fill any vacancies that arose in the future.[97]

The organization of unskilled men was, as we have seen, difficult enough; bringing women under the trade union umbrella was—Annie Besant's match girls aside—even more problematical. The explanation for this fact is quite simple. Single women with some education and polite manners could find gainful employment as clerks, teachers, nurses, and retail salespeople from the middle of the nineteenth century. Poor, uneducated women had fewer options. While young or unmarried, they were expected to contribute to the family economy; once married, they were expected merely to supplement their husband's income. In both cases, only the lowest-status, least-skilled, worst-paying occupations were open to them.[98]

Not surprisingly, a much larger proportion of women were employed in the poorer districts of east and south London than elsewhere in the Metropolis.[99] An increasing number of these women worked in the "sweated trades," particularly tailoring. During the late Victorian period, rising demand for mass-produced, ready-made clothing along with the increased utilization of sewing and material-cutting machines made the subdivision of labor in the clothing trades easier and more profitable. For large numbers of metropolitan women, however, increased job opportunities in the clothing trades led not to economic independence or security, but to a harsh and degrading existence on the margins of the Victorian

---

[97] See the (London) *Times* for a day-by-day account. See also Joan Ballhatchet, "The Police and the London Dock Strike of 1889," *History Workshop* 1991 (32): 54-68, which includes some information on the role of the police in the gasworkers' strike of December 1889.

[98] See Theresa McBride's article in Lenard Berlanstein, ed., *The Industrial Revolution and Work in the Nineteenth Century* (New York, 1992); and Wally Seecombe, "Patriarchy Stabilized: The Construction of the Male Breadwinner Wage Norm in Nineteenth Century Britain," *Social History* 1986 11 (1): 53-76.

[99] See Special Report by Clara Collet (the Labour Correspondent to the Board of Trade), "Statistics of Employment of Women and Girls," 1894 (c.7564), v. lxxxi, 80-85; and Gareth Stedman Jones, *Outcast London* (Oxford, 1971).

economy.[100]

Many Victorian social critics recognized that the poor women of the Metropolis represented an exploited class. The novelist Walter Besant commented that "Everywhere the woman gets the worst of it. She is the hardest worked, and has to do all the nastiest kinds of work; she is the worst paid; she is always bullied, scolded, threatened, nagged and sworn at; she has the worst food . . . she has no holidays; she has the fewest amusements."[101] Another social critic remarked that "children, girls and women are daily bought and sold in London, just as underpaid factory girls and shop women are constantly driven to vice by sheer want."[102] A third argued that working conditions for London women were worse than fifty years before. Women workers labored long hours either at home or in isolated, unregulated sweatshops under the most appalling conditions. Within a short period of time, all of their aspirations for a better life had been beaten out of them. Under such circumstances, was it any wonder that they neglected the moral upbringing of their children? Was it any wonder they failed to practice Christian morality?[103] Other authors, while recognizing the difficult conditions under which women labored, took a more positive view. The social investigator Clementia Black, for instance, expressed her admiration of the industry, sobriety, and courteousness displayed by the majority of poor working women.[104]

The best solution for industrial distress was, of course, for women workers to combine into their own trade unions. Unfortunately, because working women were so poorly paid, overworked, unskilled, easy to replace, and dispersed by the home work system, they found it extremely difficult to organize themselves. As one historian has noted, "outworking could not be eliminated until the trade was thoroughly organized, and the trade could never be thoroughly organized until outworking was eliminated."[105] Furthermore, they could expect little help from their male trade union counterparts; indeed, as most male unionists believed that the widespread employment of women drove down wages and reduced job opportunities for men, they wished to limit the number of women in the workplace. John A. Hobson was by no means alone in hoping "that with every future rise in the wages and industrial position of male wage-earners, there may be a growing

---

[100] For a detailed analysis of the problems of sweated labor in metropolitan London, see James Schmiechen's "State Reform and Local Economy," *Economic History Review* 1975 28 (3): 413-28; and *Sweated Industries and Sweated Labor* (Urbana, Ill., 1984).

[101] Walter Besant, *Children of Gibeon* (1886, Reprint Edition, New York, 1889), 337.

[102] *Justice*, 11 July 1885.

[103] See W. H. Wilkins, "How Long, Oh Lord, How Long," *Nineteenth Century* (August 1893); Ada Heather-Bigg, "The Cry Against Home work," *Nineteenth Century* (December 1894); and Edith Hogg, "The Fur-pullers of South London," *Nineteenth Century* (November 1897).

[104] See Clementia Black, "Some East End Workwomen," *National Review* (August 1889).

[105] James A. Schmiechen, *Sweated Industries and Sweated Labor* (Urbana, Ill., 1984), 131.

sentiment in favor of a restriction of industrial work among married women."[106] The idea that the employment of women was detrimental to the industrial position of male workers was hotly denied by the supporters of unions for women. In their estimation, the organization of women would, in fact, greatly ease economic competition between the sexes by bringing wage levels more into balance; women would no longer be hired as a cheap alternative to the employment of men.[107]

The establishment of the Women's Trade Union Provident League by Emma Paterson and Emilia Dilke—second wife of Charles Dilke, a leading member of the Liberal Party—during the mid-1870s represented an important, albeit small, first step towards the organization of working women.[108] If such private efforts proved unsuccessful, then the State might have to intervene strongly on behalf of women workers. Margaret Gladstone—a distant relation of William Gladstone, the leader of the Liberal Party, future wife of the first Labour Prime Minister, Ramsey MacDonald, and head of the Women's Industrial Council—argued strenuously that legislative protections of working women needed to be strengthened. The dangerous trades, particularly domestic workshops, had to be better regulated. The number of hours in the workday should be further limited by law; a minimum wage must be imposed. Improved technical training needed to be made available to women so as to draw them out of the unskilled labor market. In 1896 the WIC argued that increasing the school leaving age to sixteen would be highly beneficial, because it would reduce the number of teenagers flooding the labor market. Finally, the activist Janet Hogarth proposed in 1897 that the State establish a labour bureau in order to catalog and describe job opportunities for women throughout the British isles.[109]

More controversy surrounded the elimination of home work altogether. Socialist supporters of the women's movement, like John Burns and Beatrice Potter Webb, argued that as domestic manufacture so often led to excessive hours and unhealthy conditions, and as home work prevented the organization of women

---

[106] John A. Hobson, *The Problems of Poverty* (London, 1891), 170. For the opposite view, see Emilia Dilke's "Trades Unionism for Women," *New Review* (January 1890) and "The Industrial Position of Women," *Fortnightly Review* (October 1893); and Susan Jeune, ed., *Ladies at Work* (London, 1893).

[107] See Christina Bremner, "Women in the Labour Market," *National Review* (June 1888).

[108] See Clementia Black's "The Organization of Working Women," *Fortnightly Review* (November 1889) and "A Working Woman's Speech," *Nineteenth Century* (May 1889); see also Edith Shaw, "How Poor Ladies Might Live," *Nineteenth Century* (April 1897); and Eliza Orma, "How Poor Ladies Live: A Reply," *Nineteenth Century* (April 1897).

[109] See Emilia Dilke, "Trades Unionism for Women," *New Review* (January 1889); Margaret McMillan, "The Woman's Labour Day," *Westminster Review* (November 1891); Ada Heather-Bigg, "The Cry Against Home Work," *Nineteenth Century* (December 1894); and Janet Hogarth, "The Monstrous Regiment of Women," *Fortnightly Review* (December 1897). See also *Women's Industrial News* for many articles on the goals and progress of the movement.

workers, it should be made illegal.[110] Others were less enthusiastic about the immediate eradication of home work. Some women had to care for their young children or elderly parents at home; others were too young to work outside the home; many were simply more comfortable working at home. If home work was to be done away with, therefore, it should be phased out gradually over time.[111]

As none of the various metropolitan socialist organizations had proven themselves capable of attracting a mass following and as the "New Unionism" did not venture beyond the traditional aspirations of their trade union predecessors, if socialism was to emerge as a powerful force in British politics, then the Independent Labour Party, which was founded in Bradford, England, in 1893, would have to lead the way. Two questions need to be answered. First, did the ILP espouse socialist doctrine during the 1890s? Second, did the Independent Labour Party have the ability to influence the shape and direction of Victorian politics prior to the turn of the century?[112]

Although prominent socialists had often urged the formation of a trade union party in order to force parliament to consider social reform more seriously, their pleas should not be mistaken for support of the ILP.[113] The vast majority of the London socialist movement steered clear of the Independent Labour Party prior to 1900, believing that it was shot-through with "trade-union consciousness." Whether this was in fact the case remains to be seen. Socialist or not, the ILP, under the leadership of James Keir Hardie, proposed a large number of political, social, and economic reforms during the 1890s: an eight-hour workday; the abolition of overtime and piecework; the prohibition of the employment of children under fourteen; public provision for the sick, the disabled, the aged, widows, and orphans paid for by an one hundred percent tax on "unearned" income; free, nonsectarian primary, secondary, and university education; and public works, with local county councils allowed to acquire farm land for cultivation by the unemployed.[114] John Burns—the chairman of the Trade Union Congress, a member of parliament from Battersea, and a long-time supporter of the ILP—favored the establishment of a labour bureau, the municipalization of certain industries, and the extension of the franchise. On the issue of public works, Burns

---

[110] See John Burns, "The Unemployed," *Fabian Tract*, no. 47 (London, 1893); and Beatrice Potter Webb, *Women and the Factory Acts* (London, 1896). The Liberal politician Richard B. Haldane was elected president of the WIC during the mid-1890s. Sidney Webb served as treasurer, and his wife, Beatrice, was also a member of the council from 1896.

[111] See Margaret Irwin, "The Problems of Home Work," *Westminster Review* (November 1897).

[112] See Henry Pelling's *The Origins of the Labour Party, 1880-1900*, 2nd Edition (Oxford, 1965) for an informed, if old-fashioned, analysis of the founding of the Independent Labour Party.

[113] See Sidney Webb and George Bernard Shaw, "To Your Tents, O Israel," *Fortnightly Review* (November 1893).

[114] See James Keir Hardie, "The Independent Labour Party," *Nineteenth Century* (January 1895).

believed—as did most members of the ILP—in differentiating the poor. Relief in money or food was to be distributed to those who could not work; for the able-bodied, road work, sewer repairs, recreation grounds keeping, and street cleaning would provide employment during "hard times." Those who refused to work would be turned over to the Poor Law.[115] Other ILP reformers advocated the establishment of a ministry of Labour and conciliation boards to settle disputes between capital and labor. Not surprisingly, as trade unionists provided the backbone of the Independent Labour Party, most everyone supported the removal of restrictions on working class organization and agitation.[116]

Most of these reforms could be—and, in fact, eventually would be—supported by the advanced wing of the Liberal Party.[117] The minority report of the Royal Commission *On Labour* in 1894, however, represents a much more direct attack on British capitalism. Written by the secretary of the ILP, Tom Mann, the report reveals that social reform was only the first step along the road to socialism.[118] Mann called for the direct public employment of workers *whenever* it was advantageous. In addition, he hoped that public works would be made as attractive as possible; workers should, in his estimation, be guaranteed an eight-hour workday, trade union conditions, and a "moral" minimum wage. Mann also advocated the State provision of sanitary housing for all those who could not at present afford it and argued that

the whole force of democratic statesmanship must, in our opinion, henceforth be directed to the substitution, as fast as possible, of public for capitalist enterprise, and where the substitution is not yet practicable, to the strict and detailed regulation of all industrial

---

[115] See John Burns, "The Unemployed," *Fabian Tract*, no. 47 (London, 1893). Burns's division of the unemployed was popular across the Victorian political spectrum. One critic revealed that "the workhouse of today will only foreshadow in the severity of its regulations the workhouse of the future" (Beatrice Potter [Webb], "Dock Life of East London," *Nineteenth Century* [October 1887], 499). See also Sidney Webb, "The Reform of the Poor Law," *Contemporary Review* (July 1890); and R. Didden, "Individualism and Collectivism," *Westminster Review* (June 1898).

[116] See John Burns, "Labour Leaders on the Labour Question," *Nineteenth Century* (December 1892); *The Trade Unionist*, 6 February 1892; various articles in *Labour Leader* throughout the 1890s; and J.A.M. MacDonald, "The Problem of the Unemployed," *New Review* (December 1893).

[117] They were also supported by most trade unionists. One commentator remarked in 1891 that the State "may do something, much, in fact, towards putting down abuses in the industrial system, such as truck, sweating, and the like; and also in improving the conditions of labour as regards safety, sanitation, and in other ways" (George Howell, "Mistaken Labour Legislation," *New Review* [March 1891], 273).

[118] Tom Mann had long been a member of the Social Democratic Federation; was one of the organizers of the Great Dock Strike and the Gas Workers' Union in 1889; and, from 1894 until 1896, he served as secretary of the Independent Labour Party.

operations, so as to secure to every worker the conditions of efficient citizenship.[119]

As conflict between workers and employers was the inevitable result of the present system of "industrial anarchy" in Britain, the "only complete solution of the problem is, in our opinion, to be found in the progress of the industrial evolution, which will assign to the 'captains of industry,' as well as to the manual workers, their proper positions as servants of the community."[120] The proper role of "democratic Government" was, according to Mann and the ILP, therefore, the nationalization of land, industry, and the means of distribution and exchange.

Such policies could not, in the estimation of the ILP press, be expected from either the Liberal or the Conservative Party. As both were equally committed to the preservation of capitalism, neither could be expected to legislate socialism on behalf of the poor. A cartoon in the final issue of the *Workman's Times* revealed the House of Commons to be peopled by the very class of exploiters that one would expect to oppose Labour aspirations: 148 lawyers, 130 landowners, 24 brewers, 116 factory owners, and a "mixed lot of stockjobbers, merchants, [and] company promoters."[121] James Keir Hardie's *Labour Leader* argued that all workers could expect from the comfortable classes in parliament was a bunch of meaningless and condescending platitudes. As Hardie's fictional "millionaire Prime Minister" remarked in 1895 to a poor petitioner for parliamentary aid: "I'm very sorry for you. You have my full sympathy. Here's a committee for you. Now run away, there's a good man, and don't bother me again this year."[122]

Neither party represented "living political forces; no, nor even living political ideas. The division of the future lies between those who care for the interests of property, and those who care for the interests of Labour."[123] For workers to continue to support either the Conservative or the Liberal Party was, according to the ILP press, less than useless. Fortunately, more and more working class voters were beginning to recognize "how little the English worker is benefitted by voting for either Liberal or Tory;" in time, they will finally "exclaim, 'A plague on both your Parties.'"[124]

Although highly critical of both parties, the ILP and its minions in the press reserved its sharpest barbs for the Liberal Party. Of the so-called "People's William"—Prime Minister William E. Gladstone—Henry H. Champion's *Labour*

---

[119] Fifth and Final Report of the Royal Commission *On Labour*, part one, Minority Report (1894 [cd. 7421], v.70), 147.
[120] Ibid., 146.
[121] *Workman's Times*, 17 March 1894.
[122] *Labour Leader*, 23 February 1895.
[123] Clementia Black, *An Agitator* (London, 1894), 81.
[124] George Lansbury, "A Socialist View of Government," *National Review* (June 1895), 564. See also U. A. Forbes, "Social Anatomy," *London Quarterly Review* (July 1895); *Workman's Times*, 27 March 1891; and the *Labour Prophet*, a paper which expressed great distrust of both parties during the 1890s.

Elector was openly contemptuous; he "can find no wrongs that want righting, no oppression to be fought against, nearer than Crete or Ireland."[125] Whereas Gladstonian liberalism appeared impotent when faced with the problems of the modern world, the "New Liberalism" of Joseph Chamberlain, Charles Dilke, and others was widely regarded in labor circles as being merely a political maneuver to win working class votes.[126] As the Liberals, even those who said that they wished to enact serious reform, could not be trusted, it was up to the ILP to supplant them as the "real" reformist party on the political left. As one supporter of the Independent Labour Party put it: "The day for a Liberal Party has gone by. We want no buffer Party, but simply want the workers to be face to face with those who wish to keep things as they are."[127]

Notwithstanding the energy and ideas of its leadership, the ILP's prospects remained bleak during the 1890s. In 1895, for instance, all twenty-eight of its candidates for parliament, including Keir Hardie himself, were defeated. Obviously, the vast majority of enfranchised British workers continued to cast their votes for one of the two established political parties. The pro-nationalist, pro-imperial, anti-foreign rhetoric of the Conservative Party remained popular within the working classes well into the twentieth century. Even during the Liberal electoral landslide of 1906, the ILP captured only twenty-nine out of six hundred and seventy seats.[128]

Although the Independent Labour Party had few electoral successes during the late Victorian period and many of its staunchest supporters were in fact hostile to socialism, its very existence incited controversy, consternation, and, very often, contempt. The ILP attracted public censure—just as Henry Georgists, anarchists, Social Democrats, and Fabians had before them—for one simple reason. The vast majority of Victorian society loathed the idea of socialism and believed that the destruction of private property and the nationalization of the means of production, distribution, and exchange would spell disaster. "Misery, national decay and disintegration" would result, according to one critic, from such "experiments in the direction of Socialism."[129]

William Mallock, a prolific critic of modern socialism, firmly believed that the confiscation of property and investment capital would inevitably send the economy into a tailspin. Declining investment in British industry would quickly translate into industrial inefficiency, falling production, lower wages, and rising

---

[125] *Labour Elector*, 14 December 1889, 376. Champion was extremely critical of Gladstone, the Manchester liberals—particularly John Bright—and the "capitalist" press during the late 1880s.

[126] *Labour Leader*, 23 February 1895.

[127] George Lansbury, "A Socialist View of Government," *National Review* (June 1895), 569.

[128] See Henry Pelling, *The Social Geography of British Elections, 1885-1918* (London, 1967); and Robert McKenzie and Allan Silver, *Angels in Marble* (Chicago, 1968).

[129] "Socialism and Legislation," *Westminster Review* (January 1886), 32.

unemployment.[130] Entrepreneurship, he argued, must be rewarded or the economy would grind to a halt. Mallock also took issue with one of the central tenets of socialist doctrine, the idea that because labor created all wealth, those receiving the so-called "unearned" increment could be dispossessed of their capital gains with a clear conscience. Socialists did not seem to realize, Mallock complained, that labor was "no more the cause of wealth than Shakespeare's pen was the cause of his writing 'Hamlet.'"[131] The wealthy *earn* interest on their investments by providing labor with the incentive to produce something of value. Industrial "ability"—as Mallock called it—was, therefore, the crucial element in the production process. Even so, unlike many socialists, Mallock acknowledged that capital and labor had to work together to fulfill their potential; both must be willing to compromise so as to ensure industrial peace, prosperity, and productivity.[132]

In addition, most critics of socialism argued that equality was not in the interest of the human race. Competition, personal ambition, and inequality were a natural part of human existence. Inequality, indeed, was central to the human experience. As one writer noted, "the first step from savagery towards civilization brings inequality. The strong, the clever, and the thrifty get the largest share of the good things in life."[133] It was this desire for inequality that gave impetus to all economic progress and productivity. The struggle for survival weeded out the weak and allowed the strong to prosper. Socialism, therefore, was interpreted by its critics as an attempt to reverse the tide of evolution by grinding "down humanity into sausage meat."[134] By granting "an equal share of wages and of profits to the strong and to the weak, to the clever and to the stupid, to the prudent and to the improvident, to the industrious and to the idle, perhaps even to the sober and to the drunken" humanity would be committing biological suicide. The inevitable result of allowing the fit and the unfit to prosper equally was racial degeneration.[135] As a result, it was "not, then, chiefly in the interests of the employing classes that

---

[130] See William H. Mallock's "Fabian Economics," *Fortnightly Review* (February-March 1894) and "Socialist [George Bernard Shaw] in a Corner," *Fortnightly Review* (May 1894).

[131] William H. Mallock, *Social Equality* (New York, 1882), 67. See also Mallock's "Statistics of Agitation," *Quarterly Review* (January 1884).

[132] See William H. Mallock, "Wealth and the Working Classes," *Fortnightly Review* (September 1887); and U. A. Forbes, "Social Anatomy," *London Quarterly Review* (July 1895). Such writers agreed that economic value was created by neither capital nor labor; consumers in the marketplace gave value to goods by deciding whether or not to purchase them.

[133] John Martineau, "A Plea to Landlords," *Blackwood's Magazine* (February 1888), 193.

[134] Thomas Scanlon, "Merrie England," *Westminster Review* (March 1896), 295-96. See also John Grant, "Modern Socialism," *Scottish Review* (April 1891); and R. D. Melville, "The Present Socialist Position," *Westminster Review* (November 1896).

[135] See George Broderick, "Fallacies of Modern Socialism," *National Review* (May 1892), 300. See also Benjamin Kidd, *Social Evolution* (London, 1894).

socialism is to be resisted, but much more in the interests of the employed classes."[136]

Criticism of the various incarnations of Victorian socialism followed from this basic critique in due course. Opponents of Christian Socialism attempted to disassociate Jesus' teachings from socialist thought. In their estimation, Jesus was by no means a social revolutionary. He was largely unconcerned with the temporal world; his message was that everyone—both slaves and free, rich and poor—should be contented with their lot in life. It was not "His main purpose, or any part of His purpose, that everybody should have plenty to eat and drink, comfortable houses, and not too much to do."[137] Christianity had nothing to do with either capitalism or socialism; it was meant to elevate the human soul. Furthermore, considering that Christianity had been unable to transform human morality in two thousand years, would not Christian Socialism only become practicable if the State were willing to impose Christian precepts by law?[138]

For many critics of socialism, Henry George's "single tax" was a perfect example of State tyranny. At the heart of George's book, according to William Mallock, were a number of serious misconceptions. The rich were neither becoming richer nor the poor poorer; workers did not create their own wages; British population was not growing faster than its ability to feed itself; and poverty was caused neither by land ownership, rising rent, nor material progress. Furthermore, poverty would not be eliminated either by the confiscation of rent or the nationalization of land. Even if the Land Question were solved along Georgist lines, there was no assurance that capital and labor would be able to get along.[139] Even more seriously, George's writings gave credence to the idea that social distress could be alleviated by robbing the rich. For Mallock, indeed, "the danger of Mr. George's book is, that it does not appeal to thinking men. The popularity it aims at, the popularity it has attained, is due, not to the keenness of its arguments, but to the peculiar character of its rhetoric and the policy of confiscation which it advocates."[140]

Such works raised false hopes—contrary to the lessons of History—that the Social Question could be solved easily through legislation. A more complete form

---

[136] Thomas Mackay, ed., *A Plea for Liberty* (London, 1891), 26. Socialism was "an enemy of the worst kind to the great mass of working men who are steadily progressing towards social and political freedom by lawful means" (*Socialism, A Curse* [London, 1884], 24).

[137] "Christianity and 'Progress,'" *Fortnightly Review* (July 1892), 85.

[138] See W. C. Peterborough, "The State and the Sermon on the Mount," *Fortnightly Review* (January 1890).

[139] See William Mallock, "Progress and Poverty," *Quarterly Review* (January 1883); and F. J. Bruce, *Mr. Henry George's Unproved Assumption* (London, 1884).

[140] William Mallock, "Progress and Poverty," *Quarterly Review* (January 1883), 73-74. For another critic, George's work was "the most arrogant, self-sufficient performance ever seen" (Lord Bramwell, *Nationalisation of Land: A Review of Mr. Henry George's "Progress and Poverty"* [London, 1884], 15).

of State socialism—as advocated by the Social Democratic Federation, the Fabians, and the Independent Labour Party—would do even more damage to the economy than George's "single tax." Such programs would, many argued, massively disrupt the national economy and severely reduce productivity and industrial efficiency. By excusing injustice, rewarding the most selfish motives, and by making workers dependent on the State from the cradle to the grave, socialism would complete the demoralization of the working classes. For these reasons, a large number of critics concluded that the remedies proposed by the advocates of socialism were far worse than the disease.[141]

In addition, many members of the Victorian middle and upper classes agreed with Karl Marx, Henry Hyndman, and William Morris that socialism would only come to pass in Britain after a bloody civil war between the classes. This conflict would result, not from the internal dissatisfaction of the working classes with Victorian capitalism, but from the incitement of outside agitators. After all, the working classes, left to themselves, were not especially dangerous. William Mallock expressed a common view that "Like dynamite . . . they are not self-exploding. They remain dumb and impassive till the fuse is applied by the agitator. Then an explosion follows."[142] As a result, "the peripatetic agitator, with his head crammed with foolish fallacies and his wallet with plausible but lying leaflets, is one of the great dangers of the age."[143] Once he had worked his wiles upon the poorer classes, however, "the people about here will grow desperate; and they will walk westwards, cutting throats and hurling brickbats, until they are shot down by the military."[144]

Socialists did not, in the opinion of their critics, seem to realize the contradiction inherent in their desire the bring about a just society by such means. As one author noted, "Swords rent with the blood of Revolution can never open the gates of human Paradise."[145] Nor did they see that a socialist revolution was wholly unnecessary. Economic progress was, if only gradually, allowing the working classes to taste comforts that had been reserved for the chosen few only a generation or two before. As the economist Alfred Marshall explained in 1890, "social and economic forces already at work are changing the distribution of wealth

---

[141] See Leonard Courtney, "A Fair Day's Wages for a Fair Day's Work," *Fortnightly Review* (March 1879); William H. Mallock, *The Old Order Changes* (New York, 1886); Alfred E. Hake, *Suffering London* (London, 1892); and Helen Dendy, "The Socialist Propaganda," *National Review* (September 1895).

[142] William H. Mallock, *The Old Order Changes* (New York, 1886), 356. See also William Graham, "The Collectivist Prospect in England," *Nineteenth Century* (January 1895).

[143] *Primrose League Gazette*, 3 June 1893, 6.

[144] Margaret Harkness, *In Darkest London: Captain Lobe, A Story of the Salvation Army* (London, 1891), 190.

[145] W. Douglas MacKenzie, "The Socialist Agitation," *Westminster Review* (May 1890), 507.

for the better."[146] As a result, the "attempt to interfere with the progress of the nine-tenths because the one-tenth has not hitherto shared it, would be like attempting to wreck a great steamer with six hundred passengers merely because sixty of them had bad accommodation in the steerage."[147] With patience, all would experience the blessings of a rising standard of living.

The Victorians were not, of course, necessarily opposed to reform. Most believed that the State and society should act in tandem to remove the worst excesses of the industrial system. Workers deserved a clean, healthy environment and the leisure to pursue their own enlightenment and pleasure. The social philosopher Benjamin Kidd argued persuasively in 1894 that industrial competition should be "civilized." By providing equal opportunity for all, Britain would become a more just, productive, and progressive society.[148] One way to do this without increasing the size of the State was to encourage the adoption of profit-sharing within British industry. The bringing of capital and labor into partnership with each other might prove to be an effective antidote to the rise of socialism within the working classes. The masses would feel that they had more control over the means of production. Laborers would soon realize that by raising productivity in the workplace, they would be able to increase company profits and the size of their weekly wage packet. There would be less incentive for either side to resort to strikes or lock-outs; both capital and labor, under such a system, were, after all, pursuing the same goal.[149] It was, as most everyone realized, a very large leap from such modest reforms to the forced confiscation of property. "Social reform is one thing, because it is reform," noted the Liberal activist Charles Bradlaugh definitively, "Socialism is the opposite because it is revolution."[150]

In the end, all the sound and fury of the late-nineteenth-century socialist movement had not amounted to very much. In the opinion of one journalist writing in 1895, although "Socialism has been at work in London for fifteen years with an energy out of all proportion to its wisdom," it had not had "any more effect [on public opinion] than a pea-shooter on the rock of Gibraltar."[151] Socialism remained the province of an isolated, marginalized, and tiny minority of social reformers throughout the late Victorian era.

---

[146] Alfred Marshall, *Principles of Economics* (1890, Reprint Edition, London, 1922), 712.

[147] William H. Mallock, *Classes and Masses* (London, 1896), 33. See also Mallock's "The Census and the Condition of the People," *Pall Mall Magazine* (January-April 1895).

[148] See Alice Oldham, "The History of Socialism," *National Review* (January 1891); and Benjamin Kidd, *Social Evolution* (London, 1894).

[149] See William Volckman, *The Prevention of Poverty* (London, 1873); Henry Fawcett, *Labour and Wages* (London, 1884); Moritz Kaufmann, "The Alternative to Socialism," *London Quarterly Review* (January 1887); and David Schloss, "The Labour Problem," *Fortnightly Review* (October 1889).

[150] Henry Hyndman and Charles Bradlaugh, *Will Socialism Benefit the English People?* (London, 1884), 11.

[151] *The New Age*, 25 July 1895.

Chapter 6

Conservative, Liberal, and Radical Responses to the Social Question

However peripheral socialism may have been to the British political mainstream, it did reflect the increasingly common Victorian attitude that sweeping social reform was in the offing. In January 1883, *The Economist* noted that "it required very little observation of current politics to see that the principle of *laissez-faire* is no longer in the ascendent."[1] *The Graphic* agreed, stating further that "whatever may be said for it on theoretical grounds [*laissez-faire*] has practically not worked well, and that it may at any rate be worthwhile to try what can be effected by means of the Government acting as the organ of the community as a whole."[2] Shortly before the publication of Andrew Mearns's "Bitter Cry of Outcast London" in October 1883, another *Economist* editorial proclaimed, "When once it has been conceded that the functions of the State are not to be strictly limited to those simpler duties . . . it is wonderful how soon and how rapidly the number of the outlets in which it is thought that State aid may be advantageously applied becomes increased and multiplied."[3] The problem is that *laissez-faire*, if it had ever existed,

---

[1] "The New Radicalism," *The Economist* (20 January 1883), 62. According to one journalist, "the *laissez-faire* of competition and the devil-take-the-hindmost maxims that have hitherto held almost undisputed sway are giving way to nobler and more humane principles" (*Jewish Standard*, 30 August 1890, 7). See also (London) *Times*, 15 February 1883, for an editorial on the "death" of *laissez-faire*.

[2] *The Graphic*, 28 February 1891, 226.

[3] "State Aid," *The Economist* (29 September 1883), 1132. The novelist George Gissing asked whether "anyone [would] attempt to persuade me that the duties of a Government are composed in the narrow bounds of paltry diplomacy; that the etiquette of courts should take precedence in the minds of statesmen [over] a people's wail for food, food for body and food for mind" (George Gissing, *Workers in the Dawn* [London, 1880], 1:166).

had been definitely discarded as a practical philosophy of government some fifty years before. It had been half a century since the British State first "awakened to the fact that it is essentially part of [its] duty to forward the mental and physical state of those under [its] charge."[4]

The Factory Act of 1833 had established an inspectorate to insure that children under nine would no longer work in textile mills. Children between the ages of nine and thirteen were limited to an eight-hour workday, while those up to eighteen could be legally employed for nine hours on any given day and forty-eight hours a week. The Mines Act of 1842 had made it illegal for women and boys under ten to work below ground. The Ten Hour Act of 1847 further limited the workday for both women and adolescent males. Each act set an important precedent for the future by allowing the State to intervene in the economy in order to protect the most vulnerable portion of the British workforce.[5] By the late Victorian period, an increasing number of reformers began to question whether "the protection of the State" should be extended "not only to women and children, but, if need be, to men."[6]

It was, of course, very much in the interest of the two Victorian political parties to address the needs of the less fortunate, especially after the Reform Act of 1867 widened the franchise to include elements of the laboring classes. For emigration reformer Reginald Brabazon, indeed, a great political opportunity awaited whichever party had the boldness "to break loose from superstitious worship of *laissez-faire*," and recognize "that the happiness of the people is the true end and aim of its existence"; the party that raised the standard of social reform would inevitably, in his estimation, "obtain a lengthened monopoly of political power."[7] Setting aside parliamentary partisanship, social reform might serve a very useful purpose by shoring up the Victorian *status quo*. Bismarck's social reforms in Germany during the 1880s—particularly his old age pensions and national insurance programs—were worthy of notice in this regard as they were "in the highest degree conservative in their influence and results and their enactment consequently is the best guarantee for the peace, prosperity, and solidarity of the

---

[4] G. Rome Hall, "Public Health and Politics," *National Review* (January 1890), 61.

[5] For this reason, a number of historians have located the "origins" of the British Welfare State in the period between 1830 and 1850. See, for instance, David Roberts, *Victorian Origins of the British Welfare State* (New Haven, Conn., 1961).

[6] Arnold Toynbee, *"Progress and Poverty": A Criticism of Mr. Henry George* (London, 1883), 24.

[7] Reginald Brabazon, *Social Arrows* (London, 1886), 352. The novelist George Gissing saw the adoption of social reform as mere opportunism. He asked, "who are the real social reformers? The men who don't care a scrap for the people, but take up ideas because they can make capital out of them" (George Gissing, *Thyrza* [1887, Reprint Edition, New York, 1900], 140).

empire."[8] Through responsible reform, the Demos could be kept in its place; the newly enfranchised working class voters, who were like "the captain of a ship, who is taller and stronger than any of the crew, but is a little deaf, and has weak sight and little knowledge of navigation," needed to be shown that their interests would best be served by leaving politics in the hands of the politicians.[9] Also, as noted above, widespread concern about national decline in an era of increased international industrial and imperial competition, forced many members of the Victorian political elite to consider social reform more seriously. One critic feared that "unless we can give more attention to the vital questions which concern the welfare of the masses, our country must go down in the scale of nations."[10]

It was, quite simply, increasingly difficult for a "man who has a heart as well as a head to look at the present state of society and not feel inclined to be *as much of a Socialist as his knowledge of facts and human nature will allow him to be*" (emphasis added).[11] We should not forget, however, that much as many wished to ameliorate the worst excesses of industrial capitalism, the Victorians' "knowledge of facts and human nature" prevented them from adopting a truly socialist course. The vast majority of the Victorian political elite were willing to accept the limits the influential historian and social reformer Arnold Toynbee placed upon what he liked to call the "New Political Economy."

Toynbee stipulated a number of prerequisites for governmental intervention in the economy. The problem to be addressed had to be of sufficient size to warrant the expansion of State power into the private sector. Second, the State's solution needed to be both practicable and to have a reasonable chance for success. Most important, State social reform must never demoralize the poor. On the contrary, the aid and oversight of the Victorian State should further enlightenment, self-reliance, and morality within the poorer classes; in so doing, the State would encourage increased productivity, better parenting, an active and informed citizenry, and a more stable social and political environment. Any reform that tended to the demoralization of the poor was to be resisted at all costs.[12] Finally,

---

[8] George Howell, "The Dwellings of the Poor," *Nineteenth Century* (June 1883), 1007.

[9] F. C. Conybere, "On Professor Green's Political Philosophy," *National Review* (August 1889), 771.

[10] Quote by Samuel Smith in Reginald Brabazon, ed., *Prosperity or Pauperism: Physical, Industrial, and Technical Training* (London, 1888), 332.

[11] "Panaceas for Poverty," *Saturday Review* (20 February 1886), 252. See also George Howell, "The Dwellings of the Poor," *Nineteenth Century* (June 1883); and F. W. Haine, "Common Sense," *Westminster Review* (September 1890).

[12] See Arnold Toynbee, *The Industrial Revolution* (London, 1884). See also Earl Pembroke, "Liberty and Socialism," *National Review* (May 1883) on the inevitability of increased State regulation of the economy as Britain became more populous; and G. Vere Benson, "The Social Problem," *Westminster Review* (August 1887) on the awakened belief that the condition of the poor might be sensibly raised through the reform of laws and institutions.

State intervention "must not take place until every effort has been made, every expedient exhausted, and indisputable proof given that, if the State does not do the work, it will never be done at all."[13]

Such restrictions, of course, still left a broad field open to social reformers in both political parties. For an appreciation of the reformist ideology of the late Victorian Conservative Party, one must examine the ideas of Benjamin Disraeli, Lord Randolph Churchill, John Gorst, Joseph Chamberlain, and Lord Salisbury. Disraeli explained his conception of domestic reform in a rare public appearance at Free Trade Hall in Manchester on 3 April 1872.[14] Although devoting merely five minutes of a three-hour speech to the issue of social reform, Disraeli defined clearly what he would and would not do if elected to office. He first recognized that the Conservative Party was often

accused of having no programme of policy. If by a programme is meant a plan to despoil churches and plunder landlords, I admit we have no programme. If by a programme is meant a policy which assails or menaces every institution and every interest, every class and every calling in the country, I admit we have no programme.[15]

What Disraeli did advocate was the maintenance of the "Constitution of the Country" and sanitary legislation. According to Disraeli, "Pure air, pure water, the inspection of unhealthy habitations, the adulteration of food, these and many kindred matters may be legitimately dealt with by the Legislature."[16]

Upon finally attaining the office of prime minister at the head of a majority party in 1874, Disraeli helped to pass a number of important pieces of social legislation. The Trades Union Act of 1875 repealed earlier statutory and judicial restrictions on picketing. An Employers and Workmen Act made breach of contract no longer punishable as a criminal offense. The Factory Act of 1874 once again attempted to reduce the number of hours women and children spent in the workplace. A Food and Drug Act tried to reduce the risk of poisoning from tainted goods. The Public Health Act of 1875 gave municipalities the authority to insist on the maintenance of proper sanitary water, sewer, and drainage facilities.

---

[13] Lord Shaftesbury, "Common Sense and the Dwellings of the Poor," *Nineteenth Century* (December 1883), 938.

[14] Disraeli wrote a number of social novels during the 1840s, most famously *Coningsby* (Philadelphia, 1844) and *Sybil* (London, 1845). His flamboyant personality, unnerving political oscillations, and dramatic rise to power have made Disraeli an extremely fascinating and controversial historical figure. The best modern biography is still Robert Blake's magisterial *Disraeli* (New York, 1966).

[15] Benjamin Disraeli, *Selected Speeches of the Late Right Honourable the Earl of Beaconsfield*, edited by T. E. Kebbel (London, 1882), 2: 491-92.

[16] Ibid., 510-12. Disraeli's speech at Free Trade Hall is perhaps best known for his description of the Liberal front bench as being "a range of exhausted volcanoes."

Finally, the Artisans' Dwellings Act of 1875 represented another attempt to encourage the provision of safe, clean homes to the working classes. (It will be discussed at some length in the next chapter.) In no way did the reforms passed by Disraeli's government during the mid-1870s reflect a new attitude towards State intervention. Paul Smith, the author of the best book on Disraelian conservatism, views Tory social reform at this time as "empiricism in the face of concrete problems."[17] Another well-respected historian, Robert K. Webb, sees the Disraelian era "as the end of a long phase of social reform that had begun in the 1820s."[18]

Lord Randolph Churchill, who had been first elected to parliament in 1874, never attempted to hide his admiration for Benjamin Disraeli. With the Conservative Party out of power between 1880 and 1885, Churchill often argued that it must adhere to Disraeli's idea of "Tory Democracy" if it was to return to office in the near future.[19] Churchill did not, however, seem to have a clear idea of what "Tory Democracy" meant. According to one historian, he viewed it "as little more than popular support for the traditional props of Toryism: the Monarchy, the House of Lords, and the Church of England."[20] He was not at all interested in social legislation of the sort that would "follow the whole course of the life of the citizen from the cradle to the grave."[21] In addition, having attained office as chancellor of the exchequer in 1886 through sheer force of character, Churchill soon resigned from Lord Salisbury's government, citing differences over the budget. Although in the political wilderness from 1886 until his premature death from syphilis in 1895, Churchill did have an important impact on Conservative thought. He may have frightened and alienated many of his colleagues by his vague references to "Tory Democracy," but for those Conservatives seeking an antidote to socialism, his words brought inspiration. Churchill's goal, like theirs, was to strengthen ties and dampen class conflict by pursuing a policy of gradual, modest reform.[22]

It was left to John Gorst, one of Churchill's closest allies in parliament, to distinguish the progressive wing of the Conservative Party from its less ambitious colleagues; in 1895, he proposed a series of far-reaching reforms: conciliation boards for the arbitration of industrial grievances; labor registries; strengthened

---

[17] Paul Smith, *Disraelian Conservatism and Social Reform* (London, 1967), 323. Smith argues that Disraeli was too old, sick, and preoccupied with the Eastern Question to devote much attention to domestic reform between 1874 and 1880; he did not play an active role in either the formulation or passage of many of the social reforms enacted during his tenure in office.

[18] Robert K. Webb, *Modern England*, 2nd Edition (New York, 1980), 352.

[19] See, especially, Lord Randolph Churchill, "Elijah's Mantle," *Fortnightly Review* (May 1883)

[20] See R. E. Quinault, "Randolph Churchill and Tory Democracy," *Historical Journal* 1979 22 (1): 143.

[21] Reginald Brabazon, "Great Cities and Social Reform," *Nineteenth Century* (November 1883), 800.

[22] See *The Primrose Record*, 19 November 1885, 180.

employers' liability legislation; public works—as long as they did not compete with private industry; moral education for the unemployed; and houses of "wholesome correction" for the willfully idle. In addition, Gorst believed that pauper children should be placed in cottage homes; the sick poor be treated in private hospitals; and the aged be separated from their demoralized workhouse companions, and, perhaps, even be given a pension.[23]

Joseph Chamberlain, a wealthy screw manufacturer who had made his reputation as a social reformer while mayor of Birmingham during the 1870s and who had continued to press for a host of reforms while a member of William Gladstone's cabinet in the 1880s, deserted the Liberal Party over Home Rule for Ireland in 1886. Along with other disaffected Liberal Unionists, Chamberlain soon gravitated to the Conservative Party. While not joining Lord Salisbury's cabinet until 1895, Chamberlain became, almost by default, one of the leading proponents of Tory social reform. By 1892, Chamberlain was arguing that the Conservatives, not the Liberals, were the reformist party *par excellence*; in consequence, Chamberlain advocated a host of reforms: reduced hours for miners and workers in other "dangerous trades"; local enforcement of trade regulations; arbitration tribunals; employers' compensation for those injured on the job; old age pensions for the deserving poor; the limitation of pauper immigration; increased local government power to improve working class housing; and legislation making it easier for workers to receive municipal home loans.[24]

Last, we must give the most important Conservative politician of the late Victorian period, Lord Salisbury, his due. Prime Minister from 1885 to 1886, 1886 to 1892, and from 1895 until his retirement in 1902, Salisbury dominated Tory politics in much the same way as did his rival and Liberal counterpart, William Gladstone, during the same period. Salisbury's attitude towards social reform was controlled by three separate considerations. First, he realized that his primary task was to hold the Conservative Party together. In a letter dated 7 November 1886, Salisbury cautioned Randolph Churchill that

The Tory party is composed of very varying elements; and there is much trouble and vexation of spirit in trying to make them work together.... It is evident, therefore, that we must work at less speed and at a lower temperature than our opponents. Our Bills must be

---

[23] See John Gorst, "The Conservative Programme of Social Reform," *Nineteenth Century* (July 1895); Gorst also supported the opening of foreign markets and the protection of British trade. See also William H. Mallock, "Conservatism and Socialism," *National Review* (January 1884); and Robert A. Woods, *English Social Movements*, 2nd Edition (New York, 1894).

[24] See Joseph Chamberlain, "The Labour Question," *Nineteenth Century* (November 1892). In December 1892 the *Primrose League Gazette* revealed, for example, that twenty-two of the thirty-five pieces of factory legislation passed between 1802 and 1892 had been initiated by a member of the Conservative Party.

tentative and cautious, not sweeping and dramatic.[25]

Second, Salisbury feared that "sweeping and dramatic" reform might pose a threat to private property, individualism, and liberty. In a speech to the House of Lords on 29 July 1897, Salisbury noted that although

> in no well-governed State, in no State governed according to the principles of common humanity are the claims of mere liberty allowed to endanger the lives of the citizens . . . Where property is in question I am guilty . . . of erecting individual liberty as an idol, and of resenting all attempts to destroy or fetter it.[26]

Third, Salisbury, who served as both prime minister and foreign secretary during thirteen of his sixteen years in office, was often distracted by imperial and diplomatic squabbles overseas.

Not surprisingly, therefore, Salisbury's initiatives in the realm of social reform were cautious, gradualist, and, for the most part, sterile. His administration did establish county councils under the Local Government Act in 1888, abolish primary school fees in 1891, and strengthen employers' compensation legislation in 1897. Other than these rather modest accomplishments, Salisbury had little to show domestically for his long years at the helm of the British nation. He wholeheartedly agreed with the writer for the *Primrose League Gazette* who commented that what Britain wants is "a period of rest; we need have no definite policy, but one of strength abroad and peace at home, one of protection and conservatism."[27]

In many ways, William Gladstone played much the same role towards the Radical wing of the Liberal Party as Lord Salisbury did towards Churchill, Gorst, and, after 1886, Chamberlain. Gladstone, according to the *Economist*, "though recognizing that the reforms [the Radicals] approve will in some way or other be much discussed in 'Parliaments of the future,' relegates them to a distance which, to eager Democrats, will seem very far indeed."[28] For the present, Gladstone would continue to adhere to the props of traditional liberalism: the dismantling of internal and external obstacles to competitive free enterprise; the opening of careers to talent; the provision of a free market in land; judicial equality; the separation of Church and State; and some commitment to representative government. The liberal ideal was a meritocratic society consisting of self-reliant and responsible individuals capable of benefitting from a policy of religious toleration, free trade, political liberty, and economical government. At the root of traditional liberalism was a deep suspicion of the State, of the Church, and of those who wished to

---

[25] Cited in J.P.D. Dunbabin, "The Politics of the Establishment of County Councils," *Historical Journal* 1963 6 (2): 251-52.

[26] Quoted in Peter Marsh, *The Discipline of Popular Government: Lord Salisbury's Domestic Statecraft* (Sussex, England, 1978), 267.

[27] *Primrose League Gazette*, August 1896, 6. See also Peter Marsh, *The Discipline of Popular Government: Lord Salisbury's Domestic Statecraft* (Sussex, England, 1978).

[28] "Mr. Gladstone on Radical Proposals," *The Economist* (7 December 1889), 1563.

control the economy through protectionist policies. At the same time, liberals retained great faith in economic progress, reason, volunteerism, the ultimate goodness of the British citizenry, and the efficiency of the private sector.[29]

While, perhaps, recognizing that the "function of true Liberalism in the future will be that of putting a limit to the powers of Parliament," Gladstone did support the passage of a number of pieces of significant social legislation.[30] During his ministry of 1868-1874, Gladstone backed an Irish Land Act, legislation to legalize trade unions and grant them the protection of the courts, the secret ballot, and various reforms of the British military, civil service, and legal system. Most important, William E. Forster's Education Act of 1870 authorized the election of local nondenominational school boards and gave them the power to levy rates, build schools, and hire teachers. During his second ministry between 1880 and 1885, however, Gladstone was too preoccupied with crises overseas, particularly in Egypt and Ireland, and the further extension of the franchise under the Third Great Reform Act of 1884 to give much thought to social reform. Nevertheless, even this government passed several important reforms. In addition to another Irish Land Act, Gladstone insured that, after 1880, elementary school attendance would be compulsory. His Employers' Liability Act of that same year allowed employees to sue for damages if they were injured on the job. Finally, from 1885, those receiving free medical relief from the Poor Law no longer risked being disenfranchised.

The departure of Chamberlain and some of his followers after Gladstone's conversion to Irish Home Rule in 1886 temporarily drained the Liberal Party of its reformist impulse. By 1891, the emergence of new leaders—Herbert Asquith, Henry Campbell-Bannerman, and John Morley to name but a few—had more than filled the void left by the departing Unionists. The "Newcastle Programme" of that year stated forthrightly what the Liberal Party would do when it returned to power; the "Programme" voiced support for, among other things, triennial parliaments, an end to plural voting, local government reform, land allotments, strengthened employers' liability legislation, and Irish Home Rule. Because of Gladstone's absorption with Home Rule for Ireland, however, little by way of significant social reform was enacted by the Liberal Party after its return to power in 1893, with the possible exception of William Harcourt's budget of 1894.[31] All other reforms—the

---

[29] See Michael Barker, *Gladstone and Radicalism* (Sussex, England, 1975); Ian Bradley, *The Optimists* (London, 1980); Richard Bellamy, ed., *Victorian Liberalism* (London, 1990); and Eugenio Biagini, *Liberty, Retrenchment, and Reform* (New York, 1992).

[30] Herbert Spencer, *Man versus the State* (1884, Reprint Edition, Caldwell, Idaho, 1940), 403.

[31] Lord Randolph Churchill and the Liberal Unionist George Goschen had both attempted to raise death duties on estates during the last half of the 1880s. In 1894, Harcourt eliminated the distinction between landed and personal property and introduced a system of graduated death duties. In the future, heirs would pay from one to eight percent of their inheritance, depending on its value. Fifteen years later, David Lloyd George's "People's Budget" raised death duties further and introduced a progressive income tax.

establishment of a Labour Department, the hiring of additional factory inspectors, the tightening of regulations concerning sweated labor, the passage of a mild Factory and Workshop Act in 1895, and the granting of the eight-hour day to all War Office and Admiralty factories—merely built upon past precedent.[32]

Gladstone's lack of ambition in the realm of social policy was very troubling to many of the Radicals within his party. Increasingly during the 1880s, they came to view Gladstone and the traditional liberalism he represented as "a spent projectile."[33] Like their counterparts in the Conservative Party, the "New Liberals" believed that the State should be much more aggressive in its promotion of social reform. Unlike Gladstone, they did not fear the consequences of State power. The Radical Liberal Richard Haldane commented in 1888 that the "mere removal of obstacles which used to block the highway of human progress in this country has been pretty well completed. We are face to face with a new kind of social problem. Liberalism has passed from the destructive into the constructive stage in its history."[34] Frank Harris agreed, arguing further that the "State has too long made itself the champion of the rights of the individual; it must now assert the rights of the many—of all."[35]

The goals of the "New Liberalism" were many. Haldane desired to lessen societal inequality, widen the distribution of wealth, and elevate the poor. John A. Hobson hoped that State intervention in the economy would make capitalism efficient by preventing recurrent cycles of surplus, over-investment, under-consumption, and mass unemployment. L. T. Hobhouse argued that, as private citizens had both rights and duties towards one another, the State should dedicate itself to the promotion of humanity and ethics.[36] Haldane, Hobson, and Hobhouse

---

[32] See Michael Barker, *Gladstone and Radicalism* (Sussex, England, 1975). Barker vastly overstates the importance of the social reforms of Gladstone's 1893-1894 government.

[33] George Bernard Shaw, "What Mr. Gladstone Ought to Do," *Fortnightly Review* (February 1893), 280.

[34] Richard Haldane, "The Liberal Creed," *Contemporary Review* (October 1888), 463. The *Progressive Review* noted that "because State activity under ill-informed and class governments has often proved injurious [in the past], it does not follow that the action of the State as it exists to-day will of necessity be ill-advised" (*Progressive Review*, May 1897, 126). See also *Progressive Review*, October 1896, 4.

[35] Frank Harris, "The Radical Programme—The Housing of the Poor in Towns," *Fortnightly Review* (1883), 600. As one critic asked, "what in all the world is the banding together of men good, if not for that?" (N. Kempner, *Common Sense Socialism* [London, 1887], 299). See also Robert Eccleshall, *British Liberalism* (London, 1986), 3.

[36] See John Allet, *The New Liberalism: The Political Economy of J. A. Hobson* (Toronto, 1981); and L. T. Hobhouse, *The Labour Movement* (London, 1893). Hobhouse's adherence to the principle of "utility" convinced him that "Collectivism" was the most rational and ethical organization for the modern industrial economy.

all believed that *"laissez-faire"* economics and small-state liberalism sapped the physical strength and destroyed the morals of the nation. All were concerned with the removal of economic injustice, championed the cause of the productive classes, and had faith in the innate wisdom of the people. Each firmly believed in Bentham's principle of "utility"—the greatest good for the greatest number—with regard to legislation. None accepted social misery and inequality as inevitable; by improving material conditions, the State could both reduce poverty and raise the morality of the poorest classes as well.[37]

By no means, of course, did the "New Liberals" intend to overturn capitalism; their reforms were meant to render it secure by cushioning workers from the accidents, unemployment, sickness, and old age that all too often rendered their lives a misery. As one journalist reported, the "measures now contemplated, would preserve in their normal vigour and freshness all the individual activities of English citizenship, and would do nothing more spoliatory than tax . . . aggregations of wealth for the good of the community."[38] State aid, control, and management could be relied upon to check the abuses of private enterprise without impairing initiative, creativity, or productivity. Finally, parroting what Lord Shaftesbury had written seven years before, the economist John Rae forcefully contended that although the State should be allowed to do what it does best, it should "leave to the individual the things the individual can do best."[39]

Within these parameters, Joseph Chamberlain—at least prior to his defection from the Liberal Party in 1886—cast a long shadow. Indeed, his influence over British radicalism reached its height with his "unauthorized programme" of 1885. Chamberlain included a number of long-standing Radical proposals: universal manhood suffrage, an end to plural voting, and the payment of members of parliament. In addition, he emphasized the need for local government reform, better housing for the working classes, free secular primary education, and land reform.

Chamberlain explained his philosophy of social reform in a series of campaign speeches he delivered in 1885. While in his hometown of Birmingham on 5 January, he argued that parliament must promote the general happiness and welfare of the people, "the aim and end of all our Liberal policy—the greatest

---

[37] See William Graham, *The Social Problem* (London, 1886); and James Holms, "Is This a 'New Liberalism,' " *Westminster Review* (September 1890).

[38] "The Revolution of 1884," *Fortnightly Review* (January 1885), 7. See also "Socialism and Legislation," *Westminster Review* (January 1886).

[39] John Rae, "State Socialism and Popular Right," *Contemporary Review* (December 1890), 876.

happiness of the greatest number."[40] In late April, Chamberlain commented specifically that the State needed to "protect the weak, and to provide for the poor, to redress the inequalities of our social system, to alleviate the harsh conditions of the struggle for existence, and to raise the average enjoyment of the majority of the population."[41]

Chamberlain knew, of course, that the State could not and, indeed, should not try to do everything. He often challenged his audiences to think more about the duties they owed to their neighbors and to their country, and less about their own rights. Furthermore, Chamberlain stated that he did not want his listeners "to think that I suggest to you that legislation can accomplish all that we desire . . . above all, I would not lead you into wild and revolutionary projects, which would upset unnecessarily the existing order of things."[42] The "existing order of things" included, for Chamberlain, the capitalist free enterprise system. Chamberlain's important speech at Hull on 5 August 1885 should, in consequence, be quoted at some length.

I am not a Communist, although some people will have it that I am. Considering the difference in the character and the capacity of men, I do not believe that there can ever be an absolute equality of conditions, and I think that nothing would be more undesirable than that we should remove the stimulus to industry and thrift and exertion which is afforded by the security given to every man in the enjoyment of the fruits of his own individual exertions. I am opposed to confiscation in every shape or form, because I believe that it would destroy that security and lessen that stimulus.[43]

Even with this disclaimer, Chamberlain and his fellow Radicals had a reputation—perhaps undeserved—for favoring excessive State intervention in the economy. A journalist for *The Economist* warned in 1889 that

At the present moment the dominant idea of the Radical party is, that there is nothing that the State cannot do by legislation to improve the general condition, that it can secure 'fair' wages and short hours to all workers, that it can ensure decent lodging to the entire population, that it can make the whole people temperate, thrifty, and chaste, and that it can extinguish . . . poverty.[44]

In fact, their ambitions were of a more modest nature. For example, Arnold Toynbee favored the nationalization of gas, water, and railroads; he was also

---

[40] Joseph Chamberlain, *Mr. Chamberlain's Speeches*, edited by Charles Boyd (New York, 1970), 139.

[41] Ibid., 165-66. See also "The Trades Unions and Socialism," *The Economist* (11 September 1886), 1132.

[42] Joseph Chamberlain, *Speeches of the Right Hon. Joseph Chamberlain, M.P.*, edited by Henry W. Lucy (London, 1885), 161-64.

[43] Ibid., 164.

[44] "The Debate on Tuesday on the Poor," *The Economist* (6 April 1889), 430.

willing to allow municipalities to buy land and to let it out at reduced rates to societies building for the working classes. The Liberal Charles Bradlaugh supported progressive taxation, taxation of the "unearned" increment in land, the establishment of courts of arbitration to settle labor disputes and a bureau of labor statistics, and increased factory and sanitary inspections. Furthermore, Bradlaugh believed that the State should be willing to take possession of uncultivated lands and lease them out in small parcels to the underemployed.[45] The Radical newspaperman Henry Massingham in 1893 approved of the eight-hour day for workers, strengthened employers' liability legislation, the equalization of the London rates, the restoration of Trafalgar Square to the people, better administration of the factory acts, scrupulous inquiries into the "dangerous" trades, the appointment of workers as justices of the peace, the lowering of the property qualification for Poor Law Guardians to £5, a Royal Commission on the aged poor, the establishment of a Labour Department, and the imposition of death duties. *The New Age* newspaper agreed with most of Massingham's proposals and added in 1899 that the State should ensure the payment of members of parliament and their election expenses; abolish child labor under the age of fourteen; municipalize the drink traffic; tax ground values; and institute a progressive income tax. In addition, according to *The New Age*, "progressives" should advocate old age pensions; the municipalization of land, water, gas, and trams; public works for the unemployed; and universal suffrage.[46]

Gladstone and his allies within the Liberal Party could, of course, be expected to resist many of these reforms. At the same time, however, it was very much in their interest to adopt a more positive attitude towards the "New Liberalism." As Henry Massingham noted in 1893, if the Liberal Party did not soon discard its shopworn individualism, "it may be Toryism for the rest of the century, and a Radical-Labour-Collectivist opposition to face it."[47] The Fabian Socialist Sidney Webb agreed with Massingham that if Gladstone did not enact the "Newcastle Programme," legislate an eight-hour day, provide a minimum wage for public servants, humanize the Poor Law and the penal system, and comfort the aged, the Liberal Party would in the near future be "reconstituted as a mainly working-class organization on a frankly collectivist basis."[48]

Whatever their aspirations, Radical Liberals accomplished little in the realm

---

[45] See Arnold Toynbee, *The Industrial Revolution* (London, 1884); and Charles Bradlaugh's answers in *Will Socialism Benefit the English People?* (London, 1884).

[46] See Henry W. Massingham, "What Mr. Gladstone Ought to Do," *Fortnightly Review* (February 1893); and *The New Age* (9 February 1899).

[47] Henry W. Massingham, "What Mr. Gladstone Ought to Do," *Fortnightly Review* (February 1893), 275. See also L. A. Atherley-Jones's "The New Liberalism," *Nineteenth Century* (August 1889) and "Liberalism and Social Reform," *New Review* (December 1893); and George W. E. Russell, "The New Liberalism: A Response," *Nineteenth Century* (September 1889).

[48] Sidney Webb, "What Mr. Gladstone Ought to Do," *Fortnightly Review* (February 1893), 287.

of parliamentary social reform during the late Victorian period. At the local level, however, they did achieve a number of notable successes. Not surprisingly, Joseph Chamberlain played a pivotal role in the municipal reform movement. While mayor of Birmingham from 1873 until 1876, Chamberlain had overseen the purchase of gas and water companies, the demolition of forty acres of slums, and the construction, at municipal expense, of large numbers of model dwellings for the poor. He clearly agreed with Reverend Samuel Barnett that the task of municipal government was "not to protect the pockets of the rich, but to save the people."[49] Upon entering Gladstone's administration in 1880, Chamberlain argued persuasively in favor of local government reform, especially for metropolitan London; in his estimation, "the want of an efficient and thoroughly representative municipal government [in London] stands in the way of reform."[50]

Nor was Chamberlain alone in his condemnation of the misadministration of the Metropolis. Sir Edwin Chadwick (1800-1890), an associate of Jeremy Bentham who had fought for factory and public health legislation since the 1830s, warned that it was difficult "to tell the price London pays for its disunity, which has retarded improvements, diminished efficiency, and increased cost in every branch of local service."[51] Pollution, infectious disease, overcrowding, urban decay, and political apathy would continue to stalk the Metropolis until it had been given a central government of its own. J.F.B. Firth of the Municipal Reform League agreed whole-heartedly with Chamberlain and Chadwick about the necessity for London municipal reform. Under a supreme municipal council, London would be able to obtain cheaper water and gas, better sanitation and drainage, superior police and fire protection, and more public markets, baths, wash houses, parks, and libraries. Homes would be better built; pubs would be licensed; and country workhouses would be available for the use of the aged poor. As important, a single authority would henceforth speak for and command the respect of the community.[52]

Having agitated for London government reform since the late 1860s, however, Firth recognized how difficult it would be to bring their desires to fruition. London, although the capital of the British Empire and the largest city in the world, was woefully under-represented in parliament during the Victorian era. If the Metropolis had been represented in proportion to its population, it would

---

[49] Samuel A. Barnett, "Great Cities and Social Reform," *Nineteenth Century* (November 1883), 816.

[50] Joseph Chamberlain, "Labourers' and Artisans' Dwellings," *Fortnightly Review* (December 1883), 765-66.

[51] Edwin Chadwick, "London Centralized," *Contemporary Review* (June 1884), 794. Chadwick believed that the lack of a strong central administration had retarded sanitary reform in the Metropolis by at least a quarter century.

[52] See Joseph F. B. Firth, *Municipal London* (London, 1876).

have sent seventy-three members to parliament; in 1883, it only sent twenty-two.[53] As a result, its needs were often, in Firth's opinion, overlooked. Second, the chaotic, conflicting, and overlapping nature of London's government ensured a great deal of internal bureaucratic resistance to change.[54] The City of London—formerly the parishes encompassed by the medieval city walls and during the modern era London's financial district—lobbied particularly aggressively for the preservation of its prerogatives and independence. Furthermore, many members of parliament feared that the establishment of a unified county council for London would lead directly to the worst excesses of Continental socialism. First, Firth and his supporters would purchase the water and gas companies. Then they would gain control over the Metropolitan Police. Finally, the "Commune of London" would enact socialistic legislation within the heart of the British Empire.[55]

In addition, many Victorians agreed with the novelist Margaret Harkness that the centralization of London government was both "unenglish" and "experimental." She favored the establishment of four metropolitan municipalities headed by the Lord Mayor of the City. Another critic complained that gas and water would not be cheaper under municipal control; improvements would not be made any faster; and Londoners would not become more interested in their local government following the passage of reform. The immense bureaucracy established in London would be expensive, extravagant, and inefficient. Because of its proximity to Westminster, it would be able to put pressure on parliament to enact unwise social legislation.[56] Finally, contrary to what Firth had been saying for years, "there was no genuine public opinion in London on the subject of Municipal Reform"; consequently, many believed the subject could be shelved for the time being.[57]

Unfortunately for those who preferred the *status quo* in London, the advocates of change had by the 1880s won important allies within the halls of parliament. In December 1881, the Liberal Home Secretary William Harcourt, prompted by Chamberlain at the Board of Trade, brought the issue of a unified county council for the Metropolis before the cabinet. Widespread unrest in Ireland, Gladstone's consuming interest in electoral reform, and disagreement in the cabinet over whether the Metropolitan Police should be transferred to local control or remain in the hands of the Home Office ensured that municipal reform would not be given

---

[53] If London were represented like Scotland, it would send sixty; like Ireland, seventy; and like Wales, ninety representatives to Westminster (Joseph F. B. Firth, "The Fate of the London Bill," *Fortnightly Review* [July 1883], 98).

[54] For example, eight water companies, ten postal divisions, thirty Poor Law unions, and thirty-nine local governments served the Metropolis prior to the Local Government Act of 1888.

[55] See George Salisbury, "Municipal London," *Quarterly Review* (July 1884).

[56] See Margaret Harkness, "The Municipality of London," *National Review* (May and September 1883); J. Whittaker Ellis, "The Government of London Bill," *National Review* (June 1884); and George Salisbury, "Municipal London," *Quarterly Review* (July 1884).

[57] Arthur Baumann, "The London Clauses of the Local Government Bill," *National Review* (June 1888), 539.

a high priority by this particular Liberal government, however.[58] Local government reform would only be enacted after the Conservatives under Lord Salisbury had come to power.

Although the passage of the Local Government Act of 1888 has often been interpreted as no more than an inevitable sequel to Gladstone's Third Reform Act of 1884, there was much more to it than that. The support Salisbury received from Chamberlain and other Liberal Unionists after the Home Rule crisis of 1886, unrest in the Metropolis in 1886-1887, and the persuasiveness of Firth's attacks on the Metropolitan Board of Works and other vested interests in London all combined to induce a serious consideration of municipal reform at the close of the 1880s.[59]

Furthermore, the desertion of London, a former bastion of the Liberal Party, to the Tories after 1886 may have made some Conservative parliamentarians less anxious about municipal reform in the Metropolis. After winning only twenty-one percent of all parliamentary seats in London from 1859 until 1880, the Conservatives claimed seventy-five percent between 1885 and 1900. In the elections of 1886, 1895, and 1900, indeed, the Tories captured between eighty and eighty-six percent of all metropolitan seats. The reasons for this dramatic electoral shift are clear: low voter turnout; Liberal opposition to the Independent Labour Party and the drink trade; a chronic lack of funds within the Liberal camp; Tory "generosity" and their ability to take advantage of anti-alien and anti-Irish sentiment. In essence, "the upper and middle class had a strong propensity to vote Conservative," while "the working class had a much less marked tendency to vote Liberal."[60]

Whatever the reason for its passage, the Local Government Act of 1888 represented a giant, if incomplete, step forward in the administration of metropolitan London. Although only two of its one hundred and twenty-seven articles actually dealt with London, each was important. The first disbanded the Metropolitan Board of Works; the second founded the London County Council. The establishment of the LCC provided Firth and his followers with the means to

---

[58] Not surprisingly, Home Secretary Harcourt favored the retention of the police by the Home Office; Gladstone wished it to be turned over to the London County Council. For more information, see Ken Young and Patricia Garside, *Metropolitan London: Politics and Urban Change, 1837-1981* (London, 1982).

[59] See "The Government of London," *The Economist* (31 January 1874); "The Doings of the Metropolitan Board of Works," *Westminster Review* (November 1888); and J.P.D. Dunbabin, "The Politics of the Establishment of County Councils," *Historical Journal* 1963 6 (2): 226-52. The historian David Owen has argued that many of the criticisms levied against the Metropolitan Board of Works were patently unfair. He determined on closer examination that the MBW was not corruption-ridden, wasteful, or particularly inefficient. See David Owen, *The Government of Victorian London, 1855-1889*, edited by Donald Olsen and David Reeder (Cambridge, Mass., 1982).

[60] Henry Pelling, *The Social Geography of British Elections, 1885-1918* (London, 1967), 56. See also Paul Thompson, "Liberals, Radicals, and Labor in London, 1880-1900," *Past and Present* 1964 (27): 73-101.

enact substantive reform in the Metropolis in the future. "Important therefore as this body will be, and enormous as will be the initial powers conferred upon it," Firth commented, "there will be more power and greater responsibility to follow."[61] Firth believed that the London vestries needed to be reformed and the City abolished as a separate administrative entity; their funds could then be dedicated to improving education, hospitals, museums, parks, libraries, and housing in the Metropolis. Owner and occupier taxation must be introduced. The LCC needed to gain control of the Metropolitan Police and the London gas and water companies. Finally, the number of representatives on the LCC needed to be raised to around three hundred; at present the electoral districts were far too large in Firth's opinion.[62] Such reforms became even more practicable after Firth's Progressive Party won an electoral landslide in the LCC election of January 1889, capturing seventy-three of the one hundred and eighteen seats.[63] After electing the future Liberal Prime Minister Lord Rosebery chairman, the London County Council got down to the task of governing the vast city under its charge.

The abolition of the City of London as a separate political unit and the reclamation of the endowments of the City Guilds were, as noted above, important parts of the Progressive program. In the estimation of Firth and his supporters, there was no good reason for the City to retain its privileged status; it was simply an anachronism from a bygone era. As it drew much of its revenue—in tolls, rents, fees, and stallage dues in London markets—from outside its territorial boundaries, critics could argue that the wealthy City drained much-needed income from its poorer neighbors. Furthermore, few could understand how the £900,000 the City spent annually on itself benefitted the Metropolis as a whole.[64]

Surprisingly, the City was able to ward off the blows directed against it with

---

[61] Joseph F. B. Firth, *London Government under the Local Government Act, 1888* (London, 1888), v. According to one member of the Municipal Reform League, "Regarded as a complete plan for meeting the wants of local government in London it is very defective. Regarded as a step towards such a plan, it is a bold and important one, in the right direction" (Arthur Hobhouse, "Local Self-Government for London," *Contemporary Review* [June 1888], 773).

[62] See "The Local Government Act," *Westminster Review* (September 1888); and Joseph F. B. Firth, *The Reform of London Government and of the City Guilds* (London, 1888). The goals of the Progressive Party were, thus, "to disestablish and disendow the City one day, to take over the control of the police the next, and to introduce the millennium before the close of the year" (W. M. Acworth, "The London County Council," *Nineteenth Century* [March 1889], 426).

[63] For the election of the London County Council, the Metropolis was divided into fifty-seven districts, each to provide two councillors. The City was entitled to send four representatives to the LCC as well. Elections were to take place every three years.

[64] See Frederic Harrison, "The Amalgamation of London," *Contemporary Review* (November 1894); G. Laurence Gomme, "The Future Government of London," *Contemporary Review* (November 1894); and J. F. Oakeshott, "The London County Council: What It Is and What It Does," *Fabian Tract*, no. 61 (London, 1895).

relative ease. By cloaking itself in "ancient" ritual, costume, ceremony, and symbolism—particularly during the popular annual Lord Mayor's Show—the City proved that its traditions were worthy of preservation. The generosity displayed by the City charities, especially the Mansion House Relief Fund during the mid-1880s, won much support. Finally, the City collected signatures, published pamphlets, disrupted reform meetings, and used its political slush fund to propagate its views to the people of the Metropolis and within parliament. Consequently, despite the best efforts of Progressives within the London County Council, the City was allowed to retain its independence.[65]

Although prevented from draining the coffers of the City to pay for metropolitan improvements, the Progressives forged ahead. As London desperately needed additional parks and recreation areas, one commentator advocated the purchase and administration of the more than two hundred disused burial grounds and neglected squares of the Metropolis. County Council control would ensure a clean, healthy environment and, during the summer months, public concerts.[66] As London also required wider streets to ease congestion and to improve trade and communication within the Metropolis, and as better cleaning, lighting, and paving of its streets would make London a more healthful, less crime-ridden city, the Progressives were staunch advocates of metropolitan improvements and the strict enforcement of the sanitary laws.[67]

The Progressive Party also favored the imposition of a tax on metropolitan real estate which had increased in value as a result of public improvements. Supporters could cite many historical precedents. Henry I, Henry VIII, Edward VI, Elizabeth I, James I, and Charles II had all imposed similar taxes at various times. In the modern era, the United States, Canada, Australia, New Zealand, and Gibraltar all had placed "betterment" taxes on the books. The LCC was, indeed, willing in 1890 to refuse to vote funds for metropolitan improvements until parliament allowed it to impose "betterment" taxes. Even after this problem had been resolved, another remained; owners often passed land and "betterment" taxes along to their tenants through increased rent. According to one author, by collecting such taxes from occupiers while allowing them, by law, to deduct these

---

[65] See Timothy Smith, "In Defense of Privilege: The City of London and the Challenge of Municipal Reform, 1875-1890," *Journal of Social History* 1993 27 (1): 59-83.

[66] See M. J. Meath's "Lungs for Our Great Cities," *New Review* (May 1890) and "The London County Council and Open Spaces," *New Review* (December 1892); and Frederic Harrison, "Sir John Lubbock and the London County Council," *New Review* (November 1891). In 1892, the LCC controlled only sixty-seven of the two hundred and fifty-eight parks and playgrounds within the Metropolis.

[67] See Frederic Harrison, "London Improvements," *New Review* (October 1892); and J. F. Oakeshott, "The London County Council: What It Is and What It Does," *Fabian Tract*, no. 61 (London, 1895).

charges from their rent, this difficulty might be overcome.[68] The Progressive Party program of 1895 expanded upon these early ideas. In addition to "betterment" taxes, revenue could be raised by taxing the owners of ground rents and by levying municipal death duties on local real estate. The metropolitan tax system would be made fairer by equalizing local rates through the municipal common fund and by insisting upon a proper evaluation of house and land values.[69]

The question of who was to control the Metropolitan Police was, as we have already seen, also highly controversial. According to the Progressives, placing the police under the jurisdiction of the London County Council would make it more efficient and much less expensive. Supporters could cite statistics to bolster their claim that Home Office administration of the police was something less than cost-effective. Between 1878 and 1888, the population of the Metropolitan Police Area grew by twenty-three percent and its rateable value rose by thirty-eight percent; the cost of police protection, however, increased by forty-four percent. The Metropolitan Police were more expensive than those of any other city, whether judged by population, miles of street, or number of inhabited houses. Nevertheless, critics remained suspicious of LCC control of the police. Some, indeed, invoked the specter of the French Revolution; if the LCC controlled the police, it might, by allowing widespread rioting and looting to proceed unchecked in the Metropolis, be able to coerce parliament. London's "capture by a hostile force would not only paralyze the whole government of the empire, but possibly lead to its overthrow."[70] Not surprisingly under the circumstances, the Government preferred to retain control of the Metropolitan Police under the Home Office.

The Progressives also supported the further democratization of the London County Council electorate. It made little sense to them that the parliamentary franchise was in 1888 less restrictive than that of the LCC. Only ratepayers and occupiers possessing land worth £10 per annum and who met strict residency requirements—usually one year—were allowed to vote in local elections in the Metropolis. Unlike parliament, however, women, if unmarried and otherwise eligible, were allowed to vote for borough or county councillors. What was unclear was whether women could actually sit on the London County Council. In January 1889, Lady Margaret Sandhurst and Jane Cobden won election from Brixton and Bow & Bromley respectively on the Progressive ticket. Although supported by the majority of the LCC, both of their elections were soon under attack in the House

---

[68] See Arthur Baumann, "The London County Council," *Universal Review* (1890); B.F.C. Costelloe, "The Bitter Cry of the London Rate-payer," *Contemporary Review* (February 1894); and Hugh H. L. Bellot, "The Principles of Betterment," *Westminster Review* (April 1894).

[69] See J. F. Oakeshott, "The London County Council: What It Is and What It Does," *Fabian Tract*, no. 61 (London, 1895).

[70] Howard Evans, "The London County Council and Its Police," *Contemporary Review* (March 1889), 448. See also James Stuart, "The Metropolitan Police," *Contemporary Review* (April 1889).

of Lords. Sandhurst was replaced almost immediately; Cobden, because she refused to speak in the LCC, was allowed to retain her seat. Upon breaking her vow of silence in February 1890, she was thrown off the London County Council. Though the Progressives continued to support a woman's right to stand for election to the LCC, only in 1907 were women allowed to sit legally as councillors.[71]

Nor were the Progressives much more successful in the realm of "municipal socialism" during the late Victorian period. The question of whether the London gas or water companies should be brought under municipal control had been a matter of some debate since the 1870s. As with the Metropolitan Police, the Progressives believed that they could provide more efficient and cheaper service than could be furnished by the private sector. They were not alone in this belief. The parliamentary select committee on the "London Water Supply" commented in 1880 that, for the health of the community, "it is expedient that the supply of water to the Metropolis should be placed under the control of some Public Body."[72] London's eight water companies—five north of the Thames and three south—were accused by the committee and others of gouging their customers. Water rates appeared to rise with rising property values, not as a result of increasing costs to the water companies. Parliamentary investigators found many instances of illegal overcharging or charging for services not rendered by the water companies.[73]

Conservative Home Secretary Richard A. Cross's Bill to acquire the London water companies in 1880, unfortunately, went nowhere. The cost, some £31 million, seemed an extremely high price to pay for such defective property. Although "the present water supply is so bad and deficient that it cannot be tolerated much longer," widespread opposition to higher taxes made the municipalization of the London water supply appear unattractive.[74] Later attempts

---

[71] See "Local Government and the Franchise Question," *Westminster Review* (July 1888); J. F. Oakeshott, "The London County Council: What It Is and What It Does," *Fabian Tract*, no. 61 (London, 1895); and Jonathon Schneer, "Politics and Feminism in 'Outcast London,'" *Journal of British Studies* 1991 30 (1): 63-82.

[72] The committee included William Harcourt, Joseph Chamberlain, Joseph F. B. Firth, and Home Secretary Richard A. Cross. See the report from the Select Committee, House of Commons, on "The London Water Supply" (1880 [329], v. x, sess. 2, iii).

[73] See "The Metropolitan Water Companies," *The Economist* (11 April 1885); and Archibald Dobbs, "The London Water Companies: A Review and an Impeachment," *Westminster Review* (May 1892). While the number of houses in London supplied with water rose by thirty-two percent between 1872 and 1883, the water rate increased by fifty-nine percent. Average water consumption per home not only did not increase, it decreased slightly. Shortages in both summer and winter were common.

[74] "The Purchase of the London Water Companies," *The Economist* (6 March 1880), 261. See also "The Water Supply of the Metropolis," *The Economist* (19 June 1880); and John Lubbock, "London Government," *National Review* (December 1895). As purchase seemed out of the question, some members of the LCC argued during the next twenty years that the municipality should be allowed to place a director on the board of each of the water companies to protect the public interest.

to buy the London water companies in 1891, 1895, and 1896 failed as well for one reason or another.

In addition, the Progressives found it impossible to bring the London gas companies under municipal control during the late Victorian era. In this case, the issue was not quite so clear. As many believed that electric lighting—a cheaper, safer, and healthier form of illumination—would supersede coal-gas in the near future, it made little sense for the LCC to purchase the gas companies. When the time came, the municipality would, many hoped, gain control of electricity in the Metropolis.[75]

Although spectacularly unsuccessful in the realm of "municipal socialism," the Progressive Party—following the example of Glasgow, Birmingham, Liverpool, Manchester, Leeds, Bradford, and other British cities—continued to attempt to expand the areas under its control. London markets, hospitals, cabs, and trams were all considered targets for municipalization. Indeed, in 1891, over the objections of the press, opponents in parliament, and Moderates within the London County Council, the LCC passed a resolution to buy a portion of the London Street Tramways Company.[76] Most Progressives also favored the eight hour workday with one day off per week, unionization, and the increased regulation of sweated labor, particularly among workers employed by the LCC. A smaller number proposed improved—perhaps even public—housing for the poor and the direct employment of labor by the LCC during periods of economic distress. A handful supported the municipal ownership of land. But little was done, in the final analysis, to bring these dreams to fruition.[77]

Although the Progressive Party's legislative record in the London County Council was spotty, they were able to win further electoral victories in 1892, 1895, and 1898.[78] Contrary to public fears, rates had only risen by 1.5d. per pound

---

[75] See R. H. Patterson, "London Gas," *British Quarterly Review* (January 1879); W. H. Dickenson, "The Water Supply of London," *Contemporary Review* (February 1897); and G. Shaw Lefevre, "The London Water Supply," *Nineteenth Century* (December 1898).

[76] See Robert Collier, "The London County Council and the Tramways," *New Review* (December 1891). See also Joseph Chamberlain, "Municipal Government," *New Review* (June 1894). Not surprisingly, considering his record as mayor of Birmingham in the 1870s, Chamberlain believed that municipalities should be allowed to do all that could not be effectively done by the private sector.

[77] See Frederick Dolman, *Municipalities at Work* (1895, Reprint Edition, New York, 1985); Joseph Chamberlain, "Municipal Government," *New Review* (June 1894); J. F. Oakeshott, "The London County Council: What It Is and What It Does," *Fabian Tract*, no. 61 (London, 1895). The danger was that "if the county council possesses the machinery for employing large bodies of men, irresistible pressure will be put on it in times of distress to find relief for the unemployed" ("London Questions," *The Economist* [22 October 1892], 1323).

[78] Indeed, their margin of victory increased from 10,000 in 1889 to 31,000 votes in 1892.

sterling between 1889 and 1895. Even so, much, according to the Fabian Socialist Sidney Webb, had been accomplished. The LCC had purchased one thousand acres for open spaces, purified the Thames, and improved sanitation, working class housing, and the fire-watch. It had provided eight hundred scholarships to poor children, forced slum lords to repair their buildings, constructed large common lodging houses for the homeless, and begun work on the Thames tunnel. In essence, the Progressives had proven themselves, in the opinion of many impartial observers, to be efficient, responsible administrators of the public interest.[79]

As a result, many Progressives were openly contemptuous of the conservatism of their opponents on the LCC, the Moderate Party. John Burns, a member of the LCC from Battersea, argued that the Moderates must be crushed because of their unholy alliance with land speculators, jerry-builders, house-farmers, monopolists, jobbers, and publicans. Long-time social critic Robert Collier characterized the typical Moderate as "a vacuous dandy who never tried to do a good day's work of any kind in his life, and finds quite enough to do in enduring the boredom of doing nothing, presuming to employ the few stock phrases of fashionable slang at his command in abuse of the world's workers."[80] Much of this campaign-style rhetoric should not be taken too seriously. In reality, there was not as wide a gulf between the two parties as Burns and others liked to believe. The Progressives were not, by and large, socialists intent on dismantling capitalism, but reformers interested in gradual, ameliorative reform. The Moderates were just that, conservatives resistant to rising rates and government intervention in the economy. Not surprisingly, the decade following the Local Government Act of 1888 "tended to confirm the . . . belief that the change [in London government was] more apparent than real."[81]

Still, the Moderate Party, like their Progressive counterparts, had to make an effort to distinguish themselves from their opponents. Unfortunately, their opposition to the

excessive centralization of London Government, indifference to local aspirations, a costly Works Department, ill-considered projects of municipalization, interference with private enterprise, a rising rate, neglect of public improvements, impracticable schemes of taxation, and a generally aggressive policy

did not resonate with the London populace, largely because the Progressives'

---

[79] See William Saunders, *History of the First London County Council, 1889-1891* (London, 1892); T. G. Fardell and Charles Harrison, "The London County Council," *New Review* (March 1892); James Stuart, "The London Progressives," *Contemporary Review* (April 1892); and Sidney Webb, "The Work of the London County Council," *Contemporary Review* (January 1895).

[80] Robert Collier, "The London County Council," *New Review* (December 1891), 493. See also John Burns's "Towards a Commune," *Nineteenth Century* (March 1892) and "Let London Live," *Nineteenth Century* (April 1892).

[81] J.P.D. Dunbabin, "Expectations of the New County Councils and Their Realization," *Historical Journal* 1965 8 (3): 370. See also R. E. Prothero, "Towards Common Sense," *Nineteenth Century* (March 1892).

accomplishments had been so modest.[82] Neither did the Moderates' complaints that the Progressives had introduced party spirit into the LCC seem particularly impressive. Finally, most Londoners scoffed at the Moderates' fears that the transfer of control over the Metropolitan Police from the Home Office to the London County Council might prove dangerous.[83] The perception, perhaps correct, remained that the choice fell between modest, gradual, incremental change under the Progressives or the *status quo* under the Moderate Party.[84] In that contest, the Moderates had little chance of victory.

Having lost four straight elections between 1889 and 1898, an increasing number of Moderates realized that only by breaking the "excessive centralization of London government" would they be able to unseat their Progressive rivals. Critics of the LCC, such as Joseph Chamberlain, had long argued that its districts were far too large for any one councillor to represent. John Lubbock, a member of the LCC, agreed, stating further that no duty should be given to the central authority that could best be handled at the local level. In consequence, the Moderate C. A. Whitmore favored the creation of twenty-eight independent municipal boroughs to bring local government closer to the people and raise popular interest in London affairs.[85]

By November 1897, Conservative Prime Minister Lord Salisbury—who increasingly regretted his part in the birth of the London County Council in 1888—had come to the conclusion that Chamberlain, Lubbock, and Whitmore were correct. In his estimation, metropolitan London *was* ten or twelve times too large to be properly administered as a single unit. The vast size and complexity of London local government resulted, almost inevitably, in the neglect of much necessary work. To remedy this situation, a large portion of the LCC's duties should, in Salisbury's opinion, be delegated to a number of smaller municipalities within the Metropolis.[86]

In the past the Progressive Party had battled ministerial neglect, overcome the press's attempts to discredit and demean their accomplishments, and had, albeit

---

[82] R. Melville and H. Percy Harris Beachcroft, "The Work and Policy of the London County Council," *National Review* (February 1895), 836.

[83] Henry Clarke, *London Government* (London, 1888); "Party Government in London," *The Economist* (16 January 1892); and C. A. Whitmore, "The London Programme," *National Review* (May 1893).

[84] See C. A. Whitmore, "Our Defeat and Some Morals," *National Review* (April 1898). Whitmore believed that the Moderates would never gain power on the LCC unless they adopted a more positive program.

[85] See Joseph Chamberlain, "Municipal Government," *New Review* (June 1894); John Lubbock, Edward Clarke, and C. A. Whitmore, "London Government," *National Review* (December 1894); and Frederick Whelen, *London Government* (London, 1898). John Leighton, in his *The Unification of London* (London, 1895), proposed the creation of nineteen boroughs, each a two-mile hexagon with about 80,000 inhabitants (iii).

[86] In addition, "There can be no doubt that many conservatives . . . regard the LCC with grave dislike, as a body which might develop into a Commune on the continental model" ("Lord Salisbury on the LCC," *The Economist* [20 November 1897], 1622).

Responses to the Social Question 139

only occasionally, even triumphed over the obstructionist Moderates in the County Council. Throughout 1898 and into 1899, they faced a new challenge, that Lord Salisbury would use his parliamentary majority to emasculate the LCC by dispersing its powers among a number of independent borough councils.[87] This may, in fact, have been Salisbury's original intention. The London Government Act passed at Salisbury's request in 1899, however, fulfilled neither the expectations of many Conservatives nor the fears of the Progressive Party. Although twenty-eight new borough councils were created within metropolitan London, the LCC remained the center of local government in the Metropolis. Once again, change, when it did come, was more cosmetic than real.[88] As such, it conformed to late Victorian politics as a whole. Many people—Conservatives, Liberals, Radicals, Progressives, and Moderates—had ideas about how to use the State to better the lives of the citizenry; no one, it seems, had the political clout to enact any but the most modest of reforms.

The next chapter—a thematic companion to this one—will explore the limits of State intervention in Victorian society. Moving from moral reform to restrictions on foreign immigration, from the regulation of sweated labor to housing legislation, from public works for the unemployed to pensions for the aged, we will try to understand the factors that connect the various social reforms of the late nineteenth century. Having done so, we will have grasped the essence of Victorian social politics.

---

[87] See Arthur Hobhouse, "The London County Council and Its Assailants," *Contemporary Review* (March 1892); Sidney Lee, "The London County Council," *Quarterly Review* (January 1898); and T. McKinnon Wood, "The Attack on the London County Council," *Contemporary Review* (February 1898).

[88] See C. A. Whitmore, "The Government of London," *Quarterly Review* (April 1899); J. Renwick Seager, *The Government of London under the London Government Act, 1899* (London, 1899); and Ken Young and Patricia Garside, *Metropolitan London: Politics and Urban Change, 1837-1981* (London, 1982).

Chapter 7

The Limits of Governmental Intervention during the Victorian Era

Having examined the social policies pursued by the major Victorian political parties, we must now broaden our discussion to include those areas that attracted widespread popular support during the late nineteenth century. The first of these, the education—moral and otherwise—of the poorer classes grew naturally out of the common Victorian assumption that working class sexuality, intemperance, and industrial inefficiency inhibited their ability to lead happy, productive lives. Unlike most of their compeers within the ranks of Victorian philanthropy, however, the supporters of "social purity" and education reform tended to insist that the State actively intervene in the promotion of a moral, efficient citizenry.

The multi-faceted "social purity" movement, for instance, hoped to raise working class morality through the passage of legislative restrictions upon indecent or unhealthy behavior. "Social purity" advocates called on parliament to criminalize the marriage of those under eighteen years of age and argued that engaged couples should be required to prove themselves to be self-sufficient prior to receiving a marriage license. Both of these suggestions grew out of the common perception that early or ill-considered marriages within the working classes were a major cause of poverty.[1] Public morality was another issue of great and growing concern within the ranks of the "social purity" movement. For half a century, the Metropolitan Police had overseen, albeit in a cursory fashion, the numerous hotels, theaters, pubs, and common lodging houses of London; now "social purity"

---

[1] See Countess Cowper, "Some Experiences of Work in an East End District," *Nineteenth Century* (November 1885); and F. W. Farrar, "Social Problems and Remedies," *Fortnightly Review* (March 1888).

enthusiasts insisted that the police actively suppress "disorderly" houses, and eliminate street prostitution, gambling, and public drunkenness.[2] In this case, the State responded with alacrity. Between 1885 and 1914, roughly twelve hundred English and Welsh brothels were prosecuted each year, fourteen times as many per year as between 1875 and 1884. Attempts to end street-walking were much less successful. Public prostitution was not, in and of itself, a crime during the Victorian period, although prostitutes could be arrested for disturbing the peace or under the Vagrants' Act of 1824. Still, parliament's refusal to make prostitution illegal in explicit terms ensured the failure of the "social purity" movement's attempts to rid Britain of this moral evil. Although public outbursts against streetwalkers continued to attest to widespread Victorian interest in the suppression of prostitution, only with the Street Offenses Act of 1959 was public solicitation finally made illegal.[3]

While the "social purity" movement's efforts to outlaw street prostitution proved unavailing, parliament did follow their lead in other areas. The Criminal Law Amendment Act of 1885 prohibited homosexual "indecencies" between males; it was under this act that the poet, novelist, and playwright Oscar Wilde was charged, convicted, and sentenced to two years in Reading jail in 1895. Furthermore, William Stead's campaign against "White Slavery"—the supposed traffic in young English girls to brothels on the Continent—during the summer of 1885 inspired an outcry of public indignation. The "Maiden Tribute of Modern Babylon" articles published in the *Pall Mall Gazette*, Stead's audacious "purchase" of a thirteen-year-old virgin for £5 to prove his point, and the popular agitation conducted by Catherine and Bramwell Booth of the Salvation Army, Josephine Butler, and the National Vigilance Association put great pressure on parliament to raise the age of consent. Although it had been lifted from twelve to thirteen as recently as 1875, the Criminal Law Amendment Act raised the age of consent further to sixteen. For many supporters of the "social purity" agenda even this was not enough; in their estimation, parliament should have raised the age of consent to eighteen or even twenty-one.[4]

---

[2] See Arthur Sherwell, *Life in West London*, 2nd Edition (London, 1897); and Stefan Petrow, *Policing Morals: The Metropolitan Police and the Home Office, 1870-1914* (Oxford, 1994).

[3] See Judith Walkowitz's *Prostitution and Victorian Society* (New York, 1980) and "Jack the Ripper and the Myth of Male Violence," *Feminist Studies* 1982 8 (3): 543-74; and Robert Storch, "Police Control of Street Prostitution in Victorian London," in *Police and Society* (Beverly Hills, Calif., 1977).

[4] See Deborah Gorham, "The 'Maiden Tribute of Modern Babylon' Reexamined," *Victorian Studies* 1978 21 (3): 353-79; and Edward Bristow, *Vice and Vigilance: Purity Movements in Britain since 1700* (Totowa, N.J., 1977). Stead, charged with abduction and indecent assault for his "purchase," was imprisoned briefly. Josephine Butler had been an impassioned opponent of the Contagious Diseases acts of the 1860s; these acts, which required arbitrary and intrusive examinations of prostitutes in certain port cities for venereal disease, represented for Butler a threat to personal liberty and reflected a sexual double standard. The acts were finally repealed in 1886.

This particular piece of legislation did not go wholly unopposed. Critics pointed out that very few prostitutes were under sixteen, that nearly all entered their chosen profession voluntarily, and that large-scale "White Slavery" was a figment of William Stead's imagination. An Oxford graduate writing anonymously to the *Pall Mall Gazette* in 1885 argued further that raising of the age of consent to sixteen was completely illogical. At present, he argued, a British girl could not marry without parental consent until she was twenty-one years old; how then could parliament justify her being allowed to consent to have sexual relations at sixteen, but still be unable to marry without consent until she was five years older?[5]

Temperance reform was yet another *cause célèbre* of the late Victorian "social purity" movement. Reformers proposed restricting the hours of sale, closing public houses on Sunday, and reducing the number of licenses issued by the State for the sale of alcoholic beverages. Also, as noted above, moral reformers expected the police to enforce public decency by curbing gambling, swearing, and drunkenness in and around British public houses.[6] Going further, one innovative author called for the "moralization" of British pubs. By removing the bar; ensuring proper ventilation; insisting on large rooms for dining, smoking, and conversation; requiring public houses to offer newspapers, magazines, and a library of one hundred or more books drawn from a list provided by a competent "Board"; and prohibiting the sale of wine or spirits, public houses would be transformed into family recreation centers. Individuals who paid a small fee would be allowed to visit these reformed "pubs" without being required to eat or drink anything. Any public house that did not comply with such regulations after a grace period of five to ten years would have its license revoked.[7]

A few writers suggested even more dramatic reforms. Joseph Rowntree and Arthur Sherwell, for example, advocated the municipalization of the drink traffic with all profits from the sale of alcohol going to the State; the government would then be able to provide additional parks and improve the quality of British education without raising taxes.[8] For the vast majority of moral and temperance reformers, however, such innovations smacked of socialism. Most were unwilling

---

[5] See *Letter to the Editor of the Pall Mall Gazette* (London, 1885); and Deborah Gorham, "The 'Maiden Tribute of Modern Babylon' Reexamined," *Victorian Studies* 1978 21 (3): 353-79.

[6] See George M'Cree, *Sweet Herbs for the Bitter Cry, or Remedies for Horrible and Outcast London* (London, 1884); Arnold White, "The Nomad Poor of London," *Contemporary Review* (May 1885); F. W. Farrar, "Social Problems and Remedies," *Fortnightly Review* (March 1888); and David Jones, "The New Police, Crime, and People in England and Wales, 1829-1888," *Transactions of the Royal Historical Society* 1983 (33): 151-68.

[7] See R. E. MacNaughten, "Temperance and Public Houses," *National Review* (February 1890).

[8] See Joseph Rowntree and Arthur Sherwell, *The Temperance Problem and Social Reform* (London, 1899).

to go beyond the policing of working class morals. Not surprisingly, as one historian has commented, the "social purity" movement "used interventionist language without ever clothing it with administrative reality."[9]

Still, Rowntree and Sherwell had touched on an issue that was extraordinarily important to most Victorians, the elevation of the working classes through education. Many writers believed that impressionable British youths might have to be shielded from the pernicious influences of the so-called penny dreadfuls by State censorship or the prosecution of a few selected authors and publishers. In addition, most hoped that public and board schools, by exposing their students to alternative reading material, specifically the classics of English and European literature, would inspire a taste for higher things. State schools needed to do much more than just instill patriotism and an appreciation for British culture; they had to train their students to succeed in an increasingly competitive world economy.[10]

Such education and training was, according to the noted Victorian economist Alfred Marshall, essential to the continued prosperity of the British nation. Considering the increased industrial competitiveness of the United States and Germany during the final third of the nineteenth century, the need for improved technical education was widely recognized.[11] The United States and Germany were thought, with good reason, to possess a better system of industrial education than did Britain. Both nations, one commentator noted, "bring science to bear upon every department of the national life; whereas we, up till lately, resented all State interference, and so exaggerated the doctrines of freedom as almost to glory in our abuses."[12] What Britain needed above all, according to Walter Besant, was a program of continuing education that would extend the technical training of working class children beyond the primary school level. Besant argued that if the government provided facilities and supplies, private volunteers could be found in most cities to continue the training of young workers between the ages of thirteen

---

[9] Brian Harrison, "State Intervention and Moral Reform," in *Pressure from Without* (London, 1974), 316.

[10] See Francis Peek, "In Darkest England and a Way Out," *Contemporary Review* (December 1890); Hugh Chisholm, "How to Counteract the Penny Dreadful," *Fortnightly Review* (November 1895); and Reginald Brabazon, "The Depreciators of the Nation," *Fortnightly Review* (January 1899).

[11] See Alfred Marshall, *Principles of Economics* (1890, Reprint Edition, London, 1922). The Royal Commission *On the Depression of Trade and Industry* (1886 [c.4893], v. 23); Lord Compton, "Distress in London," *Fortnightly Review* (January 1888); and Ernest E. Williams, *Made in Germany* (London, 1896) all stressed the importance of technical education and the study of foreign languages.

[12] Reginald Brabazon, ed., *Prosperity or Pauperism: Physical, Industrial, and Technical Training* (London, 1888), 333.

and seventeen.[13]

The provision of nutritious meals to British schoolchildren—already a part of the French and German curriculum of the 1880s—was also vitally important to many reformers. Ill-fed students, stunted in mind and body, could not be expected to learn or develop properly; many would inevitably fall into the ranks of either the pauper or the criminal classes.[14] The solution was both simple and relatively inexpensive. As only between four and eight percent of all pupils were under-fed, State provision of reduced-price or free meals would increase the annual cost of British public education by only about five percent. Because teachers and school board members had personal knowledge of which students were truly in need of assistance, the additional monies would be well spent. Nor did such public aid have to take the form of an outright grant; at least one author argued that children receiving free or subsidized meals should be required to work—cleaning classrooms for instance—before or after school so that they could dine with "honor."[15]

For other social commentators, imperial colonization provided the best remedy for the "Condition of England."[16] Many private organizations, including the Charity Organisation Society and the Primrose League, already collected monies for the migration of the "deserving" poor to Britain's overseas empire. Even so, the efforts of the private sector had done little to induce the sort of large-scale emigration necessary to eliminate British poverty. Inevitably, a few reformers began to look to the State for the establishment of a comprehensive program. For Reginald Brabazon, the head of the National Association for the Promotion of State-Aided Colonization, Arnold White, Henry Cardinal Manning, and others during the late 1880s, it was clear that the State needed to take a more activist role in the directing and financing of British colonization. Large-scale overseas colonization was expected to benefit Britain in many different ways. By diverting surplus agricultural labor, it would ease overcrowding in English cities, strengthen the colonies, undercut support for socialism, and improve the condition

---

[13] See Walter Besant, "From Thirteen to Seventeen," *Contemporary Review* (March 1886).

[14] See Reginald Brabazon's "The Decay of Bodily Health in Towns," *Nineteenth Century* (May 1887) and *Prosperity or Pauperism: Physical, Industrial, and Technical Training* (London, 1888); and Joseph Diggle, "Child Distress and State Socialism," *National Review* (December 1895).

[15] See Eric Robertson, "Education for the Hungry," *Fortnightly Review* (January 1885); and George Sargent, "Free Dinners at National Schools," *Fortnightly Review* (September 1887). Sargent estimated that about three hundred and thirty thousand students went hungry year-round, with twice that number in want during the winter months (377). See also Margaret Harkness, "Children of the Unemployed," *New Review* (February 1893).

[16] Although a small number of Victorians favored imperial tariffs as a way to protect domestic industry, lessen poverty, and eliminate the threat of revolution in Britain, they did not pose a serious challenge to the "Free Trade" *status quo* prior to World War I. See *Fair Trade* (1885-1891) and A. S. Krausse, *Starving London* (London, 1886), 165-66.

of British labor. Furthermore, by opening new markets to British manufactures abroad, colonization would also be good for the national economy.[17]

State aid was expected to take a variety of forms. Brabazon suggested that each emigrant family be advanced £120 for transportation overseas, housing, and tools; the State should also induce the various colonies to grant previously uncultivated land for their use. The British government could ensure prompt repayment of the loan by retaining a mortgage on colonial land grants and, after three or five years, by charging six percent interest on the principal outstanding.[18] Arnold White proposed further that the State establish an information bureau for emigrants, a national council to receive and distribute contributions to proven emigration societies and "deserving" individuals, and that it make revisions to the Passenger Act of 1855 in order to limit the damage done by fraudulent transportation agencies.[19] By the late 1880s, in response to the arguments of Brabazon, White, and others, the State had instituted a number of reforms. It expanded, if only slightly, the amount of assistance given for the emigration of pauper children. It established an Emigrants' Information Office in October 1886 to provide reliable data on the cost of passage to and the demand for labor in the various British colonies. Finally, under section 69 of the Local Government Act of 1888, the new county councils were authorized to borrow money from the Local Government Board in order to assist citizens to emigrate; the only stipulation was that all LGB loans be repaid within a short period of time.

Unfortunately, a number of factors prevented these reforms from having any real effect during the final decades of the nineteenth century. The LGB staunchly resisted doing anything beyond the approval of likely candidates for emigration overseas. The Poor Law Guardians proved extremely reluctant to pay passage to the colonies on their own or to assume responsibility if the settlers defaulted on their loans. The colonies themselves increasingly resented what they viewed as the "dumping" of British paupers onto their shores. Finally, by the time the select committee on "Colonization" issued its report in 1891, Britain's rebounding economy made State-directed colonization seem largely unnecessary. The committee's report commented that there were "no grounds for thinking that the present condition of the United Kingdom generally calls for any general scheme

---

[17] Several reformers hoped to establish a comprehensive system of State-aided colonies in Canada and Australia—with the goal of doubling the population of those colonies in ten years. See, for instance, J. F. Boyd, "The Depression of Trade and State-Directed Colonization," *National Review* (March 1886); and G. Osbourne Morgan, "Well-meant Nonsense About Emigration," *Nineteenth Century* (April 1887).

[18] See Reginald Brabazon's "State-Directed Emigration," *Nineteenth Century* (November 1884) and *Prosperity or Pauperism: Physical, Industrial, and Technical Training* (London, 1888); and H. S. Worthcote, "Work for Willing Hands," *Blackwood's Magazine* (February 1888).

[19] See Arnold White, "Common Sense of Colonial Emigration," *Contemporary Review* (March 1886).

of State-organized colonization or emigration."[20] The committee, believing that local councils and private organizations already had the power to assist those who wished to leave Britain, was, therefore, unwilling to consider meaningful reform.

The reverse side of the equation, the immigration of foreign nationals into Britain, caused much more concern during the late Victorian period. It was commonly believed that immigrants were flooding into England during the "Great Depression" and taking jobs away from honest British workers. This view was, as is so often the case, belied by the facts. Between 1870 and 1900, more than five million more Britons left the United Kingdom than arrived from overseas.

Net Migrations Out of the United Kingdom
1870-1879 1.41 million
1880-1889 2.50 million
1890-1899 1.11 million

This trend was only reversed during the 1930s.[21] Furthermore, foreign immigration into London, the focal point of domestic discontent on this issue, made up only a small proportion of the total number of new arrivals in the Metropolis.

	Foreign Immigrants	Total	Percent[22]
1851-1860	29,000	352,000	8.2%
1861-1871	36,000	471,000	7.6%
1871-1881	39,000	661,000	5.9%
1881-1891	48,000	487,000	9.9%

Even so, the contention that pauper immigration was damaging the London economy garnered great support both within and outside of parliament. The report of the Board of Trade on sweated labor in east London in 1887 remarked that "matters have been rendered infinitely worse to the native workers during the last few years by an enormous influx of pauper foreigners from other European nations."[23] Four years later, the noted economist John A. Hobson argued that the "constant infiltration of cheap immigrant labour is in large measure responsible for the existence of the 'sweating workshops' and the survival of a low form of

---

[20] Report of the Select Committee, House of Commons, "Colonization" (1890-1891 [152], v. xi), xvi. See also the Report of the Select Committee, House of Commons, "Emigration and Immigration" (1889 [311], v. x); and "The London Poor: Suggestions How to Help Them," *Westminster Review* (March 1890). For a full discussion of the issue of colonization, see Howard L. Malchow, *Population Pressures: Emigration and Government in Late Nineteenth Century Britain* (Palo Alto, Calif., 1979).

[21] Peter Mathias, *The First Industrial Nation* (New York, 1969), 452.

[22] H. Shannon, "Migration and the Growth of London, 1841-1891," *Economic History Review* 1935 5 (2): 84.

[23] Labour Correspondent, "Special Report to the Board of Trade on the Sweating System at the East End of London" (1887 [331], v. lxxxix), 4.

industrial development" in London.[24] Not surprisingly, an increasing number of writers began to call on parliament to restrict immigration into Britain. No other nation, they argued with powerful effect, takes in our outcasts, lunatics, criminals, and paupers. The reasons why were, in their opinion, plain to see. Pauper foreigners

> contribute nothing to our taxes, nothing to our national welfare, nothing to our national defense; they take everything and give nothing in return, even worse than nothing, since their habits and their customs exercise a most injurious effect upon the English community with whom they come into contact.[25]

Why should Britain continue to poison its industry and society by importing the refuse of Europe?

Of special concern was the immigration of large numbers of Jewish refugees to the East End of London after 1880. Although the Jewish Board of Guardians,[26] in an attempt to prevent an upsurge of native anti-Semitism, warned Jews fleeing persecution in Russia and Germany at this time to go elsewhere, roughly ninety thousand of them settled in the Metropolis between 1880 and 1900.[27] As had been feared by the leaders of the London Jewish community, these new immigrants were often blamed for the loss of "English" jobs, the prevalence of sweated labor in the East End, and the sub-standard sanitary condition of many poor metropolitan neighborhoods. Indeed, according to some critics, unskilled English workers had only three options for survival in the saturated London labor market of the 1880s: private charity, public assistance, or migration overseas.[28]

Furthermore, the concentration of large numbers of Jewish workers in certain London industries—such as tailoring, boot and shoe-making, and cabinet-making—and districts—particularly in the East End—made the problem of foreign immigration seem especially acute. In response, the select committee on "Emigration and Immigration" commented in 1889 that restrictions on the arrival of destitute foreigners might become necessary in the near future because of their

---

[24] John A. Hobson, *The Problems of Poverty* (London, 1891), 63.

[25] W. H. Wilkins, *The Alien Invasion* (London, 1892), 4.

[26] The Jewish Board of Guardians—administered by and for the Jewish population of the Metropolis—was not a part of the Victorian Poor Law.

[27] See Lloyd Gartner, *The Jewish Immigrant in England, 1870-1914* (London, 1960); Geoffrey Alderman, *London Jewry and London Politics* (London, 1989); and William Fishman, *Jewish Radicals* (New York, 1974). Pogroms in Russia in 1881 and 1882, the expulsion of Jews from Kiev, Moscow and other large Russian cities in 1890, and Bismarck's eviction of Polish aliens from Prussia in 1886 prompted a wave of Jewish immigration to Great Britain.

[28] See Arnold White's "The Invasion of Pauper Foreigners," *Nineteenth Century* (March 1888) and *The Destitute Alien in Great Britain* (London, 1892); and W. H. Wilkins, "The Immigration of Destitute Foreigners," *National Review* (September 1890).

tendency "to reduce still lower the social and material condition of our own poor."[29] Nor was the committee alone in this opinion. During the previous year, Arthur Baumann of the London County Council advocated the payment of a poll-tax of £10 by each person attempting to immigrate into Britain; Baumann also suggested the passage of legislation that would limit the number of foreign settlers by linking immigration to foreign trade—one immigrant allowed for every one hundred tons of goods imported into Britain from a foreign country.[30] Hermann Adler, the chief rabbi in London between 1891 and 1911, also pushed for restrictionist legislation because pauper refugees fostered both anti-Semitism and, in his estimation, socialism. Following Adler's lead, the Jewish Board of Guardians required immigrants to have resided in Britain for at least six months in order to qualify for their relief.[31]

Popular resentment of Jewish immigration remained strong throughout the 1890s. The Trade Union Congress voted resolutions against it in 1892, 1894, and 1895. Conservative Prime Minister Lord Salisbury proposed an Aliens Bill in July 1894; private members submitted similar bills in 1897 and 1898. As one historian has noted, "All evidence to the contrary, English trade unionists and much of the public continued to see the Jewish immigrants as the cause of sweating and lower wages" throughout the late Victorian period.[32]

By the late 1880s, however, the evidence was quite clear for those who wished to consider the issue rationally. The select committee on "Emigration and Immigration" stated in 1889 that although "the proportion of the alien to the native population has been for many years and is on the increase . . . the number is not sufficiently large to create alarm."[33] The influx of so-called pauper foreigners had, in fact, been greatly exaggerated during the mid-to-late 1880s. Few Jewish immigrants were actually destitute on their arrival in Britain. Quite the contrary, the vast majority were an important economic asset to the British community. As chaste, sober, industrious, and thrifty workers, they, much like their Huguenot predecessors, helped to increase British productivity, exports, and profits. Furthermore, because of the actions taken by the Jewish Board of Guardians,

---

[29] Report of the Select Committee, House of Commons, "Emigration and Immigration" (1889 [311], v. x], xi.

[30] See Arthur Baumann, "Possible Remedies for the Sweating System," *National Review* (November 1888).

[31] See Geoffrey Alderman, *London Jewry and London Politics* (London, 1989); and Lloyd Gartner, *The Jewish Immigrant in England, 1870-1914* (London, 1960). Nor was the aid provided by the Jewish Board of Guardians particularly generous; relief was only granted to the respectable and, even then, only for a fortnight.

[32] J. M. Pilzer, "The Jews and the Great Sweated Debate," *Jewish Social Studies* 1979 41 (3-4): 271. See also William Fishman, *Jewish Radicals* (New York, 1974); J. A. Dyche, "The Jewish Immigrant" *Contemporary Review* (March 1899); and John Smith, "The Jewish Immigrant," *Contemporary Review* (September 1899).

[33] Report of the Select Committee, House of Commons, "Emigration and Immigration" (1889 [311], v. x], xi.

metropolitan Jews did not place a significant burden on the poor rates. Finally, according to one critic of the anti-alien movement, it did not befit the prestige of a Great Power that "a nation pouring forth every year from our shores over 300,000 emigrants, are asked to close our ports to the free entry of eight thousand per annum more or less indigent foreigners, less than 2000 of whom are members of the Semitic faith."[34] Although the arrival of immigrants might have a small impact on certain cities—such as London, Liverpool, Leeds, and Manchester—and within select trades, they did not pose a general threat to British jobs or to the national economy. There was no rational reason for Britain to stray from its traditionally liberal policy towards alien immigration.[35]

Still, something needed to be done to relieve the worst excesses of the sweating system: work at home or in small workshops, the subdivision of labor and sub-contracting, excessive hours, starvation wages, and unsanitary conditions. The sweater, whether Jewish or not, represented a clear physical and moral danger to the community. Unfortunately, he was, as one Victorian novelist noted, attached to the economy "faster than a barnacle to a ship's bottom, and he's not to be dislodged for the present. All you can do is to see he doesn't draw too much blood with his pound of flesh."[36] State intervention was necessary, in the opinion of many reformers, to protect this most exploited portion of the British working classes.

The problem lay in the fact that prior to the late Victorian era, factory and workshop acts pertained exclusively to female and child labor, were often vaguely written, and were rarely rigorously enforced. The Factory and Workshop Act of 1878 passed during Benjamin Disraeli's tenure in office did not, for instance, clearly define what was meant by either overcrowding or "proper" ventilation. To remedy these ills, the *Anti-Sweater*, a weekly London paper edited by Lewis Lyons, proposed a number of reforms in October 1886. Lyons argued that the State should require the registration of all workshops, periodic inspections to ensure proper sanitation, a nine-hour day for all adults, the elimination of child laborers under fifteen, the blacklisting of firms that sold sweated goods, and that those who "put-out" work possess at least £100 of capital. The following year, a Board of Trade report on sweating in east London stipulated that limitations ought to be placed on the workday; the factory acts should be made to include male workers; and sweated laborers should no longer be used to fill government contracts. The report also emphasized the need for additional factory inspectors in order to enforce the public health and workshop regulations already in existence. Finally, workers should be

---

[34] Stephen N. Fox, "The Invasion of Pauper Foreigners," *Contemporary Review* (June 1888), 865. See also the positive interpretation provided by two of Charles Booth's investigators, David Schloss and Beatrice Potter (Webb), in Booth's *Life and Labour of the London Poor: Poverty Series*, 4 vols. (London, 1889-1893). Potter only found one character flaw among the Jews of east London: a love of gambling.

[35] See Geoffrey Drage, "Alien Immigration," *Journal of the Royal Statistical Society* (March 1895).

[36] J. A. Steuart, *Wine on the Lees* (New York, 1899), 340.

encouraged to organize themselves and industry be induced to concentrate into larger factories.[37]

Public and parliamentary pressure culminated in the appointment in 1888 of a select committee of the House of Lords to consider the problem of sweating, first in London and, later, throughout the United Kingdom. As the committee conducted its researches, popular concern continued to mount. David Schloss, one of Charles Booth's investigators, advocated the passage of strict air and ventilation standards and insisted that all workers be employed directly by their employers. No longer should companies be allowed to contract work out to sweating middlemen.[38] Arthur Baumann of the London County Council urged metropolitan parishes to act more quickly upon the recommendation of local sanitary inspectors and supported a twelve-hour workday for women and a six-hour day for children. In addition, for Baumann, the State should not hesitate to fine employers who failed to register their outworkers, enforce factory standards in all workshops, and ensure that their workers were properly compensated for overtime labor.[39]

The publication of the much-anticipated Final Report of the committee on the sweating system in April 1890, however, offered little to those who expected substantive reform. The committee found that sweating was not unique to east London or to the clothing trades; it existed in most large cities and in a host of different industries. As a result, the committee could see no connection between foreign immigration and the existence of sweated labor. In the realm of social reform, the committee proposed that all workshops be regulated under the factory acts, that more inspectors be hired, and that outwork premises be open to sanitary inspection at all times. It also suggested that employers be forced to keep an up-to-date list of the addresses of all their employees in order to facilitate regular inspections and that future government contract work be done in factories. None of these proposals was particularly new. The committee's only truly novel recommendation was that workers filling government contracts be paid a minimum wage; the committee's expectation was that the rising cost of labor would be offset by better workmanship and higher productivity. In general, though, the committee remained unconvinced that parliament could do much to improve the industrial conditions of the poorest class of workers. As the Final Report concluded: "When

---

[37] See the *Anti-Sweater*, October 1886; Labour Correspondent, "Special Report to the Board of Trade on the Sweating System at the East End of London" (1887 [331], v.lxxxix); and Arthur Baumann, "Possible Remedies for the Sweating System," *National Review* (November 1888).

[38] Schloss considered two hundred and fifty cubic feet of air space per worker—four hundred feet for overtime with gas burners counted as three workers—to be sufficient for a healthy work environment (David Schloss, "The Sweating System," *Fortnightly Review* [April 1890], 550).

[39] See Arthur Baumann, "Needed Amendments to the Factory Act," *National Review* (April 1890); and Beatrice Potter (Webb), "The Lords and the Sweating System," *Nineteenth Century* (June 1890).

legislation has reached the limit up to which it is effective, the real amelioration of the conditions must be due to an increased sense of responsibility in the employer and improved habits in the employed."[40]

Later parliamentary attempts in 1891 and 1895 to protect members of the sweated and "dangerous" trades—those, such as potters, cutlery makers, grinders, file cutters, glass polishers, printers, paper stainers, and electrical workers, who worked with dangerous materials or under injurious conditions—were no more successful. Throughout the late Victorian era, social critics continued to call for the appointment of additional sanitary inspectors, tighter control of factory and workshop conditions, and the regulation of outwork; still, little was accomplished in any of these areas. "The legislative and administrative labour policy of the State" continued to fail to protect "women and children and the weak and disorganized classes of workmen."[41] Government contracts continued to be filled by sweated laborers; most egregiously, some of the workers hired to alter army uniforms under unhealthy conditions during the 1890s were directly employed by the War Office. Government studies, such as the "Sweating Report" of 1890 and the Royal Commission *On Labour* of 1894, produced precious little by way of real reform. Prior to 1900, the State simply refused to devote the resources necessary to punish violators of the sanitary, health, and factory acts; until it was willing to do so, sweated labor would remain an important part of the industrial economy in London and in other large cities.[42]

With regard to housing reform, the Victorian State *was* willing to act with dispatch. As with sweated labor, the problem was plain to see. How was "the moral elevation of the people" practicable "among classes who have to herd together in vile abodes?"[43] Also, as was so often the case, it was overcrowding in London that received the lion's share of the public's attention. This should not be surprising as crowding in the Metropolis was especially severe. Some four hundred thousand Londoners rented one-room apartments during the late Victorian era. Almost fifty percent of metropolitan inhabitants lived in three-room apartments or smaller in 1891; a third had to make do with either one or two rooms. Furthermore, few Londoners residing within the poorest parts of the inner industrial

---

[40] Report of the Select Committee, House of Lords, "The Sweating System in the United Kingdom" (1890 [(169], v. xvii], xlv. See also "The Sweating Report," *Saturday Review* (10 May 1890); and "Sweating: The Two Reports," *New Review* (June 1890).

[41] "The Labour Commission," *National Review* (April 1894), 211. See also Vaughan Nash, "The Home Office and the Deadly Trades," *Fortnightly Review* (February 1893); and James A. Schmiechen, "State Reform and Local Economy," *Economic History Review* 1975 28 (3): 413-28.

[42] See Beatrice Webb, "The Failure of the Labour Commission," *Nineteenth Century* (July 1894); Geoffrey Drage, "Mrs. Sidney Webb's Attack on the Labour Commission," *Nineteenth Century* (September 1894); J.A.M. MacDonald, "Government Sweating in the Clothing Contracts," *New Review* (November 1894); and Henry Macrosty, "Sweating: Its Cause and Remedy," *Fabian Tract*, no.50 (London, 1895).

[43] *The Graphic*, 26 April 1879, 403.

perimeter had easy access to a private garden, yard, or park for recreation.[44] Furthermore, overcrowding in the Metropolis seemed to be getting worse. According to the housing reformer and Liberal politician William Torrens, "the congestion of work-a-day life in great tracts of London has under our eyes sensibly increased, is dangerously increasing, and ought, without further paltering, to be effectually diminished."[45]

Unfortunately, Victorian efforts to alleviate overcrowding in London represented an almost unmitigated failure. This was largely because of the fact that although "it behooves the state [both] to destroy the localities which are the centres of disease and death, and to provide healthier accommodation for the inhabitants of them," the Victorians found slum clearance much more to its liking than the provision of "healthier" accommodations.[46] Improvement schemes—street widening, dock extensions, and the demolition of slum rookeries in order to open land for new railway lines for instance—in the poorer districts of the Metropolis had an enormous, although not necessarily positive, impact upon the London working classes. Almost 70,000 Londoners were displaced by the construction of new rail lines alone after 1860.

	Projects	People Displaced
1860s	24	30,000
1870s	17	15,000
1880s	4	4,000
1890s	12	18,000

In addition, between 1853 and 1901 at least 30,000 people were evicted because of metropolitan street and dock improvements. Thus, between 1850 and 1900, perhaps 100,000 Londoners were forced out of their homes, with some seventy percent of the displacements occurring between 1860 and 1880.[47]

Far from actually alleviating overcrowding in the Metropolis, such improve-

---

[44] See Robert Williams, *The Face of the Poor, or the Crowding of London's Labourers* (London, 1897); and William H. Mallock, "The Census and the Condition of the People," *Pall Mall Magazine* (January-April 1895).

[45] William Torrens, "What Is to Be Done with the Slums?" *MacMillan's Magazine* (April 1879), 533. This quote is an obvious reference to John Dunning's famous resolution of April 1780 concerning the growth of royal political power.

[46] S. C. Paul, "Evictions in London," *MacMillan's Magazine* (October 1882), 498. Consequently, the "interests of the ratepayers are, therefore, best consulted by the removal of those causes which tend to produce ill-health and its companion, poverty"—the slums ("London," *The Lancet* [26 March 1887], 632).

[47] See Henry J. Dyos, "Railways and Housing in Victorian London," *Journal of Transport History* 1955 2:11-21, 90-100, "Some Social Costs of Railway Building in London," *Journal of Transport History* 1957 3 (1): 23-30; and "The Slums of Victorian London," *Victorian Studies* 1967 11 (1): 5-40. See also Gareth Stedman Jones, *Outcast London* (Oxford, 1971).

ments appear to have led to higher rents and more crowding within the poorest inner city districts.[48] Many displaced workers were unable to migrate to the suburbs as they needed to be within walking distance of their place of employment; furthermore, as family and neighborhood ties provided an, albeit rudimentary, social safety net for the inhabitants of the slums, most did not want to cast themselves solely upon their own resources in an unknown environment, even if only a few miles away.

Not surprisingly, therefore, most evicted tenants tended to crowd into adjoining neighborhoods, a fact which helps to explain the twenty-five percent rise in room rents in east London between 1880 and 1900.[49] As one contemporary novelist stated: although some "of these clotted spiders'-webs have since been swept away by the besom of the social reformer," most of "the spiders have scurried off into darker crannies."[50] The moral impact of additional overcrowding was quite clear to many reformers; town improvements had, in their estimation, actually increased the level of "vice, intemperance, and unchastity, and pauperism" in many slum neighborhoods.[51]

Not only had metropolitan improvements failed to remove "the poor from our gates" so that the well-to-do would "not feel the danger of contagion from their nearness" or "be shocked or made sentimental by the sight of their patient and pitiful misery"; they had also proved to be extremely expensive.[52] The primary culprit behind the high cost of urban improvements was the necessity of compensating the owners of demolished slum tenements. As the saying went, while in "India one treads on diamonds and gold," in London land "costs diamonds and gold."[53] Under the Cross acts of 1875 and 1879, the public sale of land opened by slum clearance did not come close to repaying the combined cost of demolition and compensation to the owners. The State, indeed, took a seventy percent loss on every acre "improved" under the Cross acts. Between 1875 and 1884, some forty-two acres of slum had been cleared at a cost of £1.6 million; the State's net loss approached £1.1 million. Under such conditions, one would think that enthusiasm

---

[48] Albeit, in retrospect. Conservative Home Secretary Richard A. Cross noted two years later that of "those who are displaced, probably many will settle themselves in the suburbs or elsewhere" (Richard A. Cross, "Homes of the Poor," *Nineteenth Century* [January 1884], 160). In 1882, the "Report of the Select Committee on Artisans' and Labourers' Dwellings" commented that "Many without any special calling may live in one place as well as in another" (1882 [235] v. vii), ix.

[49] Rents in the rest of London rose by eleven percent during the same period (Gareth Stedman Jones, *Outcast London* [Oxford, 1971], 325). See also Henry J. Dyos, "Railways and Housing in Victorian London," *Journal of Transport History* 1955 2:11-21, 90-100; and William Torrens, "Artisans Dwellings," *British Quarterly Review* (April 1870).

[50] Israel Zangwill, *Children of the Ghetto* (1892, Reprint Edition, Philadelphia, 1938), 3.

[51] John Storr, "The Anarchy of London," *Fortnightly Review* (June 1873), 760.

[52] Hugh MacCallam, *The Distribution of the Poor in London* (London, 1883), 4.

[53] Israel Zangwill, *Ghetto Tragedies* (1899, Reprint Edition, Philadelphia, 1938), 42.

for metropolitan slum clearance would have waned dramatically within a few years.[54] In reality, demolitions continued throughout the late Victorian era. While the Metropolitan Board of Works destroyed fifty acres of housing between 1875 and 1888, the London County Council leveled sixty-five acres during the quarter century preceding World War I.[55]

For this reason, it was extremely important for the Cross acts to be made more efficient and less expensive. During the late 1870s, critics of the Cross acts insisted upon the appointment of more sanitary inspectors, the establishment of an independent administrative commission, and vast alterations in the ways in which compensation was determined. The select committee on "Artisans' and Labourers' Dwellings" of 1882, which included both Richard A. Cross and William Torrens as members, attempted to reduce the delay in the implementation of the acts, lower compensation costs, and lessen various procedural expenses. For example, by refusing to allow changes in the term or tenure of rental agreements to have an effect on compensation values after a certain date prior to demolition, the State could dramatically reduce the cost of administering the Cross acts. Another idea broached by the committee was that the State should base its determination of house rents on the size of the building, not on the number of persons living there.[56]

Still, as these recommendations could not be put into effect immediately, public opinion began to swing strongly against the owners of metropolitan slum tenements. As early as 1870, a commentator for *The Lancet* remarked that a "house proprietor has no more right to let out fever-producing houses than a butcher has to sell unwholesome meat; in fact, far less, for the butcher at worse poisons the individual, the house proprietor the whole neighborhood."[57] As the condition of many slum landlords' properties fostered misery, disease, and pauperism, they should, in the opinion of many critics, receive only modest compensation. Furthermore, according to Joseph Chamberlain, the State should fine those who owned dilapidated houses, insist that owners make suitable repairs,

---

[54] See "The Artisans' Dwellings Acts Relating to the Metropolis—Their Total Failure and Enormous Cost," *The Economist* (27 November 1882); and Richard A. Cross, "Homes of the Poor," *Nineteenth Century* (January 1884). The much less ambitious Torrens Act of 1868 failed for a different reason. As it levied most of its costs on the inhabitants of the district to be "improved," few well-to-do residents saw any reason to insist upon the rigorous enforcement of the act.

[55] See Anthony Wohl's "The Housing of the Working Classes in London, 1815-1914," in *The History of Working Class Housing* (Totowa, N.J., 1971) and *The Eternal Slum* (London, 1977); R. Vladimir Steffel, "The Slum Question," *Albion* 1973 5 (4): 314-25; and Enid Gaudie, *Cruel Habitations: A History of Working Class Housing, 1780-1918* (London, 1974).

[56] See the Report of the Select Committee, House of Commons, "Artisans' and Labourers' Dwellings Improvement" (1882 [235] vii); and "Dwellings of the Poor," *Westminster Review* (January 1884).

[57] "Dwellings of the London Poor," *The Lancet* (10 December 1870), 827.

and place a "betterment" tax upon owners of adjacent real estate.[58] A number of critics went even further, arguing that, as slum landlords represented an affront to public health, parliament should seize their property and refuse to pay any compensation at all. In their estimation, the "remedy is [the owner's] to apply, and if he apply it not in time the power of doing so will be taken out of his hands."[59] Although unwilling to go this far, parliament did strive to limit the compensation paid to slum landowners under the Working Class Housing Act of 1890.

However difficult, the cost of compensation was not the worst problem faced by housing reformers at this time. By the 1880s, most agreed with William Torrens that "Town improvements with their cumbrous preliminaries, vast expense, and the aggravation of misery they for the time entail, can never furnish a generally applicable resource against the weed-like growth of slum."[60] An attempt, therefore, would have to be made to replace working class housing destroyed both by the public and by the private sector. Unfortunately, prior to 1882, only 23,000 displaced Londoners had been provided with new homes near their former residences by the private sector.[61] Areas cleared were often left empty while overcrowding worsened in adjacent districts. In response, the reformer Henry Brand proposed in 1881 that the State prohibit demolitions if it was uncertain new housing would be provided nearby and also set aside a portion of the land cleared for sale or lease to philanthropic housing agencies. Brand argued that housing reform in London should follow the precedent set by the Glasgow Improvement Act of 1865. In that city, displaced workers had been accommodated away from improved areas; provision had been made, prior to demolition, for all of those evicted from their homes; and sanitary inspectors had ensured that adjacent districts did not become more crowded as a result of the slum clearance. The former Conservative Home Secretary Richard A. Cross concurred with many of Brand's proposals, particularly those regarding gradual displacement and the rebuilding of improved areas.[62]

Cross, Salisbury, and many others also favored the provision of inexpensive working class trains, trams, and electric underground service to the London suburbs. The decentralization of population and industry to the outskirts of the

---

[58] See Joseph Chamberlain, "Labourers' and Artisans' Dwellings," *Fortnightly Review* (December 1883); and Henry Clarke, *Dwellings for the Poor* (London, 1884).

[59] B. L. Farjeon, *Toilers of Babylon* (London, 1888), 2:231. See also Henry Lazurus, *Landlordism* (London, 1892).

[60] William Torrens, "What Is to Be Done with the Slums?" *MacMillan's Magazine* (April 1879), 545. See also Henry Harrod, "The Dwellings of the Poor," *Dublin Review* (April 1884).

[61] Many writers were critical of the Cross acts. For example, see "The Artisans' Dwellings Acts," *Saturday Review* (24 June 1882); and "The Housing of the London Poor," *Saturday Review* (3 February 1883).

[62] See Henry Brand, "The Dwellings of the Poor in London," *Fortnightly Review* (February 1881); and Richard A. Cross, "Homes of the Poor," *Nineteenth Century* (January 1884).

Metropolis would allow for a more healthy and spacious home and work environment. Because land values were much lower in the suburbs of London, workers would not have to pay such a large portion of their weekly wages in rent. Many workers, indeed, would be able to afford to own their own homes. Unfortunately, prior to 1900, the vast majority of those aided by the Cheap Trains Act of 1883 were skilled artisans and members of the lower middle classes, not those recently displaced by slum clearance in inner city London.[63]

As most of those evicted from their homes were unable or unwilling to move to the suburbs, they needed to be provided with working class housing within the improved areas. For the vast majority of Victorian social reformers, this did not mean that the State should build and rent homes to the poor. Such tasks could be performed far better, most believed, by private enterprise and philanthropy. The State could, however, do much to encourage the private sector. Arnold Toynbee argued that the municipality of London should be allowed to buy land and rent it to various philanthropic building societies for the construction of working class housing. Lord Salisbury proposed that the State might also provide public loans at a low rate of interest to accelerate the building process. *The Economist* agreed, stipulating rates of between 3.5 percent for a twenty-year and 4.5 percent for a fifty-year loan. Although the State might take a loss in the short term, the long-term moral and material benefits of such actions would, in the opinion of many observers, be well worth the cost.[64]

Salisbury, Cross, and others also believed that a number of metropolitan prison sites could be transferred to municipal control for the provision of working class housing. Other reform proposals included the granting of three percent fifteen-year government loans to allow tenants to purchase their own homes; encouraging large companies to provide affordable housing for their workers; the establishment of local registers listing rooms and houses for rent; and the creation

---

[63] See the Report of the Select Committee, House of Commons, "Artisans' and Labourers' Dwellings Improvement" (1882 [235] vii); Robert Cecil, Lord Salisbury, "Labourers and Artisans Dwellings," *National Review* (December 1883); Richard A. Cross, "Homes for the Poor," *Nineteenth Century* (January 1884); T. Locke Worthington, *The Dwellings of the Poor and Weekly Wage-earners* (London, 1893); Edward Bowmaker, *The Housing of the Working Classes* (London, 1895); and Gareth Stedman Jones, *Outcast London* (Oxford, 1971).

[64] See Arnold Toynbee, *"Progress and Poverty": A Criticism of Mr. Henry George* (London, 1883); Robert Cecil, Lord Salisbury, "Labourers and Artisans Dwellings," *National Review* (December 1883); Report of the Select Committee, House of Commons, "Artisans' and Labourers' Dwellings Improvement" (1882 [235] vii); George Howell, "The Dwellings of the Poor," *Nineteenth Century* (June 1883); "The Slum and the Cellar," *Saturday Review* (27 October 1883); Richard A. Cross, "The Homes of the Poor," *Nineteenth Century* (January 1884); M. G. Mulhall, "Dwellings of the Poor in London," *Contemporary Review* (February 1884); Earl Meath, "Work for the London County Council," *Nineteenth Century* (April 1889); and "The Housing of the Working Classes," *The Economist* (18 October 1890).

of a system of fair rent courts. Finally, in a few instances, the local municipality could, under the Cross Act of 1875, construct working class housing; the general expectation was, however, that such properties would be sold upon completion.[65]

As it became increasingly clear that the private sector could not be induced to build a sufficient quantity of homes to reduce overcrowding in the poorest metropolitan districts, a few reformers shifted their emphasis to the public provision of dwellings for the working classes. After all, according to the Radical Liberal Frank Harris, while "re-housing may be looked upon as an insurance paid by the better classes against disease, it may also be regarded as an insurance paid by the rich against revolution."[66] Nor were such ideas, as indicated above, entirely new. One author had remarked as early as 1873 that the State should be allowed to build, manage, and sublet artisans' dwellings; after five years, the State would sell its properties to private philanthropists. A decade later, Lord Salisbury argued that some State employees—postal, police, and customs workers for instance—should be provided with low-cost housing. In 1889, the housing reformer Earl Compton stated further that the State must be prepared in the future to rent out dwellings and model lodging houses without the thought of making a profit if it was to accommodate the thousands of citizens living below the poverty line. In 1896, one social critic went so far as to advocate that all houses below a stated rent be placed under government control and rented to the poorest segment of British society; if a family could not pay its rent, the government would assist them to do so.[67]

Each of the preceding authors "had all along opposed interference with private enterprise"; by the last decades of the nineteenth century, however, they "saw no private arrangement existing for supplying" housing to the working classes.[68] However passionate their pleas for active State intervention in the housing market were, such critics remained a distinct minority. The Housing Act of 1885, which has been widely cited by historians—such as Anthony Wohl—as marking a radical break with the past, and its successors were in fact quite

---

[65] See Robert Cecil, Lord Salisbury, "Labourers and Artisans Dwellings," *National Review* (December 1883); Richard A. Cross, "The Homes of the Poor," *Nineteenth Century* (January 1884); "Dwellings of the Poor," *Westminster Review* (January 1884); Viscount Lymington, "The Housing of the Poor," *National Review* (February 1889); H. M. Bompas, "The Improvement of Working Class Homes," *Fortnightly Review* (November 1895); and George Haw, *No Room to Live* (London, 1900).

[66] Frank Harris, "The Radical Programme—The Housing of the Poor in Towns," *Fortnightly Review* (October 1883), 596.

[67] See John Storr, "The Anarchy of London," *Fortnightly Review* (June 1873); Robert Cecil, Lord Salisbury, "Labourers and Artisans Dwellings," *National Review* (December 1883); Earl Compton, "Homes of the People," *New Review* (June 1889); Harold Cox, "Re-housing of the Poor of London," *Westminster Review* (December 1890); Edward Bowmaker, *The Housing of the Working Classes* (London, 1895); and Harold Thomis, "Poverty and Crime," *Westminster Review* (January 1896).

[68] "Common Lodging Houses in London," *The Lancet* (10 May 1890), 1036.

moderate and traditional. They reflected the common Victorian sentiment, voiced by the Tory housing reformer Lord Shaftesbury in 1883, that if the State provided homes for a nominal rent or free of charge, it would demoralize the poor. The provision of subsidized housing might also send Britain down the slippery slope to socialism. One writer asked "If it is the duty of the State to house the people, is it not also the duty of the State to feed and clothe them too?"[69] Not surprisingly, given the predominance of such ideas, the State did little to provide affordable housing to the working classes prior to World War I.

One task the State *could* perform with a clear conscience in the intellectual climate of the late Victorian period was to make sure that working class dwellings were maintained in a sanitary condition. Much could be accomplished in this direction through the rigorous enforcement of existing lighting, ventilation, and drainage legislation. Additional restrictions might be enacted to ensure an adequate amount of space around and between newly constructed buildings. Land adjacent to cities might be zoned so as to limit urban sprawl. Finally, lodgings—both common and furnished—could be registered and more regularly inspected by the local sanitary authority.[70]

Unfortunately, the Victorian State was unwilling to provide a sufficient number of sanitary inspectors for this task. Time after time, parliamentary committees and commissions lamented that the housing and sanitary acts would never be administered properly unless additional public health officers were appointed. Until the State employed enough medical officers to perform house-to-house inspections in the poorer parts of London and other large cities, and until they had been freed from the fear that the recommendation of costly repairs or slum clearance might cost them their jobs, serious sanitary reform would continue to be extraordinarily difficult. Such would be the case, unfortunately, until well into the twentieth century. London, for instance, employed merely twelve housing inspectors in 1887, twenty-five in 1894, and thirty-six in 1901. As late as 1914, London had hired only one inspector for every 15,000 homes.[71]

In conclusion, although the Victorians expended more effort and spilled more ink over housing reform than over any other single issue, they accomplished next

---

[69] "Dwellings of the Poor," *Westminster Review* (January 1884), 138. See also Lord Shaftesbury, "Common Sense and the Dwellings of the Poor," *Nineteenth Century* (December 1883); George Haw, *No Room to Live* (London, 1900); and Anthony S. Wohl, "The 1880s: A New Generation," *Nineteenth Century Studies* 1990 (4): 1-22.

[70] See "Dwellings of the Poor," *Westminster Review* (January 1884); C. L. Lewes, "How to Ensure Breathing Space," *Nineteenth Century* (May 1887); Earl Compton, "The Homes of the People," *New Review* (June 1889); and Samuel A. Barnett, "The Abodes of the Homeless," *Cornhill Magazine* (July 1899).

[71] See R. Vladimir Steffel, "The Slum Question," *Albion* 1973 5 (4): 314-25. For a contemporary view, see the Final Report of the Royal Commission *On the Housing of the Working Classes* (1884-1885 [cd.4402], v. 30]; the Report of the Select Committee, House of Commons, "Public Health in Metropolitan Parishes" (1886 [c.4714], v. vi); and David Schloss, "Healthy Homes for the Working Classes," *Fortnightly Review* (April 1888).

to nothing. None of the twenty-five housing acts passed between 1870 and the turn of the century significantly reduced overcrowding in British cities. The recommendations offered by numerous Victorian committees and commissions on working class housing do not reveal a real willingness to find State solutions to the problem of overcrowding. For example, even if all of the suggestions made by the Royal Commission *On Housing* of 1885 had been put into effect, they would have had little impact on the condition of urban Britain. As one contemporary noted, the Final Report "is doubtless valuable as showing how far" the Victorian political class was "willing to go in the direction of reform; unfortunately, however, it conclusively proves that the distance is very small."[72] In addition, most local authorities were unwilling, for reasons of economy, to enforce rigorously their legal obligations under the various housing and sanitary acts. As one reformer commented in 1895, "Ten years have passed since the Report of the Royal Commission on the Housing of the Working Classes, and little if anything has been done to carry out its recommendations."[73]

The complete failure of housing reform did not at all deter those interested in the second most popular form of State intervention in the national economy, the establishment of public works for the unemployed. Providing work for those suffering from economic hardship was, of course, nothing new. The Poor Law Guardians in many large urban unions had long insisted that the able-bodied perform a "labor test" before receiving aid. The "test" could take a number of different forms: breaking stones, grinding corn, and picking oakum.[74] All such labor, however, carried with it the stigma of the workhouse. Public works, on the other hand, were intended to provide employment to "deserving" laborers who had been thrown out of work during periods of economic recession. For example, the "cotton famine" brought on by the American Civil War led to the passage of the Public Works Act of 1863. This act gave local officials the power to borrow money at a low rate of interest from the State in order to finance town improvements.

During the era of the so-called "Great Depression," proposals abounded for the employment of the "deserving" poor. In the countryside, agricultural improvements would allow respectable workers to maintain their independence. In cities, mending furniture, roofing, whitewashing rooms, street cleaning, road work, and park beautification could provide temporary employment for the poor

---

[72] Henry Harrod, "The Royal Commission on the Housing of the Poor," *Dublin Review* (July 1895), 105.

[73] H. M. Bompas, "The Improvement of Working Class Homes," *Fortnightly Review* (November 1895), 738.

[74] Oakum, a hemp fiber obtained by untwisting or picking the fibers of old rope, was used for caulking the seams of wooden sailing ships.

during troubled economic times.[75] In December 1884, *The People* called on the government to provide employment through increased naval building. Similarly, Arnold White argued the following year that the State should find work for unemployed servicemen in the civil bureaucracy.[76]

In 1886, Joseph Chamberlain, the president of the Local Government Board under Prime Minister Gladstone, called upon town councils to undertake municipal works to alleviate working class distress. As honest workers were, according to Chamberlain, suffering from the worst economic downturn since the 1840s, they should be given an opportunity to maintain their respectability outside of the Poor Law. Chamberlain's only stipulations were that the public works should not compete with the private sector; that workers be paid a standard hourly wage; and that a condition of "less eligibility" be maintained by limiting the length of the workday.[77] Although its success in reducing unemployment was minimal, the Local Government Board insisted on reissuing Chamberlain's circular in 1887, 1891, 1892, and 1895.

Nor was Chamberlain alone in his wish to aid the "deserving" poor during the 1880s. One commentator argued in 1887 that 1,300 workers could lay out public parks and pleasure grounds for a mere £20,000; the local authority would, of course, insist the workers be of good character and have resided in London for at least six months. Another stated that 100,000 "deserving" laborers might be found full-time employment during the winter months doing road, canal, and sewer repairs; slum clearance; dwellings, bath, and wash-house construction; and draining the Thames marshes. Reverend Samuel A. Barnett of Toynbee Hall wrote in 1888 that the Poor Law Guardians should buy and administer farms in England or in the colonies for the unemployed. Worthy laborers would gain possession of a farm of their own after a number of years. Barnett justified his proposal under the little-known Poor Law Amendment Act of 1825, which allowed unions to purchase fifty acres of farmland for the use of impoverished cottagers. Barnett, economical as ever, hoped to defray the cost of this new program by selling the food grown on the farms to nearby cities.[78]

The discussion of public works during the 1890s, in contrast to the previous decade, however, reveals a much less sympathetic attitude towards those who had

---

[75] See R. H. Patterson, *The State, the Poor, and the Country* (London, 1870); "East and West," *Fraser's Magazine* (September-October 1870); and George S. Reaney, "Outcast London," *Fortnightly Review* (December 1886).

[76] See *The People*, 21 December 1884; and Arnold White, "The Nomad Poor of London," *Contemporary Review* (May 1885).

[77] See the "Circular Addressed by the President of the Local Government Board to the Several Boards of Guardians," 15 March 1886, *Parliamentary Papers* (69), lvi.

[78] See "The New Mansion House Fund," *Saturday Review* (24 December 1887); Bennet Burleigh, "The Unemployed," *Contemporary Review* (December 1887); Samuel A. Barnett, "A Scheme for the Unemployed," *Nineteenth Century* (November 1888); and J. A. Ingham, *City Slums* (London, 1889).

been temporarily thrown out of work. Although recent years might have restored the pre-1834 "right to labor" of the Elizabethan Poor Law, this did not mean that the unemployed were to be coddled by the State. Most critics strongly believed that laborers chosen for public works had to be selected carefully and supervised closely. The able-bodied needed to be paid subsistence wages and only employed until other work became available. The State had to ensure that workers did not come to rely upon public works every winter; they should, therefore, only be established in years of real distress. Plus, localities were not "to manufacture or create work with the view of giving employment" even during periods of economic difficulty.[79] Such limitations notwithstanding, the temporary public employment of the "deserving" poor did serve a useful purpose. Public works, if administered along liberal lines, tended to further "the elimination of the unworthy" from the ranks of the poor and remove "many of the reasons for the 'unsympathetic' treatment of the unemployed" as a whole.[80]

The problem was that public works were never employed on a wide scale during the late Victorian era. Although pilot programs were established in various metropolitan districts—in Whitechapel, Lewisham, and Wandsworth in 1886; in Camberwell in 1887 and 1888; in Abbey Mills in 1892 and 1893; and in Poplar, West Ham, and Mile End Old Town in 1893 and 1894—none provided a significant amount of relief to the unemployed. For example, in 1887 only 456 Londoners found employment with the State; in 1893 and 1894, this small number fell to 141. Furthermore, although parliament authorized the Treasury to make special loans to local authorities for public works in 1895, the Government was extraordinarily reluctant to do so. In consequence, future public works would have to be largely financed out of the local rates, an entirely unwelcome prospect for most municipal officials.[81] With the economy rebounding to a state of relative prosperity by the mid-1890s, there was even less incentive for the Victorians to establish an expensive system of public works.

While housing reform was undertaken on a vast scale and public works were at least experimented with during the late Victorian period, old age pensions failed to emerge from the realm of academic controversy. Even so, the plans offered by Reverend William Blackley, Joseph Chamberlain, and Charles Booth on this issue are important in that they set the parameters for the debate over pensions prior to their establishment by Herbert Asquith's Liberal government in 1908. Several

---

[79] W. R. Bousfield, "The Unemployed," *Contemporary Review* (December 1896), 837. See also H. Clarence Bourne, "The Unemployed," *MacMillan's Magazine* (December 1892); James Mavor, "Setting the Poor on Work," *Nineteenth Century* (October 1893); J. Theodore Dodd, "What Can the Government Do for the Poor at Once?" *New Review* (August 1893); A. Dunn-Gardner, "The Drift to Socialism," *Contemporary Review* (January 1894); and Charles S. Loch, "Manufacturing a New Pauperism," *Nineteenth Century* (April 1895).

[80] R. H. Law, "New Pleas for Old Remedies," *Westminster Review* (June 1896), 682.

[81] Jose Harris, *Unemployment and Politics* (Oxford, 1972), 96-99, 112-14. See also Charles S. Loch, "Manufacturing a New Pauperism," *Nineteenth Century* (April 1895).

factors spurred the consideration of old age pensions during the final decades of the nineteenth century. First, the financial solvency of many private insurers was very much open to doubt. Insufficient contributions and excessive promises—the result of both ill-management and rising life expectancies—had brought nearly sixty percent of all English and Welsh friendly societies to the brink of bankruptcy by the early 1880s. At the end of that decade, an investigation in *The Economist* found seventy-seven percent of the 3,500 societies it surveyed to be in a precarious financial position.[82] In addition, few societies offered portability for those changing jobs or moving from place to place.

Second, although deposits in savings banks—particularly those administered by the Post Office—government annuities and insurance, friendly societies, and union pensions had risen substantially since 1870, large numbers of working class families did not earn enough to prepare properly for their old age. Far too many low-income households "were finely balanced on a knife edge of sufficiency, always threatening to plummet into the arms of the relieving officer."[83] Financial crises—resulting from the unemployment, sickness, or death of one or both parents—were a common occurrence within the working classes; as a result, many among the poor found it extremely difficult to set aside sufficient funds for the future.[84]

Almost inevitably, therefore, a large proportion of Britain's elderly population fell into pauperism. Charles Booth found in 1891 that twenty-nine percent of all British citizens over the age of sixty-five, roughly four hundred thousand persons, received some form of relief; an even larger number, thirty-five percent, lived in poverty.

Age	Booth's Poverty Rate
65+	35%
65-70	20%
70-75	30%
75+	40%

---

[82] Of the 13,000 friendly societies contacted, only 3,500 sent in returns ("The Financial Position of Friendly Societies," *The Economist* [3 August 1889], 994). See also James Randall, "Friendly Societies: Their Position and Prospects," *Fortnightly Review* (August 1880); "Working Class Insurance As It Is," *Westminster Review* (January 1882); U. A. Forbes, "The Growth of Poor Man's Providence," *London Quarterly Review* (April 1885); and Bentley Gilbert, "The Decay of Nineteenth Century Provident Institutions and the Coming of Old Age Pensions," *Economic History Review* 1965 17 (3): 550-63.

[83] Paul Johnson, *Saving and Spending: The Working Class Economy in Britain, 1870-1939* (New York, 1985), 1. See also Brian Mitchell, *European Historical Statistics, 1750-1970* (New York, 1976), 691.

[84] See Paul Johnson, *Saving and Spending: The Working Class Economy in Britain, 1870-1939* (New York, 1985); and Clementia Black, Lady Cavendish, et al., "Thrift for the Poor," *New Review* (December 1892).

Taking into account only the working classes, between forty and forty-five percent of those over 65 lived on or below the poverty line. In addition, Booth found that the aged poor living in large British cities received less outdoor relief, had fewer employment opportunities, and could not count on their families for much financial support.[85] In essence, to quote a contemporary novelist, whereas "In savage communities, where the laws of nature are respected, the old, the ill-formed, and the helpless are mercifully slaughtered. In Christian countries they are tolerated like stray dogs, and allowed to struggle miserably against starvation, sickness, and neglect."[86] For such a situation to exist at the close of the nineteenth century was, in the opinion of many critics, intolerable. In the future, friendly societies would need to be subject to closer scrutiny. If private charity was unable to provide for the aged poor, the State might have to intervene on their behalf. Perhaps, as Arnold Toynbee believed, the State should drive down the cost of insurance and pensions through grants-in-aid to the friendly societies. Beyond this, the State might establish a pension scheme of its own outside of the friendly society system. It is to this latter task that Reverend William Blackley turned his attention during the late 1870s.[87]

Simply put, Blackley intended to compel young workers to provide for sickness and old age. Every British male would, under his scheme, be forced to contribute £15 to a national friendly society by the time he turned twenty-one. As a result, each would be entitled to eight shillings per week when sick and four shillings per week after reaching the age of seventy. Workers would be allowed to receive money from the fund in order to emigrate or to pay burial expenses. They could also, if they wished, purchase additional coverage. Public monies would be available to make up for any short-term deficiencies in the fund. Finally, as Blackley's pensions were to be distributed through the Post Office and result from the workers' own contributions, the "deserving" poor would no longer be demoralized in their old age by their association with the Poor Law.[88]

The main criticism leveled against Blackley's pension plan was that it forced workers to save. Blackley countered this argument by stating that compulsion "may interfere with [a young workers'] waste; but that does not harm him. It may interfere with his habits; but only so far as his habits are bad. It may interfere with

---

[85] See Charles Booth, *The Aged Poor in England and Wales* (1894, Reprint Edition, New York, 1985), 420; Royal Commission *On the Aged Poor* (1895 [cd.7684], v. 14-15), xiii; and "Old Age and Pauperism," *The Economist* (11 April 1891), 462.

[86] Harry Lander, *Lucky Bargee* (New York, 1898), 149.

[87] See Arnold Toynbee, *"Progress and Poverty": A Criticism of Mr. Henry George* (London, 1883).

[88] See William Blackley's "National Insurance," *Nineteenth Century* (November 1878) and "English Pauperism," *Fraser's Magazine* (October 1880).

his liberty; but only so far as his liberty is licentious."[89] However distasteful coercion might be to some observers, Blackley believed it to be both justified and necessary. He realized that "all our public and private aids to thrift, great, growing, and valuable though they be, are offered as yet to *only one class of people*, and for the rest are as utterly ineffective as if they were absolutely non-existent."[90] Without compulsion, "the rest" would never be induced to provide for sickness and old age.

Universal coverage, for Blackley a corollary of coercion, would bring great benefits to society at large. Honest, respectable workers would no longer fear falling upon the rates in old age. Those of good character, who had saved for the future, would be assured that they would not be defrauded of their savings through the financial negligence—criminal or otherwise—of private insurers and friendly societies. Furthermore, once established on a national basis, Blackley's scheme would make the division between the "deserving" and the "undeserving" poor quite clear. According to Blackley, only the most demoralized element of society would now fall under the supervision of the Poor Law; as a result, the pauper class could be treated harshly with a clear conscience.[91]

The pension plan offered by Joseph Chamberlain in 1891 was very different from that proposed by Reverend Blackley. Chamberlain envisioned a voluntary system with annuities provided at low cost through the Post Office. At twenty-five, each worker wishing to join would deposit £5; as a reward for his providence, the State would donate £15 to the fund. From that point on, the worker would pay £1 per year into his account. At sixty-five, he could begin drawing five shillings per week for the rest of his life. Obviously, Chamberlain hoped to stimulate and encourage thrift, not compel it as Blackley had wanted to do. Unlike Blackley, Chamberlain firmly believed that "our help should be given only to those who have shown their willingness to do all in their power to help themselves."[92]

Critics were not long in attacking Chamberlain's proposal. *The Economist* wailed in November 1891 that the plan would lead to higher taxes, no reduction in the cost of the Poor Law, and that it would not reach those most in need of assistance. In addition, few workers would be willing, *The Economist* reasoned, to set £5 aside for use forty years later. Not surprisingly, the friendly societies

---

[89] William Blackley, "Compulsory Providence as a Cure for Pauperism," *Contemporary Review* (July 1879), 614-15.

[90] William Blackley, "The Juggernaut of Poor Men's Providence," *Fortnightly Review* (April 1884), 68.

[91] Ibid. See also "Charity, Pauperism, and Self-Help," *Westminster Review* (January 1875); E. W. Brabrook, "The Relation of the State to Thrift," *Journal of the Royal Statistical Society* (March 1885); and W. Moore Ede, "National Pensions: One Way Out of Darkest England," *Contemporary Review* (April 1891).

[92] Joseph Chamberlain's "Old Age Pensions and Friendly Societies," *National Review* (January 1895), 615. See also Joseph Chamberlain, "Old Age Pensions," *National Review* (February 1892); J. Fletcher Moulton, "Old Age Pensions," *Fortnightly Review* (April 1892); and, for a slightly less generous proposal, U. A. Forbes, "Industrial Provision for Old Age," *London Quarterly Review* (October 1891).

opposed Chamberlain's proposal for the same reason that they had earlier agitated against Blackley's pension scheme; they believed, with some justification, that either, if successful, would cut into their profits and limit their ability to do business.[93] William Blackley, of course, agreed that while Chamberlain's plan "will be accepted by a few of our best and wisest workers it will be generally neglected by the mass of the young and inexperienced, and so that it will only benefit those who want it least and not alter the condition of those who need it most."[94] Even so, Blackley believed Chamberlain's proposal was worth trying, if only to prove that no voluntary scheme would be able to reach the masses.

In addition to Blackley and Chamberlain, a number of writers in the early 1890s proposed pension plans that were remarkably similar to that in operation in Germany since 1889. These British reformers believed that Otto von Bismarck's reforms—which linked employers, employees, and the State together to provide for the sick, the disabled, and the aged—set an important precedent for the future. *The Economist* had noted several years before that as German social reforms had "been a direct result of universal suffrage," they would "be imitated in many countries."[95] J. W. Williams, following this line of reasoning, argued that by combining individual savings—two to four pence per week depending on when one joined his program—employer contributions, and State subsidies, workers would be allowed to insure themselves against poverty in old age. Furthermore, their weekly pension of seven shillings six pence—as with Blackley and Chamberlain, paid through the Post Office—would allow friendly societies to concentrate on sickness and death insurance. In addition, unlike many earlier proposals, Williams's pension plan was open to women, although he expected their weekly subscription to be higher because of their longer life-span; women would also, of course, lose their

---

[93] See "Mr. Chamberlain on Old Age Pensions," *The Economist* (21 November 1891); George Holloway, Thomas Mackay, et al., "Old Age Pensions," *National Review* (March 1892); and Thomas Scanlon, "Mr. Chamberlain's Pension Scheme," *Westminster Review* (April 1892). Holloway and Mackay believed that friendly societies should be allowed to provide sickness, old age, and death insurance with the size of one's contribution determined on the basis of age.

[94] William Blackley, "Mr. Chamberlain's Pension Scheme," *Contemporary Review* (March 1892), 395.

[95] "Prince Bismarck's Poor Law," *The Economist* (19 February 1881), 218. Contrary to what some historians—such as E. P. Hennock—have written, the Victorians were well aware of political and social developments in Germany. Most believed, however, that such legislation would depress wages, raise taxes, and pauperize the British working classes. Many were also concerned about the compulsory aspects of Bismarck's reforms. See "Mr. Chamberlain on Old Age Pensions," *The Economist* (21 November 1891); Henry Wolff, "Old Age Pensions in Practice," *Contemporary Review* (June 1894); and, for a historical interpretation, E. P. Hennock, *British Social Reform and the German Precedents* (New York, 1987).

employers' contributions if they left the workforce upon marriage.[96]

Each of the pension plans considered thus far had one common component; workers were expected to contribute a portion or, in Blackley's case all, of the funds for their upkeep in old age. As the Old Age Pensions Act of 1908 did not require such contributions, it is important to examine those writers whose ideas had a more direct impact on the Liberal reforms of the Edwardian era. Reverend Samuel A. Barnett called in 1883 for the government to provide a pension of between eight and ten shillings per week to all those over sixty who had never received Poor Law relief. Money for this program could, according to Barnett, be raised by raiding the "endowed charities" of the City of London, by making a new assessment for the land tax, and by cutting waste in government. Seven years later, the Fabian Socialist Sidney Webb argued that the State should establish a universal pension of around four shillings a week for those over sixty-five. In 1893, Edith Sellers, a noted investigator of the sweated trades, published a fascinating article on the way the Viennese Poor Law dealt with the aged; she found that since 1781, all those over sixty could claim one-third of their average daily wage as a reward for past services to the State. Sellers clearly implied that such a system should be established in Britain as well.[97]

Each of these authors believed that most poverty among the elderly was unavoidable, that friendly societies' use of sick funds for the aged placed a dangerous strain on their resources, and that neither voluntary schemes nor "universal" compulsion would reach those most in need. The only viable alternative, in their estimation, was for the State to provide pensions without requiring workers' contributions. Each writer represented the "revival of the almost forgotten duty of the young and the working to provide for the aged and the past-working—a social duty as clear as that of providing for the infant and the child."[98] Unfortunately, none of these reformers had the name recognition necessary to propel their proposals to the forefront of the national debate. Once joined by Charles Booth, the famed investigator of metropolitan poverty, in 1891, however, they had to be taken much more seriously.

Even so, Booth realized, more than any of his predecessors, how difficult it would be to sell universal, noncontributory pensions to the British people. Booth knew that he had first to convince public opinion that the granting of pensions was morally justifiable. His argument, like Sellers', was that pensions were not charity, but a reward for one's past services to the country. Second, Booth needed to show

---

[96] See J. W. Williams, "Old Age Pensions," *Westminster Review* (August 1895). The National Provident League and the Poor Law Reform Association also argued in favor of government supplements to those willing to save for the future.

[97] See Samuel A. Barnett, "Practicable Socialism," *Nineteenth Century* (April 1883); Sidney Webb, "Reform of the Poor Law," *Contemporary Review* (July 1890); and Edith Sellers, "A Humane Poor Law," *MacMillan's Magazine* (February 1893).

[98] J. Frome Wilkinson, "The Endowment of Old Age," *Contemporary Review* (April 1892), 562.

that his "endowment"—five shillings per week paid by the State to all those who did not otherwise fall upon the rates—would actually aid in the moralization of the poor by stimulating thrift within the working classes. As laborers who fell upon the rates in old age would lose their £13 annual pension, those living on the brink of poverty had an added incentive to save while they were young. Because pensions were paid through the Post Office or savings banks, workers would not be demoralized or degraded. In addition, in Booth's opinion, his pensions would neither reduce wages nor damage private insurance companies. Finally, Booth's scheme would make the differences between the "deserving" and the "undeserving" poor that much easier to recognize.[99]

Critics attacked Booth's plan on a number of grounds. Would not taxes have to be raised to pay for this new, expensive program? Even one of Booth's supporters argued in 1892 that a graduated income tax plus steep death duties would be needed to defray the additional costs, some £20 million, of his pension program. Seven years later, another commentator stated that it would be necessary to raise taxes on beer, spirits, and wine, great incomes, grand establishments, and land to pay for universal pensions.[100] Second, would not universal, noncontributory pensions, whatever Booth might say to the contrary, increase improvidence within the working classes? Finally, would not later parliaments be sorely tempted to increase benefits for political reasons? Might not, in other words, Booth's socialistic proposals prove infectious?[101]

If parliamentary investigations of old-age pensions are any guide, there was little chance of this, at least in the near future. Select committee consideration of national provident insurance—specifically, William Blackley's scheme and social insurance in Germany—between 1885 and 1887 followed a traditional path. The committee argued that although voluntary plans did not reach the unemployed or the demoralized poor, many respectable workers could not save the £10 stipulated by Blackley by the time they were twenty-one. Furthermore, "the great majority of the working classes would prefer to provide their own insurance in their own way, rather than be parties to any compulsory scheme."[102] Although the committee did support making the inclusion of information about thrift and insurance a part of a child's education and insisted that friendly societies should put their financial

---

[99] See Charles Booth's "Enumeration and Classification of Paupers, and State Pensions for the Aged," *Journal of the Royal Statistical Society* (December 1891) and *Pauperism: A Picture and an Endowment of Old Age* (London, 1892); and J. A. Spender, *The State and Pensions in Old Age* (London, 1892).

[100] See J. Frome Wilkinson, "The Endowment of Old Age," *Contemporary Review* (April 1892); and Vaughan Nash, "The Old Age Pension Movement," *Contemporary Review* (April 1899).

[101] See William Blackley, "Mr. Chamberlain's Pension Scheme," *Contemporary Review* (March 1892); "Old Age Pensions and Pauperism," *London Quarterly Review* (July 1892); and Spencer Walpole, "Old Age Pensions: A Suggestion," *Nineteenth Century* (April 1899).

[102] Report of the Select Committee, House of Commons, "National Provident Insurance" (1887 [257], v. xi], v.

house in order, such reforms could not be expected to strike at the heart of old age pauperism.

The Royal Commission *On the Aged Poor*—which included the Prince of Wales, Charles Loch of the Charity Organisation Society, Joseph Chamberlain, Charles Booth, and many others—unfortunately, fared no better. After two years' study between 1893 and 1895, the commissioners seemed "to come out much as they went in."[103] The Final Report of the Royal Commission did not suggest fundamental change for a number of reasons. First, the number of non-able-bodied paupers had diminished greatly overall, an indication of rising thrift within the working classes. Second, as most of the aged poor were able to receive outdoor relief through the Poor Law, an elaborate pension system seemed superfluous. The Majority Report did call on the Poor Law Guardians to be more discriminating, to ensure that the relief they distributed was adequate, and to reform the workhouse environment. In addition, the majority encouraged private charity to provide pensions for the "deserving" on a case-by-case basis. The Minority Report—signed by Chamberlain, Booth, and three others—argued that the Majority Report's summary was far too optimistic and that its "remedies" would do little to reduce old age pauperism.[104]

A further select committee report on old age pensions in 1898 did little to address the concerns of Booth, Chamberlain, and the rest. Indeed, it came to the same tired conclusions. As thrift and self-denial rose, the poor would be better able to provide for themselves. In fact, the committee noted, all statistical evidence to the contrary, the number of people "in a position to require assistance must, in any case, form but a small proportion of the industrial population."[105] Of the elderly housed within Poor Law workhouses or infirmaries, the committee argued, few would be able to support themselves even if they had a pension. Furthermore, pensions would be costly and difficult to administer, and they would not reach those most in need of help.[106] Despite the lack of progress, parliamentary interest in the issue of old age pensions continued unabated. In 1899, the Board of Trade sponsored an extensive study of old age pensions in various European countries. Only two nations were found to make a general provision for the elderly, Germany and Denmark, both of which provided compulsory insurance against sickness, accidents, and old age.[107]

By 1899, however, public opinion had grown quite weary of such endless, yet essentially meaningless, parliamentary discussions of old age pensions. It was

---

[103] *The Graphic*, 6 April 1895, 403.

[104] See the Majority and Minority reports of the Royal Commission *On the Aged Poor* (1895 [cd.7684], v. 14-15).

[105] Report of the Select Committee, House of Commons, "Old Age Pensions" (1898 [c.8911], v. xlv), 14.

[106] Ibid.

[107] In addition, pensions had been established in New Zealand in 1898, in New South Wales and Victoria by 1901, and in all of Australia in 1908.

becoming increasingly clear that, however much Joseph Chamberlain and Arthur Balfour—Prime Minister Salisbury's nephew—might agitate for State-aided pensions at election time, the Conservative Party was unwilling even to present a bill for parliamentary consideration.[108] The establishment of yet another select committee on the aged poor in May 1899 might have been expected merely to regurgitate the same old conservative formula. Such was not the case, however.

The committee—headed by the Tory Lionel Holland and the Liberal David Lloyd George—proposed that British subjects who were at least sixty-five years old, had not been imprisoned for a crime or received Poor Law relief (other than medical aid) in the past twenty years "except under circumstances of a wholly exceptional character," had an income of ten shillings or less per week, and had "endeavored to the best of [their] ability, by [their] industry or by the exercise of reasonable providence, to make provision for [themselves] and those immediately dependent on [them]" should receive a pension of between five and seven shillings per week.[109] Pensions were to be awarded for three years; after that period, they could be either renewed or withdrawn. To the untrained eye, it would seem that the select committee on the "Aged Deserving Poor" of 1899 had traversed a significant distance between Chamberlain's State-aided scheme and the universal, noncontributory pensions advocated by Charles Booth. That the committee—and other Victorian social reformers—did not go further was due in large part to the strong opposition of those marshaled against the expansion of the British State.

Opponents vilified the various late Victorian pension schemes on a number of different grounds. First, they argued that few workers favored their establishment.[110] Second, a large portion of the Labour movement viewed the political class's endless arguments over the establishment of national pensions as a way to prevent the consideration of more substantive reform. The *Labour Leader*, for example, contended in 1899 that "Old Age Pensions had been selected

---

[108] See Lionel Holland, "The Problem of Poverty in Old Age," *National Review* (February 1896); and Bernard Holland, "Old Age Relief," *Edinburgh Review* (October 1899). One critic complained in 1889 that "Royal Commissions are no doubt, in their intention, often a convenient political method for appeasing a popular agitation, which is too strong to be snubbed and too vague or uninformed to admit of an immediate and definite legislative remedy" (Viscount Lymington, "Housing of the Poor," *National Review* [February 1889], 830).

[109] Report of the Select Committee, House of Commons, "Aged Deserving Poor" (1899 [296], v. viii], ix. See also Henry Burdett, "Old Age Pensions," *Journal of the Royal Statistical Society* (December 1898). Burdett thought that pensions should only be distributed to those among the "deserving" whose earnings did not allow them to save for old age, about one-quarter of all adult wage-earners. For Burdett, local and endowed charities, not the State, should pay most, if not all, of the cost of these stipends.

[110] Not everyone agreed, of course. One author argued in 1899 that the "whole country is crying in silence" for contributory pensions. In his estimation, what was important was that there was no popular *opposition* to their establishment (A. Edmund Spender, "A State Crutch for Old Age Pensions," *Westminster Review* [July 1899], 49).

as a battle-cry, because it meant least of all in the matter of social reform and offered facilities for hoodwinking the unwary."[111] Third, pensions would not substantially reduce the overall poverty rate. Seebohm Rowntree discovered in 1901 that, as only 3.62 percent of those in poverty in the city of York were over sixty-five, the establishment of universal pensions for the elderly would reduce the overall poverty rate in York by only about one percent. The problem—a 25.59 percent poverty rate in York and, by extrapolation, in all English cities—would remain daunting.[112]

Fourth, most critics believed that poverty amongst the aged was being—and would continue to be—alleviated by other means. Self-help and thrift allowed the "better class of workmen" to prepare for the future. Friendly societies, union funds, and other private insurers provided ample opportunities for those who wished to save against sickness and old age. The evidence was clear that more and more workers were doing so. During the last half of the nineteenth century, pauperism among those over sixty had decreased by a third. Many writers assumed that future moral and material progress within the working classes would make old age pauperism less and less of a problem. The "residuum" could rely, as it had in the past, on the Poor Law and private charity.[113] The distribution of outdoor relief to the elderly, although roundly condemned by the Charity Organisation Society and others, continued to be widely practiced. For those housed within the workhouse, improved conditions allowed those over sixty-five—one-quarter of those receiving indoor relief in 1892—to enjoy a more comfortable, less degrading existence as wards of the State. Furthermore, private philanthropy had the power to award substantial pensions to the "deserving" poor.[114] Finally, according to the head of the Charity Organisation Society, Charles Loch, State-aided annuities and universal, noncontributory pensions would not only fail to address the true causes of British pauperism, but also demoralize the poor by taking the disgrace out of public assistance. Pensions of this kind, in Loch's estimation, discouraged thrift, increased pauperism, and induced an unhealthy reliance on the State.[115]

---

[111] *Labour Leader*, 8 April 1899, 107.

[112] See B. Seebohm Rowntree, *Poverty: A Study of Town Life* (1901, Reprint Edition, New York, 1971).

[113] See "Old Age Pensions and Poor Relief," *The Economist* (14 November 1891); H. Clarence Bourne, "National Pensions," *MacMillan's Magazine* (February 1892); and J. Lister Stead, "Friendly Societies and Old Age Pensions: A Reply to Mr. Chamberlain," *National Review* (March 1895).

[114] See Geoffrey Drage's *The Problem of the Aged Poor* (London, 1895) and "The Problem of the Aged Poor," *Fortnightly Review* (October 1899); and J. Tyrell Baylee, "The Problems of Pauperism and Old Age," *Westminster Review* (January 1896); and Charles S. Loch, "Fallacies about Old Age Pensions," *Nineteenth Century* (November 1898).

[115] See Charles S. Loch's *Old Age Pensions and Pauperism* (London, 1892), *Pauperism and Old Age Pensions* (London, 1892), and "Fallacies About Old Age Pensions," *Nineteenth Century* (November 1898). See also William Chance, *Our Treatment of the Poor* (London, 1879); and *Insurance and Saving* (London, 1892).

In addition, for some critics, the national debate within the middle and upper classes regarding pensions for the aged poor represented the thin end of the wedge. Once parliamentary politicians began to press upon the electorate "that they are—or may in course of time become—entitled to an unearned, unexpected, five shillings a week the honeyed suggestion makes way, and produces expectations which are capable of being represented as a popular demand which the Government is bound to reckon."[116] Furthermore, the people, "like a drunkard whose craving for drink grows with every potation," thirst for ever "larger doses of paternal legislation."[117] In time, the British people will, one writer warned, lose all sense of providence, discipline, and self-reliance.[118]

Once the majority of Britons came to expect that "it is the business of the Government to provide work at suitable wages for all who apply to it for employment," food for the hungry, shelter for the homeless, medical care for the sick, and pensions for the elderly, Britain would be, in the opinion of many observers, well on its way to national ruin.[119] According to the noted housing reformer Lord Shaftesbury, "State benevolence is a melancholy system that tends to debase a large mass of people to the condition of the nursery, where the children look to the father and mother, and do nothing for themselves."[120] For many critics, such State intervention in the economy softened unduly the workings of natural selection and sapped at the nation's spirit by coddling the weak, the unfit, the degenerate, and other "delicate organisms."[121] Material progress, in their estimation, arose from liberty, inequality and social Darwinism, not from pensions, public works, and subsidized housing. In brief, government paternalism—sometimes known as "grandmotherly" legislation—reduced national enterprise, energy, wealth, and character. In the competitive international economy of the late nineteenth century, Great Britain "least of all nations can risk any experiment which can bring with it a relaxation of mental and moral fibre."[122]

---

[116] Edward Bond, "Is the Unionist Party Committed to Old Age Pensions?" *National Review* (July 1899), 732.

[117] Alfred Hake and O. E. Wesslau, *The Coming Individualism* (Westminster, England, 1895), 23. According to such authors, "State Socialism" was contrary to the "great energy," "impatience of interference," and "tolerance of everything until it becomes an abuse" of the national character ("The Advance towards State Socialism," *The Economist* [7 April 1894], 417).

[118] See Thomas Mackay, *The State and Charity* (London, 1898).

[119] See the Report of the Select Committee, House of Lords, "Poor Law Relief" (1888 [363] v. xv], vii.

[120] Lord Shaftesbury, "Common Sense and the Dwellings of the Poor," *Nineteenth Century* (December 1883), 938-39.

[121] J. Milner Fothergill, *The Town Dweller* (1889, Reprint Edition, New York, 1985), 108. See also "Panaceas for Poverty," *Saturday Review* (20 February 1886); and G. P. MacDonell, "The State and the Unemployed," *British Quarterly Review* (April 1886).

[122] *Charity Organisation Review*, April 1893, 118. See also David Field, *The Duties of the State* (London, 1890) on the impact of governmental paternalism.

A number of societies—the Industrial Freedom League, the Middle Class Defense Organization, the London Ratepayers League, and, most famous, the Liberty and Property Defense League—were established during the early 1880s to guard against this eventuality. Each society was vehemently anti-socialist, and all recognized that the real danger came from the State, not from the fragmented socialist organizations outside of the British political mainstream. Gladstone's land legislation, Chamberlain's Radicalism, the popularity of Henry George's writings, and growing fears that both parliamentary parties would use social legislation as a way to woo newly enfranchised working class voters inspired great concern. The Liberty and Property Defense League—founded in July 1882 by Lord Wemyss, William Mallock, and Albert V. Dicey—was particularly active in the struggle against State socialism. The LPDL set up federated societies throughout Britain and the Empire, and in the United States, France, Italy, Germany, and Switzerland. It espoused its views through a number of journals: *The Liberty Review*, *The Free Life*, *The Personal Rights Journal*, and *The Trumphet* among others. The LPDL also established a parliamentary pressure group to agitate against undesirable pieces of legislation.[123]

The LPDL's definition of what was "undesirable" was quite broad; their dedication to *laissez-faire* economics, indeed, exceeded that of the Manchester liberals. Society must not, they believed, under most circumstances, protect the weak through legislation; it should reward the strong, the enterprising, and the intelligent. Herbert Spencer, the ideological godfather of the LPDL, clearly stated that the government should play only a limited role in society: defend the national borders, punish crime, enforce contractual obligations, and make justice accessible to the people. The "New Toryism," which according to Spencer began around 1860, had brought increased social legislation, regulation of the economy, and bureaucratic red-tape in its train. The citizen of the modern era would, in his opinion, soon learn to fear the tyrannous "divine right of parliaments."[124]

What social reformers in parliament did not seem to realize was that "the habits of a vast working population are not to be changed" for the better "by an Act of Parliament"; in most cases, they would merely "become the victims of hasty and

---

[123] The seminal study of the LPDL is Edward Bristow's *Individualism versus Socialism in Britain, 1880-1914* (New York, 1987). See also Bristow's "The Liberty and Property Defense League and Individualism," *Historical Journal* 1975 18 (4): 761-89.

[124] See Herbert Spencer, *Man versus the State* (1884, Reprint Edition, Caldwell, Idaho, 1940). See also William H. Mallock's "Radicalism and the Working Classes," *National Review* (September 1883), *Property and Progress* (London, 1884) and *Aristocracy and Evolution* (London, 1898); Sir Henry Maine, *Popular Government* (London, 1885); and J. H. Rigg, "The Social Horizon," *London Quarterly Review* (October 1892). None of this was particularly new or unique to Britain. One author, comparing the "New Liberalism" in Britain to Bismarck's policies in Germany, remarked that "they are really nothing more than the oldest and most arrogant principles of despotism served up on a new dish" (Edward Jenkins, "Bismarckism in England," *Contemporary Review* [June 1873], 107).

mistaken legislation."[125] Character and self-reliance would only be strengthened and disciplined by the painful struggle for survival. In order to ensure economic progress in the future, Britain should, therefore, place its trust in the private sector. Even when the State could perform a task cheaper, faster, and more effectively than private industry, it should be extraordinarily reluctant to do so. Put simply, for the supporters of the LPDL, the "utility of every increment of governmental work rapidly diminishes," while "the disutility of every increment of taxation rapidly increases."[126]

One should not, however, infer from the extreme *laissez-faire* ideology of the LPDL that it was completely outside of the Victorian mainstream. Their belief that government programs and regulations tended to limit individual freedom, demean character, reduce industrial competitiveness, decrease wealth, and increase pauperism resonated widely throughout the Victorian political class. Their faith in the ability of the private sector and individual initiative to shape a better future was strongly seconded by the vast majority of British society. As a result, no one should be particularly surprised at the inability of either the Liberal or the Conservative parties to pass substantial—or even meaningful—social reform during the late Victorian era. An ideollogy of small-government, liberal individualism continued to dominate British politics, as it had since the 1830s, down to World War I.

---

[125] Joseph G. Horner, "State Pensions for Old Age," *Quarterly Review* (April 1892), 533.

[126] J. S. Nicholson, "The Reaction in Favour of the Classical Political Economy," *Journal of the Royal Statistical Society* (December 1893), 638.

Chapter 8

The Strange Vitality of Liberal England

Our examination of middle and upper class opinion between 1870 and 1900 reveals a very different picture from that commonly portrayed by historians of nineteenth-century Britain. The late Victorians, while recognizing new challenges at home and abroad, did not cast aside their traditional faith in national progress. Widespread concern about the poor during the "Great Depression in Trade and Agriculture" did not cause the Victorians to abandon their belief in self-help, character, private charity, and local initiative. The revival of the "Condition of England" question during the 1880s did not increase public confidence that poverty could be ameliorated through social legislation. The emergence of the London socialist movement and the Independent Labour Party, far from spurring social reform, served to energize and focus the attention of those opposed to the expansion of the State. The "New Unionism" largely concerned itself with traditional working class issues—wages, hours, and factory conditions—not with the overthrow of capitalism or the establishment of the Welfare State. Neither the Conservative nor the Liberal Party proposed ambitious social programs to reduce poverty prior to the turn of the century. Nor did the discussion of social reform within the late Victorian public sphere stray far from the classical liberal path. The poor were to be left to fend for themselves for the most part, although the "deserving" could expect some aid from private charity and, to a far lesser extent, the State. The "undeserving," however, were to be punished for their lack of character through the rigorous enforcement of the Poor Law and the withholding of societal largesse. Those proposals that ran counter to the dominant liberal paradigm had little chance of being enacted into law or even of attracting a popular following prior to 1900.

The traditional view is further undermined by the unwillingness or inability of its proponents to answer explicitly several difficult questions. First, what precisely do they mean by the "ideological" origins of the Welfare State? Is it the period when someone first conceived of the Welfare State as we know it today? Or should we date the "ideological" origins to those who first advocated large-scale State intervention in the economy in a more general sense? Furthermore, do they intend to imply causality when they speak of the Victorian "origins" of the Welfare State? Or is it enough to say that as the Welfare State exists, it must have had origins of some kind in the nineteenth century?

Several things should be made clear. First, it is not enough to assume that because the late Victorians were more willing than their predecessors to consider the expansion of State power, they willed the Welfare State into existence. Nor is it enough to say that the twentieth-century Welfare State was inevitable by 1900 because it was conceivable to a handful of Victorian writers. Historians should not dismiss as unimportant the continued allegiance of the vast majority of British society to the tenets of classical liberal philosophy with the argument that "the cultural and ideological trends that mattered most were those affecting well-educated minorities of upper and middle class people."[1] One should never forget that a "revolution" might be accomplished in the minds of a segment of the political elite without ever being translated into actual fact.

Second, historians should stop exaggerating the shift between "*laissez-faire*" and "collectivist" thought during the late Victorian era. It had long been recognized that the State had a responsibility to protect the interests of the most vulnerable. Furthermore, most prominent British social theorists had long favored the use of State power to curb the worst excesses of modern, industrial society. Thomas Paine, for instance, in the second part of the *Rights of Man* (1792) advocated an end to vast disparities of personal wealth; a progressive income tax on landed property with the funds given to poor families to raise and educate their children; a social security pension for workers over sixty; public funds for a decent burial; and the elimination of all laws which served to limit wages. As Paine grasped the essence of the social reforms of the Edwardian Liberal Party—with the exception of David Lloyd George's National Insurance program—during the 1790s, should he be considered the true ideological "founder" of the Welfare State?[2]

John Stuart Mill, following in the footsteps of Jeremy Bentham, believed that laws should be judged not upon whether they conformed to "Liberty" or some other abstract "natural right," but whether they were useful and practical. In his opinion, "Liberty" was only desirable when it produced the "greatest good for the greatest number"; when individual freedom acted contrary to the best interests of society, the State should step in to redress the balance.[3] Not surprisingly,

---

[1] Ann Orloff and Theda Skopol, "Why not Equal Protection?" *American Sociological Review* 1984 49 (6): 734.

[2] See Thomas Paine, *The Rights of Man* (1792; Reprint Edition, New York, 1985), 258-59.

[3] Mill is most famous for his *Principles of Political Economy* (1848), *On Liberty* (1859), *Utilitarianism* (1861), and *Chapters on Socialism* (posthumously published, 1879).

therefore, by the 1860s Mill had voiced support for a number of reforms: increased factory and sanitary legislation; a program of insurance against sickness, accident, and old age; the abolition of primogeniture; the appropriation by the State of the "unearned" increment in land; and voting rights for women. Furthermore, in 1869 Mill wrote that

> society is fully entitled to abrogate or alter any particular right of property which on sufficient consideration it judges to stand in the way of the public good . . . [and should demand] a full consideration of all means by which the institution may have a chance of being made to work in a manner more beneficial to the large portion of society which at present enjoys the least share of its direct benefits.[4]

That said, Mill's fundamentally optimistic beliefs about the future tempered his enthusiasm for reform. He believed that working class conditions were gradually improving, that competition helped to keep consumer prices low, and that the general tendency was towards the slow diminution of the evils and injustices which marred British society. Although Mill had a high opinion of the utopian socialism of Charles Fourier and Robert Owen, he knew that it was not practical at the present time, except among "the elite of mankind." With regard to "continental" or "revolutionary" socialism, Mill had little sympathy, believing, like most of his contemporaries, that the adoption of either would be a disaster for Britain. In addition, Mill rejected the idea that taxation should be used to redistribute wealth and opposed comprehensive social security legislation. Although favoring the elimination of primary school fees, Mill opposed universal free education. Nor was he willing to endorse legislation that would limit the workday for adult males.[5]

Neither did Mill's most important philosophical successor, Thomas H. Green, stray far from the classical liberal path. His most important works of political theory—"Liberal Legislation and Freedom of Contract" in 1881 and *The Principles of Political Obligation* published after his death in 1882—reveal the limits of his vision of the ideal State. Green advocated compulsory education, the provision of more scholarships for the poor, extension courses for adults, the founding of provincial universities, and university education for women. As a member of the Reform League, he supported the continued democratization of the British electoral system. Green also favored the more rigorous enforcement of the factory and sanitary acts, the abolition of primogeniture, the breaking up of the "great estates," the encouragement of trade unions, and the passage of temperance legislation. Although Green saw the State as a "moral" force that had an obligation to remove

---

[4] John Stuart Mill, "Chapters on Socialism," *Fortnightly Review* (April 1879), 530.
[5] See Oskar Kurer, "John Stuart Mill and the Welfare State," *History of Political Economy* 1991 23 (4): 713-30.

obstacles to freedom and opportunity and ensure minimum standards, he was by no means a nascent State socialist. He thought that voluntary action was still preferable to State paternalism; when both could perform the same task equally well, the presumption had to be against State action. Still, Green, like Mill, thought that the State could do a better job than it had in the past of allowing the people to fulfill their own unique potentialities.[6]

None of these writers believed in what is commonly known as "*laissez-faire*" economics. Essentially no one did. The term "*laissez-faire*," defined as an unalterable opposition to all State intervention in the economy, has no meaning prior to the late Victorian era. Before the 1880s,

it was a mild catchphrase, expressing approval for free trade which was quite compatible with approval of government direction of most social functions. Government direction of social functions was not only tolerated, but actively propounded by many radical theorists in an attempt to reintroduce the natural harmony of society which had been strained by private enterprise and the growth of capitalism.[7]

As both classical economists and the politicians at Westminster recognized that the State had a role to play in the economy, the debate was not, as is so often assumed, between "*laissez-faire*" and "collectivism," but over what form government intervention should take. As one Victorian contemporary noted in 1890, "if we are all Socialists now, as is so often said, it is not because we have undergone any change of principles on social legislation" but because of the recent "public awakening" to the condition of our cities.[8]

Therefore, Harold Perkin's seven types of "collectivism" are very useful in allowing us to determine just how far the Victorians were willing to go towards the Welfare State:

1. The prevention of obvious moral nuisances or physical dangers.
2. The provision of minimum standards for certain sectors of the economy.
3. The provision of State aid to private charities and programs.
4. The provision of a service for a part of the population.
5. The provision of a service for everyone.
6. The State ownership of an essential service or public utility.

---

[6] See Melvin Richter, *Politics of Conscience: T. H. Green and His Age* (Cambridge, Mass., 1964), 284. See also Stefan Collini's "Hobhouse, Bosanquet, and the State," *Past and Present* 1976 (72): 86-111; and *Liberalism and Sociology: L. T. Hobhouse and Political Argument in England, 1880-1914* (New York, 1979); and F. C. Conybere, "On Professor Green's Political Philosophy," *National Review* (August 1889).

[7] Mark Francis, "Herbert Spencer and the Myth of Laissez-Faire," *Journal of the History of Ideas* 1978 39 (2): 328. See also Colin J. Holmes, "Laissez-faire in Theory and Practice: Britain, 1800-1875," *Journal of European Economic History* 1976 5 (3): 671-88; and Frederick Dolman, "Political Economy and Social Reform," *Westminster Review* (June 1890).

[8] John Rae, "State Socialism and Social Reform," *Contemporary Review* (September 1890), 439.

7. The nationalization of the means of production, distribution and exchange.[9]

"Types" one through four—representing the crux of the social debates of the Victorian era—were fully compatible with classical liberal ideology. Only by accepting the principles behind "types" five and six would Britain make the long leap to the Welfare State. This point raises several new questions which require elaboration. What is the Welfare State? How does it differ from the classical liberal philosophy which dominated the Victorian era?

The basis of the Welfare State is the concept that the State should play a key role in the promotion of the economic and social well-being of its citizens. Its goals are equality of opportunity, a more equitable distribution of wealth, and public provision for those who cannot on their own provide themselves with a modicum of comfort. The Welfare State meets its responsibilities through an extensive program of social insurance—covering health, disability, unemployment, and old age—financed in part by forced contributions, but also by transferring wealth from healthy workers to the less fortunate. It also often provides subsidized education, food, housing, and medical care. Finally, the Welfare State spends immense sums on anti-poverty programs intended to deal not so much with absolute poverty, but with the relative deprivation felt by the poor living within the wealthy consumer-oriented societies of the post-war world. Each of these complex governmental initiatives is, by necessity, administered by a class of bureaucratic experts. Thus, the poor progress from being the passive victims of the industrial economy to the passive beneficiaries of the Welfare State.

The classical liberal State, on the other hand, was highly suspicious of government intervention in the economy; the State was expected to intervene only upon the failure of voluntary, individual, and local efforts to right particularly egregious wrongs. For all the talk of "positive" liberalism, the State was still commonly expected to set limits, not to ensure personal fulfillment, happiness, or prosperity. It was, at best, a necessary evil; what was needed was not more, but better government. Consequently, classical liberalism relied heavily on the private sector—charity, religion, trade unions, and so on—and national economic progress to ameliorate the condition of the impoverished. This reliance on private and local initiative would, its proponents believed, promote both individual self-help and a sense of community responsibility. When national solutions proved necessary, nineteenth-century liberalism advocated the provision of limited services to a select portion of the population; no one during the late Victorian era, outside of the socialists and a few Radical Liberals, spoke of universal provision for all.

Third, the question of character remained important to both the public and private sectors even after Queen Victoria's death in 1901. The Unemployed

---

[9] Harold Perkin, "Individualism versus Collectivism in Nineteenth Century Britain: A False Antithesis," *Journal of British Studies* 1977 17 (1): 114-16.

Workmen's Act of 1905, which permitted the establishment of municipal distress committees outside of the Poor Law, required that all applicants be of good character. The establishment in 1908 of noncontributory pensions for those over 70 with an income of ten shillings per week or less adhered to the same model. A pension of five shillings per week—seven shillings six pence for married couples—was far too small to do anything but supplement the savings of the "deserving" poor.

The same might be said of the most innovative piece of social legislation passed by the Edwardian Liberal Party, the National Insurance Act of 1911. This statute required that all those between the ages of sixteen and seventy who earned less than £160 a year contribute four pence per week (three pence for women) for health insurance. This contribution was added to the three pence submitted by their employers and the two pence provided by the State every week. Under this plan the sick were to receive ten shillings a week for thirteen weeks (7s. 6d. for women), five shillings a week for a further thirteen weeks, a five shilling disability benefit, and free medical care. The wife of an insured man was also entitled to a thirty shilling maternity benefit. The unemployment portion of this act was, however, not nearly so comprehensive. Only workers employed in trades which were subject to extreme economic fluctuations—such as engineering, shipbuilding, iron-founding, and construction—were covered prior to World War I.[10]

Although the contribution expected from the lowest-paid workers was quickly scrapped, the modest size of the health benefit and the fact that only people employed in certain skilled trades were entitled to receive the, again, rather limited unemployment coverage provided by the National Insurance Act ensured that it would have its greatest impact within the ranks of the "deserving" poor. With good reason, therefore, Gertrude Himmelfarb writes that it "was the poor, rather than the very poor, who were the beneficiaries of most of the reforms of the late Victorian and Edwardian periods."[11] Writers as late as 1914 could join the lament voiced by the popular journalist George R. Sims in 1889 that "Dr. State alas! Is as slow to put in an appearance as his parish *confrere* when the patient in need of his services is poor and friendless."[12]

Finally, the factors which led to the demise of nineteenth-century liberalism after the turn of the century are worth exploring. Had classical liberalism been

---

[10] Roughly two and a quarter million workers received unemployment insurance under the National Insurance Act before 1914, about one-sixth of the number entitled to health benefits. The unemployment benefit, for those who were lucky enough to have it, was seven shillings a week for fifteen weeks (Martin Pugh, *Lloyd George* [London, 1988], 54-56). Only with the passage of the Unemployment Insurance Act of 1920, which extended the scope of the 1911 act to include more than twelve million workers, would most manual laborers receive coverage.

[11] Gertrude Himmelfarb, *Poverty and Compassion: The Moral Imagination of the Late Victorians* (New York, 1991), 12.

[12] George R. Sims, *How the Poor Live and Horrible London* (1889, Reprint Edition, New York, 1985), 4.

discredited in Britain by 1900 to the point that the twentieth-century Welfare State had become a matter of historical inevitability? To ask the question another way, if the Welfare State was inevitable by 1900, why did it take two World Wars and the worst economic depression of the industrial era to bring it into existence? The answer is easy enough to see. The crises capitalism experienced during the first half of the twentieth century and the ideological challenge presented by post-war communism were necessary in order to bring the Welfare State into existence in Britain and to ensure its growth and survival thereafter. World War I and the Great Depression of the 1920s and 1930s removed the constraints which classical liberalism had placed upon government expenditure prior to 1914. Yet the emergence of the Welfare State did not, as we have seen, merely mean increased spending along the same lines, but a qualitatively different attitude towards the causes of poverty and the duties of government.[13] The revolution in political theory brought to fruition by William Beveridge, John Maynard Keynes, and Clement Atlee arose from a series of unprecedented and unforeseen political and social crises. The struggle to overhaul the British political system in the face of such massive challenges generated a new ideology, that of the modern Welfare State, which was recognizably different from anything in existence prior to the outbreak of World War I.

---

[13] See Paul Barker, ed., *Founders of the Welfare State* (London, 1984); Asa Briggs, *The Collected Essays of Asa Briggs* (Brighton, England, 1985), James E. Cronin, "The British State and the Structure of Political Opportunity," *Journal of British Studies* 1988 27 (3): 199-231; Rex Pope, Alan Pratt, and Bernard Hoyle, eds., *Social Welfare in Britain, 1885-1985* (London, 1986); and Eric Hobsbawm, *The Age of Extremes* (New York, 1994).

Bibliography

Newspapers

The Anti-Sweater
Charity Organisation Reporter/Review
The Clarion
Commonweal
Daily News
Darkest England/Social Gazette
The Democrat
Fair Trade
Freedom
The Graphic
Illustrated London News
Jewish Standard
Justice: The Organ of Social Democracy
Labour Elector
Labour Leader
Labour Prophet
The Labour Standard
Land and Labour
Liberty: A Journal of Anarchist Communism
The New Age
Pall Mall Gazette
The People
The People's Press
Primrose League Gazette
The Primrose Record
Progressive Review
The Star
The (London) Times
The Torch of Anarchy: A Revolutionary Journal of Anarchist-Communism
The Trade Unionist
War Cry
Women's Industrial News
Workman's Times

Periodicals

All the Year Round
Blackwood's Magazine
British Quarterly Review
British Weekly
Church Quarterly
Contemporary Review
Cornhill Magazine
Dark Blue
Dublin Review
The Economist
Edinburgh Review
Fortnightly Review
Fraser's Magazine
Good Words
Journal of the Royal Statistical Society
The Lancet
Leisure Hour
London Quarterly Review
Longman's Magazine
MacMillan's Magazine
Modern Review
The Month
Murray's Magazine
National Review
New Review
Nineteenth Century
Pall Mall Magazine
Pictorial World
Punch Magazine
Quarterly Review
Saint Pauls
Saturday Review
Scottish Review
Universal Review
Westminster Review

Parliamentary Sources

Select Committee, House of Commons, "Habitual Drunkards," 1872 (242) ix.
Select Committee, House of Lords, "Intemperance," 1878-1879 (113) x.
Select Committee, House of Commons, "The London Water Supply," 1880 (329) x, sess. 2.
Select Committee, House of Commons, "Artisans' and Labourers' Dwellings Improvement," 1881 (358) vii; 1882 (235) vii.
"Report from Her Majesty's Commissioners on Agriculture," *Parliamentary Papers*, 1882, xiv.
Royal Commission, *On the Housing of the Working Classes*, 1884-1885 [cd.4402], v.30.
Royal Commission, *On the Depression of Trade and Industry*, 1886 [cd.4621], v.21; 1886

[cd.4715-15i], v.21-22; 1886 [cd.4797], v.23; 1886 [cd.4893], v.23.
Select Committee, House of Commons, "Public Health in Metropolitan Parishes," 1886 (c.4714), lvi; (c.4717); (c.5707), lxxxi; (c.5688), lxv.
"Circular Addressed by the President of the Local Government Board to the Several Boards of Guardians," 15 March 1886, *Parliamentary Papers*, (69), lvi.
Select Committee, House of Commons, "London Riots," 1886 (c.4665) xxxiv; (26) liii.
Select Committee, House of Commons, "Town Holdings," 1887 (260) xiii; 1888 (313) xix; 1889 (251) xv; 1890 (341) xviii; 1890-1891 (325) xviii; 1892 (214) xviii.
Labour Correspondent, "Special Report to the Board of Trade on the Sweating System at the East End of London," 1887 (331) lxxxix.
Select Committee, House of Lords, "The Condition of the Working Classes," 1887 (c.5228) xv.
Select Committee, House of Commons, "National Provident Insurance," 1887 (257) xi.
Select Committee, House of Lords, "The Sweating System," 1887 (331) lxxxix; 1888 (c.5513) lxxvi; 1888 (361) xx; 1888 (448) xxi; 1889 (165) xiii; 1889 (331) xiv; 1890 (117) xvii.
Select Committee, House of Commons, "Emigration and Immigration," 1888 (305) xi; 1889 (311) x.
Select Committee, House of Lords, "Poor Law Relief," 1888 (363) xv.
Select Committee, House of Commons, "Colonization," 1890-1891 (152) xi.
Royal Commission, *On Labour*, 1892 [cd. 6708], v.34; 1892 [cd. 6795], v.36; 1893-1894 [cd. 6894], v. 32; 1893-1894 [cd. 7063], v.39; 1894 [cd. 7421], v.35.
Select Committee, House of Lords, "Metropolitan Hospitals," 1892 (321) xiii, sess. 1.
Special Report by Robert Giffen, "Return of Rates of Wages," 1892 (c.6715) lxviii.
Special Report by Clara Collet, "Statistics of Employment of Women and Girls," 1894 (c.7564) lxxxi.
Royal Commission, *On the Aged Poor*, 1895 [cd. 7684-84ii], v.14-15.
Select Committee, House of Commons, "Distress from Want of Employment," 1895 (111) viii; 1895 (253); 1895 (365) ix; 1896 (321) ix.
Select Committee, House of Commons, "Alien Immigration and Emigration," 1896 (137) lxvii.
Special Report of the Departmental Committee of the Local Government Board, "Maintenance and Education of Pauper Children," 1896 (c.8027) xliii; (c.8032) xliii; (c.8033).
Special Report of the Commissioners in Lunacy, "The Alleged Increase of Insanity," 1897 (87) xxxviii.
"Final Report of Her Majesty's Commissioners Appointed to Inquire into the Subject of Agricultural Depression," *Parliamentary Papers*, 1897, xv.
Select Committee, House of Commons, "Old Age Pensions," 1898 (c.8911) xlv.
Select Committee, House of Commons, "Aged Deserving Poor," 1899 (296) viii.

Monographs

Adcock, A. St. John. *East End Idylls*. London, 1897.
Archer, Thomas. *The Terrible Sights of London*. London, 1870.
Banfield, Frank. *The Great Landlords of London*. London, 1888.
Barnett, Henrietta. *What Has the Charity Organisation Society To Do With Social Reform?* London, 1884.
Barnett, Samuel and Henrietta A. *Practicable Socialism*. 1888. Reprint Edition. London, 1894.

Barrett, Alfred W. *Industrial Explorings in and Around London.* London, 1895.
Bartley, George C.T. *The Poor Law in Its Effects on Thrift.* 2nd Edition. London, 1873.
―――――. *The Work of Charity in Promoting Provident Habits.* London, 1879.
Bax, Belfort and William Morris, eds. *The Socialist Platform.* London, 1888.
Bennet, Olivia, Countess of Tankerville. *A Bright Spot in Outcast London.* London, 1884.
―――――. *From the Depths.* London, 1885.
Besant, Annie W. *Modern Socialism.* London, 1890.
―――――. *A Selection of the Social and Political Pamphlets of Annie Besant.* New York, 1970.
―――――. *The Trades Union Movement.* London, 1890.
Besant, Walter. *All Sorts and Conditions of Men.* 1882. Reprint Edition. New York, 1889.
―――――. *Children of Gibeon.* 1886. Reprint Edition. New York, 1889.
―――――. *South London.* London, 1898.
Black, Clementia. *An Agitator.* London, 1894.
Blackley, William L. *Thrift and Independence.* London, 1885.
Blatchford, Robert. *Dismal England.* London, 1899.
―――――. *Merrie England.* London, 1893.
Booth, Charles. *The Aged Poor in England and Wales.* 1894. Reprint Edition. New York, 1985.
―――――. *Life and Labour of the London Poor: Poverty Series.* 4 vols. London, 1889-1893.
―――――. *Life and Labour of the People in London.* 17 vols. London, 1889-1903.
―――――. *Pauperism: A Picture and an Endowment of Old Age.* London, 1892.
Booth, William. *In Darkest England and the Way Out.* New York, 1890.
Bosanquet, Bernard, ed. *Aspects of the Social Problem.* 1895. Reprint Edition. New York, 1968.
Bosanquet, Charles B. P. *A Handy-book for Visitors of the Poor in London.* London, 1874.
―――――. *The Organisation of Charity.* London, 1874.
Bosanquet, Helen Dendy. *Methods of Social Advance.* London, 1904.
―――――. *The Poverty Line.* London, 1902.
―――――. *Rich and Poor.* London, 1896.
―――――. *Social Work in London.* London, 1914.
Bourne, Henry R. Fox. *English Newspapers.* 2 vols. London, 1887.
Bowmaker, Edward. *The Housing of the Working Classes.* London, 1895.
Brabazon, Reginald, Earl of Meath, ed. *Prosperity or Pauperism: Physical, Industrial, and Technical Training.* London, 1888.
―――――. *Social Arrows.* London, 1886.
Bramwell, Lord. *Nationalisation of Land: A Review of Mr. Henry George's "Progress and Poverty."* London, 1884.
Brayshaw, J. Dodsworth. *Slum Silhouettes.* 1898. Reprint Edition. London, 1904.
Bruce, F. J. *Mr. Henry George's Unproved Assumption.* London, 1884.
Cantlie, James. *Degeneration Amongst Londoners.* 1885. Reprint Edition. New York, 1985.
Carruthers, Christopher. *The Root of the Matter, or the Only Cure for the Bitter Cry of Outcast London.* London, 1884.
Chamberlain, Joseph. *Mr. Chamberlain's Speeches.* Edited by Charles Boyd. New York, 1970.
―――――. *Speeches of the Right Hon. Joseph Chamberlain, M.P.* Edited by Henry W. Lucy. London, 1885.
Champion, Henry H. *The Great Dock Strike in London, August 1889.* London, 1890.
Chance, William. *The Better Administration of the Poor Law.* London, 1895.
―――――. *Our Treatment of the Poor.* London, 1879.

Bibliography

The Charity Organisation Society: Its Objects and Mode of Operation. 3rd Edition. London, 1875.
Clarke, Henry. *Dwellings for the Poor.* London, 1884.
———. *London Government.* London, 1888.
Conrad, Joseph. *Secret Agent.* London, 1907.
Crockett, S. R. *Cleg Kelly: Arab of the City.* New York, 1896.
Crory, W. Glenny. *East London Industries.* London, 1876.
Dawson, W. J. *London Idylls.* New York, 1895.
Disraeli, Benjamin. *Coningsby.* Philadelphia, 1844.
———. *Selected Speeches of the Late Right Honourable the Earl of Beaconsfield.* Edited by T. E. Kebbel. London, 1882.
———. *Sybil.* London, 1845.
Dolman, Frederick. *Municipalities at Work.* 1895. Reprint Edition. New York, 1985.
Drage, Geoffrey. *The Problem of the Aged Poor.* London, 1895.
Fabian Society. *Fabian Tracts.* No. 1-95. London, 1884-1899.
Farjeon, B. L. *Toilers of Babylon.* 3 vols. London, 1888.
Fawcett, Henry. *Labour and Wages.* London, 1884.
———. *Pauperism: Its Causes and Remedies.* London, 1871.
Field, David D. *The Duties of the State.* London, 1890.
Firth, Joseph F. B. *London Government under the Local Government Act, 1888.* London, 1888.
———. *Municipal London.* London, 1876.
———. *The Reform of London Government and of the City Guilds.* London, 1888.
Forster, E. M. *Howards End.* 1910. Reprint Edition. New York, 1948.
Fothergill, J. Milner. *The Town Dweller.* 1889. Reprint Edition. New York, 1985.
Froude, James Anthony. *Oceana, or England and Her Colonies.* London, 1886.
George, Henry. *Progress and Poverty.* New York, 1879.
———. *Social Problems.* New York, 1883.
Gissing, George. *Demos, A Story of English Socialism.* 1886. Reprint Edition. New York, 1928.
———. *In the Year of Jubilee.* 1894. Reprint Edition. Rutherford, N.J., 1976.
———. *Netherworld.* London, 1889.
———. *New Grub Street.* 1891. Reprint Edition. New York, 1968.
———. *Thyrza.* 1887. Reprint Edition. New York, 1900.
———. *The Unclassed.* 1884. Reprint Edition. New York, 1968.
———. *Workers in the Dawn.* 1880. Reprint Edition. London, 1985.
Gomme, G. Laurence. *London in the Reign of Queen Victoria.* London, 1898.
Gordon, W. J. *How London Lives.* London, 1890.
Graham, William. *The Social Problem.* London, 1886.
The Great Army of the London Poor. London, 1883.
Green, Thomas Hill. *Lectures on the Principles of Political Obligation.* London, 1882.
Greenwood, Frederick. *The Wilds of London.* 1874. Reprint Edition. New York, 1985.
Greenwood, James. *In Strange Company.* 2nd Edition. London, 1874.
———. *Odd People in Odd Places, or the Great Residuum.* London, 1883.
———. *Tag, Rag, and Co.: Sketches of the People.* London, 1883.
Greg, William R. *Rocks Ahead, or the Warnings of Cassandra.* Boston, 1875.
Hake, Alfred E. *Suffering London.* London, 1892.
Hake, Alfred and O. E. Wesslau. *The Coming Individualism.* Westminster, England, 1895.
Hamilton, H. L. *Household Management for the Labouring Classes.* London, 1882.
Harkness, Margaret. *A City Girl.* London, 1887.
———. *In Darkest London: Captain Lobe, A Story of the Salvation Army.* London, 1891.

―――――. *Out of Work*. London, 1888.
Hastings, Frederick. *Back Streets and London Slums*. London, 1889.
Hatton, Joseph. *Cruel London*. 1873. Reprint Edition. New York, 1883.
Haw, George. *No Room to Live*. London, 1900.
Hill, Octavia. *Homes of the London Poor*. 1875. Reprint Edition. London, 1970.
Hobhouse, L. T. *The Labour Movement*. London, 1893.
Hobson, John A. *The Problems of Poverty*. London, 1891.
Hocking, Joseph. *All Men Are Liars*. Boston, 1895.
Hoyle, William. *Our National Drink Bill*. London, 1884.
Hyder, Joseph. *The Curse of Landlordism and How to Remove It*. London, 1895.
Hyndman, Henry M. *The Coming Revolution in England*. London, 1884.
―――――. *The Commercial Crises of the Nineteenth Century*. 1892. Reprint Edition. London, 1902.
―――――. *The Economics of Socialism*. London, 1896.
―――――. *England for All*. London, 1881.
―――――. *The Historical Basis of Socialism in England*. 1883. Reprint Edition. New York, 1984.
―――――. *The Social Reconstruction of England*. London, 1884.
Hyndman, Henry and Charles Bradlaugh. *Will Socialism Benefit the English People?* London, 1884.
Hyndman, Henry and William Morris. *A Summary of the Principles of Socialism*. London, 1884.
Ingham, J. A. *City Slums*. London, 1889.
Insurance and Saving. London, 1892.
Jackson, Spencer. *Landlord Abuses and a Plan for the Extinction of Landlordism*. London, 1885.
James, Henry. *Essays in London and Elsewhere*. New York, 1893.
Jay, A. Osborne. *Life in Darkest London: A Hint to General Booth*. London, 1891.
Jeune, Susan, ed. *Ladies at Work*. London, 1893.
Jevons, William. *Methods of Social Reform*. London, 1883.
Jones, David Rice. *From Cellar to Garret*. London, 1876.
―――――. *In the Slums*. London, 1884.
Jones, Harry. *East and West London*. London, 1875.
Kempner, N. *Common Sense Socialism*. London, 1887.
Kidd, Benjamin. *Social Evolution*. London, 1894.
King, Henry. *Savage London*. London, 1888.
Knapp, John M., ed. *The Universities and the Social Problem*. 1895. Reprint Edition. New York, 1985.
Krausse, A. S. *Starving London*. London, 1886.
Lander, Harry. *Lucky Bargee*. New York, 1898.
Lazurus, Henry. *Landlordism*. London, 1892.
Leighton, John. *The Unification of London*. London, 1895.
Leslie, Emma. *The Seed She Sowed: A Tale of the Great Dock Strike*. London, 1891.
A Letter to the Editor of the Pall Mall Gazette. London, 1885.
Levi, Leone. *Wages and Earnings of the Working Classes*. London, 1885.
Littlewood, William E. *The Visitation of the Poor: A Practical Manual*. London, 1876.
Loch, Charles S. *Charity Organisation*. London, 1890.
―――――. *How to Help Cases of Distress*. London, 1883.
―――――. *Old Age Pensions and Pauperism*. London, 1892.
―――――. *Pauperism and Old Age Pensions*. London, 1892.
Long, J. Edmond. *The Hopeful Cry of Outcast London*. London, 1884.

Bibliography

MacCallam, Hugh. *The Distribution of the Poor in London*. London, 1883.
Mackay, Thomas. *The English Poor*. London, 1889.
―――. *Methods of Social Reform*. London, 1896.
―――, ed. *A Plea for Liberty*. London, 1891.
―――. *The State and Charity*. London, 1898.
Maine, Henry. *Popular Government*. London, 1885.
Mallock, William H. *Aristocracy and Evolution*. London, 1898.
―――. *Classes and Masses*. London, 1896.
―――. *Labour and the Popular Welfare*. London, 1893.
―――. *Labour as an Agent in the Production of the National Wealth*. London, 1894.
―――. *The Old Order Changes*. New York, 1886.
―――. *Property and Progress*. London, 1884.
―――. *Social Equality*. New York, 1882.
Marshall, Alfred. *The Early Economic Writings of Alfred Marshall, 1867-1890*. New York, 1975.
―――. *The Economics of Industry*. London, 1881.
―――. *Official Papers*. London, 1926.
―――. *Principles of Economics*. 1890. Reprint Edition. London, 1922.
Marx, Karl and Friedrich Engels. *The Communist Manifesto*. 1848. Reprint Edition. New York, 1949.
Massingham, Henry W. *The London Daily Press*. New York, 1892.
Maugham, W. Somerset. *Liza of Lambeth*. 1897. Reprint Edition. London, 1936.
Mayhew, Henry. *London Labour and the London Poor*. London, 1861.
M'Cree, George W. *Sweet Herbs for the Bitter Cry, or Remedies for Horrible and Outcast London*. London, 1884.
Mearns, Andrew. *The Bitter Cry of Outcast London*. 1883. Reprint Edition. London, 1970.
―――. *London and Its Teeming Toilers*. London, 1885.
Meyer, Frederick B. *Reveries and Realities, or Life and Work in London*. London, 1890.
Millington, F. H. *The Housing of the Poor*. London, 1891.
Moore, George. *Esther Waters*. 1894. Reprint Edition. London, 1937.
Morris, William. *News from Nowhere, or an Epoch of Rest*. Hammersmith, England, 1892.
―――. *The Political Writings of William Morris*. London, 1984.
―――. *Signs of Change*. London, 1888.
Morrison, Arthur. *Child of the Jago*. 1896. Reprint Edition. London, 1913.
―――. *To London Town*. London, 1899.
―――. *Tales of Mean Streets*. London, 1894.
Mulhall, Michael. *Fifty Years of National Progress, 1837-1887*. London, 1887.
The Need of Nerve in Charity. London, 1881.
Nevison, Henry W. *Slum Stories of London*. New York, 1895.
Oliphant, James, compiler. *The Claims of Labour*. Edinburgh, Scotland, 1886.
Paine, Thomas. *The Rights of Man*. 1792. Reprint Edition. New York, 1985.
Parker, Joseph. *Regenerated London*. London, 1898.
Party Politics and the Social Question: A Word to the Workers. London, 1885.
Patterson, R. H. *The State, the Poor, and the Country*. London, 1870.
Peek, Francis. *The Uncharitableness of Inadequate Relief*. London, 1879.
Pretyman, J. R. *Dispauperization*. London, 1876.
―――. *Voluntary Versus Legal Relief*. London, 1879.
Pugh, Edwin. *A Street in Suburbia*. London, 1895.
Rae, John. *Contemporary Socialism*. New York, 1884.
Railson, George. *Heathen England*. London, 1877.
Ridge, William Pett. *Mord Em'ly*. London, 1898.

Robinson, Frederick W. *The Hands of Justice*. London, 1883.
Rook, Clarence. *Hooligan Nights*. London, 1898.
Rowe, Richard. *Picked Up in the Streets, or Struggles for Life Amongst the London Poor*. London, 1880.
Rowntree, B. Seebohm. *Poverty: A Study of Town Life*. 1901. Reprint Edition. New York, 1971.
Rowntree, B. Seebohm and Bruno Lasker. *Unemployment: A Social Study*. 1911. Reprint Edition. New York, 1980.
Rowntree, Joseph and Arthur Sherwell. *The Temperance Problem and Social Reform*. London, 1899.
Saunders, William. *History of the First London County Council, 1889-1891*. London, 1892.
Seager, J. Renwick. *The Government of London under the London Government Act, 1899*. London, 1899.
Seeley, John Robert. *The Expansion of England*. London, 1883.
Self-Help v. State Help: Speeches Delivered at the Third Annual Meeting of the Liberty and Property Defense League. London, 1885.
Shaw, George Bernard. *The Fabian Society: Its Early History*. 1892. Reprint Edition. London, 1899.
──────. "Mrs. Warren's Profession." London, 1898.
──────. *The Road to Equality: Ten Unpublished Lectures and Essays*. Boston, 1971.
Shaw, George Bernard and Sidney Webb. *Fabian Essays in Socialism*. London, 1889.
Sherard, Robert. *White Slaves of England*. London, 1897.
Sherwell, Arthur. *Life in West London*. 2nd Edition. London, 1897.
Sims, George R. *How the Poor Live and Horrible London*. 1889. Reprint Edition. New York, 1985.
──────. *The Social Kaleidoscope*. London, 1881.
Sketches from Life, or Work Among the Poor of London. London, 1879.
Smiles, Samuel. *Character*. London, 1871.
──────. *Duty*. London, 1880.
──────. *Life and Labour, or Characteristics of Men of Industry, Culture, and Genius*. London, 1887.
──────. *Thrift*. London, 1875.
Smiley, Francis E. *The Evangelization of a Great City*. 1885. Reprint Edition. Philadelphia, 1890.
Smith, Hubert Llewellyn and Vaughn Nash. *The Story of the Dockers' Strike*. London, 1889.
Smith, R. Mudie. *The Religious Life of London*. London, 1904.
Socialism, a Curse. London, 1884.
Socialism Made Plain. London, 1883.
Spencer, Herbert. *The Man versus the State*. 1884. Reprint Edition. Caldwell, Idaho, 1940.
Spender, J. A. *The State and Pensions in Old Age*. London, 1892.
Steuart, J. A. *Wine on the Lees*. New York, 1899.
Stevenson, Robert Louis. *The Dynamiter*. London, 1885.
Tennant, Dorothy. *London Street Arabs*. London, 1890.
Tennyson, Alfred Lord. *The Works of Alfred Lord Tennyson*. New York, 1894.
Thomson, James. *The City of Dreadful Night and Other Poems*. London, 1888.
Thomson, John and Adolphe Smith. *Street Life in London*. 1877. Reprint Edition. New York, 1969.
Toynbee, Arnold. *The Industrial Revolution*. London, 1884.
──────. *"Progress and Poverty": A Criticism of Mr. Henry George*. London, 1883.
Trevelyan, Charles. *Address on the Systematic Visitation of the Poor*. London, 1870.
──────. *Metropolitan Medical Relief*. 2nd Edition. London, 1879.

———. *Seven Articles on London Pauperism*. London, 1870.
———. *Three Letters to "The Times" on London Pauperism*. London, 1870.
Twining, Louisa. *State Organisation and Voluntary Aid*. London, 1882.
Volckman, William. *The Prevention of Poverty*. London, 1873.
Walker, Henry. *East London: Sketches of Christian Work and Workers*. 1896. Reprint Edition. Bucks, England, 1987.
Ward, Mrs. Humphrey. *Robert Elsmere*. 3 vols. Leipzig, Germany, 1888.
Webb, Beatrice Potter. *My Apprenticeship*. 1926. Reprint Edition. London, 1971.
———. *Women and the Factory Acts*. London, 1896.
Webb, Sidney. *The London Programme*. London, 1891.
———. *Socialism in England*. 1891. Reprint Edition. London, 1987.
Webb, Sidney and Beatrice Potter. *The History of Trade Unionism*. London, 1894.
———. *Industrial Democracy*. London, 1898.
———. *The Public Organisation of the Labour Market*. London, 1909.
Wells, James. *Rescuers and Rescued: Experiences Among Our City Poor*. London, 1890.
Whelen, Frederick. *London Government*. London, 1898.
White, Arnold, ed. *The Destitute Alien in Great Britain*. London, 1892.
———. *Problems of a Great City*. 1886. Reprint Edition. New York, 1985.
Whiteing, Richard. *No. 5 John Street*. 1899. Reprint Edition. London, 1902.
Wilde, Oscar. *The Soul of Man under Socialism*. 1891. Reprint Edition. London, 1912.
Wilkins, W. H. *The Alien Invasion*. London, 1892.
Williams, Ernest E. *Made in Germany*. London, 1896.
Williams, Montagu. *Round London: Down East and Up West*. London, 1892.
Williams, Robert. *The Face of the Poor, or the Crowding of London's Labourers*. London, 1897.
———. *London Rookeries and Colliers' Slums, A Plea for More Breathing Room*. London, 1893.
Woods, Robert A. *English Social Movements*. 2nd Edition. New York, 1894.
———, Walter Besant, et al. *The Poor in Great Cities*. London, 1896.
Worthington, T. Locke. *The Dwellings of the Poor and Weekly Wage-earners*. London, 1893.
Wright, J. Hornsby. *Beggars and Imposters*. London, 1883.
Wright, Thomas. *Our New Masters*. 1873. Reprint Edition. New York, 1984.
———. *The Pinch of Poverty: Suffering and Heroism of the London Poor*. London, 1892.
Young, George. *Friendly Societies and the Limits of State Aid and Control in Industrial Insurance*. London, 1879.
Zangwill, Israel. *Children of the Ghetto*. 1892. Reprint Edition. Philadelphia, 1938.
———. *Ghetto Tragedies*. 1899. Reprint Edition. Philadelphia, 1938.

Secondary Sources

Alber, Jens. "Continuities and Changes in the Idea of the Welfare State." *Politics and Society* 1988 16 (4): 451-68.
Aldcroft, Derek and Harry Richardson. *The British Economy, 1870-1939*. New York, 1970.
Alderman, Geoffrey. *London Jewry and London Politics*. London, 1989.
Allett, John. *The New Liberalism: The Political Economy of J. A. Hobson*. Toronto, 1981.
Arnstein, Walter. *Britain Yesterday and Today*. 6th Edition. Lexington, Mass., 1992.
Ashford, Douglas E. "The Whig Interpretation of the Welfare State." *Journal of Policy History* 1989 1 (1): 24-43.
Ausubel, Herman. *In Hard Times*. New York, 1960.

———. *The Late Victorians: A Short History*. New York, 1955.
Bailey, Victor. "In Darkest England: The Salvation Army, Social Reform, and the Labour Movement." *International Review of Social History* 1984 29 (2): 133-71.
———. "The Metropolitan Police, the Home Office, and the Threat of Outcast London," in *Policing and Punishment*. London, 1981.
Baldwin, Peter. "The Welfare State for Historians." *Comparative Studies of Society and History* 1992 34 (4): 695-707.
Ballhatchet, Joan. "The Police and the London Dock Strike of 1889." *History Workshop* 1991 (32): 54-68.
Barker, Michael. *Gladstone and Radicalism*. Sussex, England, 1975.
Barker, Paul, ed. *Founders of the Welfare State*. London, 1984.
Barret-Ducrocq, Françoise. *Love in the Time of Victoria*. New York, 1992.
Bartrip, P.W.J. "State Intervention in Mid-Nineteenth Century Britain: Fact or Fiction?" *Journal of British Studies* 1983 23 (1): 63-83.
Beer, Samuel H. *British Politics in the Collectivist Age*. New York, 1965.
Bellamy, Richard, ed. *Victorian Liberalism*. London, 1990.
Benson, John. *The Working Class in Britain, 1850-1939*. New York, 1989.
Bentley, Michael. *The Climax of Liberal Politics: British Liberalism in Theory and Practice, 1868-1918*. London, 1987.
Berlanstein, Lenard, ed. *The Industrial Revolution and Work in the Nineteenth Century*. New York, 1992.
Bevir, Mark. "The British Social Democratic Federation, 1880-1885." *International Review of Social History* 1992 37 (2): 207-29.
Biagini, Eugenio. "British Trade Unions and Popular Political Economy, 1860-1880." *Historical Journal* 1987 30 (4): 811-40.
———. *Liberty, Retrenchment, and Reform*. New York, 1992.
Birch, R. C. *The Shaping of the Welfare State*. London, 1974.
Blaazer, David. *The Popular Front and the Progressive Tradition: Socialists, Liberals, and the Quest for Unity, 1884-1939*. New York, 1992.
Blake, Robert. *Disraeli*. New York, 1966.
Blewett, Neal. "The Franchise in the United Kingdom, 1885-1918." *Past and Present* 1965 (32): 27-56.
Boyer, George. "What Did Unions Do in Nineteenth Century Britain?" *Journal of Economic History* 1988 48 (2): 319-32.
Bradley, Ian. *The Optimists*. London, 1980.
Briggs, Asa. *The Collected Essays of Asa Briggs*. Brighton, England, 1985.
———. *Victorian Cities*. London, 1963.
———. "The Victorian City: Quantity and Quality." *Victorian Studies* 1968 (11): 711-30.
Brinton, Crane. *English Political Thought in the Nineteenth Century*. New York, 1962.
Bristow, Edward. *Individualism versus Socialism in Britain, 1880-1914*. New York, 1987.
———. "The Liberty and Property Defense League and Individualism." *Historical Journal* 1975 18 (4): 761-89.
———. *Vice and Vigilance: Purity Movements in Britain since 1700*. Totowa, N.J., 1977.
Brown, J. B. "The Pig or the Stye." *International Review of Social History* 1973 18 (3): 380-95.
Brown, John. "Charles Booth and Labour Colonies." *Economic History Review* 1968 21 (2): 349-60.
———. "Social Judgements and Social Policy." *Economic History Review* 1971 24 (1): 106-13.
Brown, Kenneth D. "Conflict in Early British Welfare Policy: The Case of the Unemployed Workman's Bill of 1905." *Journal of Modern History* 1971 43 (4): 615-29.

Bibliography

Brown, Lucy. *Victorian News and Newspapers*. Oxford, 1976.
Bruce, Maurice. *The Coming of the Welfare State*. New York, 1966.
―――, ed. *The Rise of the Welfare State: English Social Policy, 1601-1971*. London, 1973.
Burnett, John. *Plenty and Want: A Social History of Diet in England from 1815 to the Present*. London, 1966.
Cannadine, David. *The Decline and Fall of the British Aristocracy*. New York, 1990.
Clark, George Kitson. *Churchmen and the Condition of England*. London, 1973.
―――. *The Making of Victorian England*. New York, 1972.
Clarke, Peter. "The Progressive Movement in England." *Transactions of the Royal Historical Society* 1974 (24): 159-81.
Collini, Stefan. "Hobhouse, Bosanquet, and the State." *Past and Present* 1976 (72): 86-111.
―――. "The Idea of 'Character' in Victorian Political Thought." *Transactions of the Royal Historical Society* 1985 (35): 29-50.
―――. *Liberalism and Sociology: L. T. Hobhouse and Political Argument in England, 1880-1914*. New York, 1979.
Cronin, James E. "The British State and the Structure of Political Opportunity." *Journal of British Studies* 1988 27 (3): 199-231.
―――. *The Politics of State Expansion*. London, 1991.
Crowther, M. A. "Family Responsibility and State Responsibility in Britain before the Welfare State." *Historical Journal* 1982 25 (1): 131-45.
Daunton, Martin J., ed. *Charity, Self-interest, and Welfare in the English Past*. London, 1996.
―――. *House and Home in the Victorian City*. London, 1983.
Davis, Jennifer. "A Poor Man's System of Justice." *Historical Journal* 1984 27 (2): 309-35.
―――. "From Rookeries to Communities." *History Workshop* 1989 (27): 66-85.
Dennis, Richard. "The Geography of Victorian Values: Philanthropic Housing in London, 1840-1900." *Journal of Historical Geography* 1989 15 (1): 40-54.
Dicey, Albert V. *Lectures on the Relation Between Law and Public Opinion in England*. London, 1905.
Dingle, A. E. "Drink and Working class Living Standards in Britain, 1870-1914." *Economic History Review* 1972 25 (4): 608-22.
Donajgrodzki, A. P., ed. *Social Control in Nineteenth Century Britain*. London, 1977.
Dunbabin, J.P.D. "Expectations of the New County Councils and Their Realization." *Historical Journal* 1965 8 (3): 353-79.
―――. "The Politics of the Establishment of County Councils." *Historical Journal* 1963 6 (2): 226-52.
Dyos, Henry J. "Railways and Housing in Victorian London." *Journal of Transport History* 1955 2: 11-21, 90-100.
―――. "The Slums of Victorian London." *Victorian Studies* 1967 11 (1): 5-40.
―――. "Some Social Costs of Railway Building in London." *Journal of Transport History* 1957 3 (1): 23-30.
Dyos, Henry J. and David Reeder. "Slums and Suburbs," in *The Victorian City*. London, 1973.
Eccleshall, Robert. *British Liberalism*. London, 1986.
Emy, H. V. *Liberals, Radicals, and Social Politics, 1892-1914*. Cambridge, England, 1973.
Englander, David. "Booth's Jews." *Victorian Studies* 1989 32 (4): 551-71.
Evans, Eric, ed. *Social Policy, 1830-1914: Individualism, Collectivism, and the Origins of the Welfare State*. London, 1978.
Feinstein, Charles. "What Really Happened to Real Wages?" *Economic History Review* 1990 43 (3): 329-55.

Feltes, N. N. "Misery or the Production of Misery: Defining Sweated Labour in 1890." *Social History* 1992 17 (3): 441-52.
Fford, Matthew. *Conservatism and Collectivism*. Edinburgh, Scotland, 1990.
Finlayson, Geoffrey. *Citizen, State, and Social Welfare in Britain, 1830-1990*. Oxford, 1994.
Fishman, William. *Jewish Radicals*. New York, 1974.
Fletcher, T. W. "The Great Depression of English Agriculture, 1873-1896." *Economic History Review* 1961 13 (3): 417-32.
Flora, Peter and A. J. Heidenheimer, eds. *The Development of Welfare States in Europe and America*. New Brunswick, N.J., 1981.
Floud, Roderick and Donald McCloskey. *The Economic History of Britain since 1700*. New York, 1981. 2nd Edition. New York, 1994.
Francis, Mark. "Herbert Spencer and the Myth of Laissez-Faire." *Journal of the History of Ideas* 1978 39 (2): 317-28.
Fraser, Derek. *The Evolution of the British Welfare State*. London, 1973.
Fraser, W. Hamish. *The Coming of the Mass Market, 1850-1914*. Hamden, Conn., 1981.
Freeden, Michael. *The New Liberalism: An Ideology of Social Reform*. Oxford, 1978.
Fry, Geoffrey. *The Growth of Government*. London, 1979.
Gardiner, A. G. *Life of Sir William Harcourt*. London, 1923.
Gartner, Lloyd. *The Jewish Immigrant in England, 1870-1914*. London, 1960.
Gatrell, V.A.C. "The Decline of Theft and Violence in Victorian and Edwardian England," in *Crime and the Law*. London, 1980.
Gaudie, Enid. *Cruel Habitations: A History of Working Class Housing, 1780-1918*. London, 1974.
Gazeley, Ian. "The Cost of Living for Urban Workers in Late Victorian and Edwardian Britain." *Economic History Review* 1989 42 (2): 207-21.
Gilbert, Bentley. "The Decay of Nineteenth Century Provident Institutions and the Coming of Old Age Pensions in Great Britain." *Economic History Review* 1965 17 (3): 550-63.
———. *The Evolution of National Insurance in Great Britain: The Origins of the Welfare State*. London, 1966.
———. "Health and Politics." *Bulletin of the History of Medicine* 1965 39 (2): 143-53.
———. "Winston Churchill versus the Webbs: The Origins of British Unemployment Insurance." *American Historical Review* 1966 71 (3): 846-62.
Gilman, Sander and J. Edward Chamberlain, eds. *Degeneration: The Dark Side of Progress*. New York, 1985.
Gorham, Deborah. "The 'Maiden Tribute of Modern Babylon' Reexamined." *Victorian Studies* 1978 21 (3): 353-79.
Greasley, David. "British Economic Growth: The Paradox of the 1880s and the Timing of the Climacteric." *Explaining Economic History* 1986 23 (4): 416-44.
Hage, Jerald, Robert Hanneman, and Edward Gargan. *State Responsiveness and State Activism*. London, 1988.
Haggard, Robert F. "Jack the Ripper as the Threat of Outcast London." *Essays in History* 1993 (35): 1-18.
Hamer, David. *Liberal Politics in the Age of Gladstone and Rosebery*. Oxford, 1972.
Hanham, H. J. *The Reformed Electoral System in Great Britain, 1832-1914*. London, 1968.
Harris, Jose. "Political Thought and the Welfare State, 1870-1940." *Past and Present* 1992 (135): 116-41.
———. *Private Lives, Public Spirit: A Social History of Britain, 1870-1914*. New York, 1993.
———. *Unemployment and Politics*. Oxford, 1972.
Harrison, Brian. "Philanthropy and the Victorians." *Victorian Studies* 1966 9 (4): 353-74.

———. "State Intervention and Moral Reform," in *Pressure from Without*. London, 1974.
Hay, J. Roy. *The Development of the British Welfare State, 1880-1975*. London, 1978.
———. "Employers and Social Policy in Britain: The Evolution of Welfare Legislation, 1905-1914." *Social History* 1977 (4): 435-55.
———. *The Origins of the Liberal Welfare Reforms, 1906-1914*. London, 1975.
Heasman, Katherine. *Evangelicals in Action*. London, 1962.
Hennock, E. P. *British Social Reform and the German Precedents*. New York, 1987.
———. "Concepts of Poverty in the British Social Surveys from Charles Booth to Arthur Bowley," in *The Social Survey in Historical Perspective*. New York, 1991.
———. "The Measurement of Urban Poverty: From the Metropolis to the Nation, 1880-1920." *Economic History Review* 1987 40 (2): 208-27.
———. "Poverty and Social Theory in England: The Experience of the Eighteen-Eighties." *Social History* 1976 (1): 67-91.
Higginbotham, Ann R. " 'Sin of the Age': Infanticide and Illegitimacy in Victorian London." *Victorian Studies* 1989 32 (3): 319-37.
Himmelfarb, Gertrude. "The Culture of Poverty," in *The Victorian City*. London, 1973.
———. *The De-moralization of Society: From Victorian Virtues to Modern Values*. New York, 1995.
———. *The Idea of Poverty*. New York, 1984.
———. "The Idea of Poverty." *History Today* 1984 34 (April): 23-30.
———. *Marriage and Morals among the Victorians and Other Essays*. New York, 1987.
———. "Mayhew's Poor: A Problem of Identity." *Victorian Studies* 1971 14 (3): 307-20.
———. *Poverty and Compassion: The Moral Imagination of the Late Victorians*. New York, 1991.
———. "Victorian Philanthropy." *American Scholar* 1990 59 (3): 373-84.
———. "Victorian Values/Jewish Values." *Commentary* 1989 87 (2): 23-31.
Hobsbawm, Eric. *The Age of Extremes*. New York, 1994.
———. *Labouring Men*. New York, 1964.
———. *Worlds of Labour*. London, 1984.
Holmes, Colin J. "Laissez-faire in Theory and Practice: Britain, 1800-1875." *Journal of European Economic History* 1976 5 (3): 671-88.
Hughes, J.R.T. "Henry Mayhew's London." *Journal of Economic History* 1969 29 (3): 526-36.
Hulin, Jean P. and Pierre Coustillas, eds. *Victorian Writers and the City*. Lille, France, 1979.
Humphreys, Robert. *Sin, Organized Charity, and the Poor Law in Victorian England*. New York, 1995.
James, Robert. *The British Revolution, 1880-1939*. London, 1977.
Johnson, Paul. "Class Law in Victorian England." *Past and Present* 1993 (141): 147-69.
———. "Conspicuous Consumption and Working Class Culture in Late-Victorian and Edwardian Britain." *Transactions of the Royal Historical Society* 1988 (38): 27-42.
———. *Saving and Spending: The Working Class Economy in Britain, 1870-1939*. New York, 1985.
Jones, David. "Crime in London, 1831-1892," in *Crime, Protest, Community, and Police*. London, 1982.
———. "The New Police, Crime, and People in England and Wales, 1829-1888." *Transactions of the Royal Historical Society* 1983 (33): 151-68.
Jones, Gareth Stedman. "The Changing Face of Nineteenth Century Britain." *History Today* 1991 41 (May): 36-40.
———. *Outcast London*. Oxford, 1971.
———. "Working class Culture and Working class Politics in London, 1870-1900."

Journal of Social History 1974 7 (4): 460-508.
Jones, Kathleen. *The Making of Social Policy in Britain, 1830-1990*. London, 1991.
Jones, Peter d'A. *The Christian Socialist Revival*. Princeton, N.J., 1968.
―――. "Henry George and British Socialism." *American Journal of Economics and Sociology* 1988 47 (4): 473-91.
Joyce, Patrick. *Visions of the People*. New York, 1991.
Keating, P. J. "Fact and Fiction in the East End," in *The Victorian City*. London, 1973.
―――. *The Haunted Study: A Social History of the English Novel, 1875-1914*. London, 1989.
―――. *The Working Classes in Victorian Fiction*. New York, 1971.
―――, ed. *Working-class Stories of the 1890s*. New York, 1971.
Kiernan, Victor. "Victorian London: Unending Purgatory." *New Left Review* 1972 (76): 73-90.
Kirk, Neville. " 'Traditional' Working Class Culture and 'The Rise of Labour.' " *Social History* 1991 16 (2): 203-16.
Kirkham, Pat., R. Mace, and J. Porter. *Furnishing the World: The East London Furniture Trade, 1830-1980*. London, 1987.
Koven, Seth and Sonya Michel. "Womanly Duties: Maternalist Politics and the Origins of Welfare States." *American Historical Review* 1991 95 (4): 1076-1108.
Kumar, Krishan. "Social Thought and Social Action: The 'Dicey' Problem and the Role of Ideas in English Social Policy," in *History and Context in Comparative Public Policy*. Pittsburgh, Pa., 1992.
Kurer, Oskar. "John Stuart Mill and the Welfare State." *History of Political Economy* 1991 23 (4): 713-30.
Landes, David. *The Unbound Prometheus*. London, 1970.
Lee, Alan. *The Origins of the Popular Press, 1855-1914*. London, 1976.
Lee, C. H. "Regional Growth and Structural Change in Victorian Britain." *Economic History Review* 1981 34 (3): 438-52.
Lewis, William A. *Growth and Fluctuations, 1870-1913*. London, 1978.
Lummis, Trevor. "Charles Booth: Moralist or Social Scientist?" *Economic History Review* 1971 24 (1): 100-105.
Lynd, Helen. *England in the 1880s*. London, 1945.
MacBriar, Alan. *Fabian Socialism and English Politics, 1884-1918*. Cambridge, England, 1962.
MacKinnon, Mary. "English Poor Law Policy and the Crusade against Out Relief." *Journal of Economic History* 1987 47 (3): 603-25.
―――. "Poor Law Policy, Unemployment, and Pauperism." *Explorations in Economic History* 1986 23 (3): 299-336.
―――. "Poverty and Policy: The English Poor Law, 1860-1910." *Journal of Economic History* 1986 46 (2): 500-502.
MacLeod, Roy, ed. *Government and Expertise*. New York, 1988.
Malchow, Howard L. *Population Pressures: Emigration and Government in Late Nineteenth Century Britain*. Palo Alto, Calif., 1979.
―――. "Public Gardens and Social Action in Late Victorian London." *Victorian Studies* 1985 29 (1): 97-124.
―――. "A Victorian Mind: Gertrude Himmelfarb, Poverty, and the Moral Imagination." *Victorian Studies* 1992 35 (3): 309-13.
Mandler, Peter, ed. *The Uses of Charity*. Philadelphia, 1990.
Marks, Lara. "Medical Care for Pauper Mothers and Their Infants: Poor Law Provision and Local Demand in East London, 1870-1929." *Economic History Review* 1993 46 (3): 518-42.

Marsh, Peter. *The Discipline of Popular Government: Lord Salisbury's Domestic Statecraft.* Sussex, England, 1978.
Marshall, T. H. "Changing Ideas about Poverty," in *The Right to Welfare and Other Essays.* New York, 1981.
Marwick, Arthur. "The Labour Party and the Welfare State in Britain, 1900-1948." *American Historical Review* 1967 73 (2): 380-403.
Mason, John W. "Political Economy and the Response to Socialism in Britain, 1870-1914." *Historical Journal* 1980 23 (3): 565-87.
Mathias, Peter. *The First Industrial Nation.* New York, 1969.
Matthews, Derek. "1889 and All That: New Views on the New Unionism." *International Review of Social History* 1991 36 (1): 2-58.
May, Trevor. *An Economic and Social History of Britain, 1760-1970.* New York, 1987.
McCarthy, Terry, ed. *The Great Dock Strike, 1889.* London, 1988.
McCloskey, Donald. "Did Victorian Britain Fail?" *Economic History Review* 1970 23 (3): 446-59.
―――. "Victorian Growth: A Rejoinder." *Economic History Review* 1974 27 (2): 275-77.
McGregor, Oliver. "Social Research and Social Policy in the Nineteenth Century." *British Journal of Sociology* 1957 8 (2): 146-57.
McHugh, Paul. *Prostitution and Victorian Social Reform.* London, 1980.
McKenzie, Robert and Allan Silver. *Angels in Marble.* Chicago, 1968.
McKibben, Ross. *The Ideologies of Class: Social Relations in Britain, 1880-1950.* Oxford, 1990.
―――. "Why Was There No Marxism in Great Britain?" *English Historical Review* 1984 99 (391): 297-331.
McLeod, Hugh. *Class and Religion in the Late Victorian City.* Hamden, Conn., 1974.
Meacham, Standish. *A Life Apart: The British Working Class, 1890-1914.* Cambridge, Mass., 1977.
―――. *Toynbee Hall and Social Reform, 1880-1914.* New Haven, Conn., 1987.
Melling, Joseph. "Welfare Capitalism and the Origins of Welfare States." *Social History* 1992 17 (3): 453-78.
Midwinter, Eric. *Victorian Social Reform.* New York, 1968.
Mitchell, Brian R. *British Historical Statistics.* New York, 1988.
―――. *European Historical Statistics, 1750-1970.* New York, 1976.
Mommsen, Wolfgang. *The Emergence of the Welfare State in Britain and Germany, 1850-1959.* London, 1981.
Morris, Robert J. and Richard Roger. *The Victorian City.* London, 1993.
Mowat, Charles Loch. "Charity and Casework in Late Victorian London." *Social Service Review* 1957 31 (3): 258-70.
―――. *The Charity Organisation Society, 1869-1913.* London, 1961.
Musson, A. E. "British Industrial Growth during the 'Great Depression': Some Comments." *Economic History Review* 1963 15 (3): 529-33.
―――. "British Industrial Growth, 1873-1896: A Balanced View." *Economic History Review* 1964 17 (2): 397-403.
―――. "The Great Depression in Britain: A Reappraisal." *Journal of Economic History* 1959 19 (2): 199-228.
Norman, E. *Victorian Christian Socialists.* New York, 1987.
O'Day, Rosemary and David Englander. *Mr. Charles Booth's Inquiry.* London, 1993.
Olsen, Donald. *The Growth of Victorian London.* New York, 1977.
―――. "Victorian London: Specialization, Segregation, and Privacy." *Victorian Studies* 1974 17 (3): 265-78.

O'Neill, James. "The Victorian Background to the British Welfare State." *South Atlantic Quarterly* 1967 66 (2): 204-17.
Orloff, Ann and Theda Skopol. "Why not Equal Protection?" *American Sociological Review* 1984 49 (6): 726-50.
Owen, David. "The City Parochial Charities." *Journal of British Studies* 1962 1 (2): 115-35.
———. *English Philanthropy, 1660-1960*. New York, 1964.
———. *The Government of Victorian London, 1855-1889*. Edited by Donald Olsen and David Reeder. Cambridge, Mass., 1982.
Paul, Ellen F. *Moral Revolution and Economic Science: The Demise of Laissez-faire in Nineteenth Century British Political Economy*. Westport, Conn., 1979.
Pederson, Susan. *Family, Dependence, and the Origins of the Welfare State*. New York, 1993.
——— and Peter Mandler, eds. *After the Victorians: Private Conscience and Public Duty in Modern Britain*. London, 1994.
Pelling, Henry. *The Origins of the Labour Party, 1880-1900*. 2nd Edition. Oxford, 1965.
———. *The Social Geography of British Elections, 1885-1918*. London, 1967.
Perkin, Harold. "Individualism versus Collectivism in Nineteenth Century Britain: A False Antithesis." *Journal of British Studies* 1977 17 (1): 105-18.
———. *The Rise of Professional Society*. London, 1989.
Petrow, Stefan. *Policing Morals: The Metropolitan Police and the Home Office, 1870-1914*. Oxford, 1994.
Pick, Daniel. *Faces of Degeneration: A European Disorder, c.1848-c.1918*. New York, 1989.
Pilzer, J. M. "The Jews and the Great Sweated Debate." *Jewish Social Studies* 1979 41 (3-4): 257-74.
Plowright, J. "Political Economy and Christian Polity." *Victorian Studies* 1987 30 (2): 235-52.
Pollard, Sidney. *Britain's Prime and Britain's Decline*. New York, 1989.
———. *The Idea of Progress*. New York, 1968.
Pope, Rex, Alan Pratt, and Bernard Hoyle, eds. *Social Welfare in Britain, 1885-1985*. London, 1986.
Porter, Bernard. *The Lion's Share*. 2nd Edition. New York, 1984.
Powell, David. "The New Liberalism and the Rise of Labour, 1886-1906." *Historical Journal* 1986 29 (2): 369-93.
Prochaska, Frank. "Body and Soul: Bible Nurses and the Poor in Victorian London." *Historical Research* 1987 60 (143): 336-48.
———. *The Voluntary Impulse: Philanthropy in Modern Britain*. London, 1988.
———. *Women and Philanthropy in Nineteenth Century England*. Oxford, 1980.
Prothero, Iorwerth. "Chartism in London." *Past and Present* 1969 (44): 76-105.
Pugh, Martin. *Lloyd George*. London, 1988.
———. *Tories and the People*. New York, 1985.
Quinault, R. E. "Randolph Churchill and Tory Democracy." *Historical Journal* 1979 22 (1): 141-65.
Rasmussen, Steen E. *London: The Unique City*. 1934. Reprint Edition. Cambridge, Mass., 1982.
Richter, Melvin. *Politics of Conscience: T. H. Green and His Age*. Cambridge, Mass., 1964.
Rimlinger, Gaston. "Welfare Policy and Economic Development." *Journal of Economic History* 1966 26 (4): 556-71.
———. *Welfare Policy and Industrialization*. New York, 1971.
Roberts, David. "How Cruel Was the Victorian Poor Law?" *Historical Journal* 1963 6 (1): 97-107.

———. *Victorian Origins of the British Welfare State.* New Haven, Conn., 1961.
Rodger, Richard. *Housing in Urban Britain, 1780-1914.* Basingstoke, England, 1989.
———. "Political Economy, Ideology, and the Persistence of Working-Class Housing Problems in Britain, 1850-1914." *International Review of Social History* 1987 32 (2): 109-43.
Rose, Michael. "The Allowance System Under the New Poor Law." *Economic History Review* 1966 19 (3): 607-20.
———, compiler. *The English Poor Law, 1780-1930.* New York, 1971.
———, ed. *The Poor and the City.* Leicester, England, 1985.
———. *The Relief of Poverty.* London, 1972.
Ross, Ellen. "Fierce Questions and Taunts: Married Life in Working Class London, 1870-1914." *Feminist Studies* 1982 8 (3): 575-602.
———. *Love and Toil: Motherhood in Outcast London, 1870-1918.* New York, 1993.
———. "Survival Networks: Women's Neighborhood Sharing in London before World War I." *History Workshop* 1983 (15): 4-27.
Routh, Guy. *Occupations of the People of Great Britain, 1801-1981.* London, 1987.
Rowe, D. J. "The Failure of London Chartism." *Historical Journal* 1968 11 (3): 472-87.
Rudé, George. *Paris and London in the Eighteenth Century: Studies in Popular Protest.* New York, 1971.
Samuel, Raphael. "Workshop of the World: Steam Power and Hand Technology in Mid-Victorian Britain." *History Workshop* 1977 (3): 6-72.
Sankhdher, M. M. *The Concept of the Welfare State.* Delhi, India, 1975.
Satre, Lowell. "After the Matchgirls' Strike." *Victorian Studies* 1982 26 (1): 7-31.
Saul, S. B. *The Myth of the Great Depression in England.* New York, 1969.
Schmiechen, James. "State Reform and Local Economy." *Economic History Review* 1975 28 (3): 413-28.
———. *Sweated Industries and Sweated Labor.* Urbana, Ill., 1984.
Schneer, Jonathon. "Politics and Feminism in 'Outcast London.'" *Journal of British Studies* 1991 30 (1): 63-82.
Schults, Raymond L. *Crusader in Babylon: W. T. Stead and the Pall Mall Gazette.* Lincoln, Neb., 1972.
Schweinitz, Karl. *England's Road to Social Security.* London, 1943.
Seecombe, Wally. "Patriarchy Stabilized: The Construction of the Male Breadwinner Wage Norm in Nineteenth Century Britain." *Social History* 1986 11 (1): 53-76.
Shannon, H. "Migration and the Growth of London, 1841-1891." *Economic History Review* 1935 5 (2): 79-86.
Sheppard, Francis. "London and the Nation in the Nineteenth Century." *Transactions of the Royal Historical Society* 1985 (35): 51-74.
Shpayer-Markov, Haia. "Anarchism in British Public Opinion, 1880-1914." *Victorian Studies* 1988 31 (4): 487-516.
Sigsworth, E. M. and T. J. Wyke. "Victorian Prostitution and Venereal Disease," in *Suffer and Be Still.* Bloomington, Ind., 1972.
Sindall, R. "The London Garotting Panics of 1856 and 1862." *Social History* 1987 12 (3): 351-59.
Smith, Paul. *Disraelian Conservatism and Social Reform.* London, 1967.
Smith, Timothy. "In Defense of Privilege: The City of London and the Challenge of Municipal Reform, 1875-1890." *Journal of Social History* 1993 27 (1): 59-83.
Soffer, Reba. "The Revolution in English Social Thought, 1880-1914." *American Historical Review* 1970 75 (7): 1938-64.
Soloway, Richard. "Counting the Degenerates: The Statistics of Race Deterioration in Edwardian England." *Journal of Contemporary History* 1982 17 (1): 137-64.

Southall, Humphrey. "The Origins of the Depressed Areas: Unemployment, Growth, and Regional Economic Structure in Britain before 1914." *Economic History Review* 1988 41 (2): 236-58.
Steffel, R. Vladimir. "The Slum Question." *Albion* 1973 5 (4): 314-25.
Stokes, John. *Fin de Siecle, Fin de Globe: Fears and Fantasies of the Late Nineteenth Century*. New York, 1982.
Storch, Robert. "Police Control of Street Prostitution in Victorian London," in *Police and Society*. Beverly Hills, Calif., 1977.
Summers, Anne. "A Home from Home–Women's Philanthropic Work in the Nineteenth Century," in *Fit Work for Women*. New York, 1979.
Swaan, Abram de. *In the Care of the State*. New York, 1988.
Tarn, John N. "The Peabody Donation Fund." *Victorian Studies* 1966 10 (1): 7-38.
Taylor, Arthur J. *Laissez-faire and State Intervention in Nineteenth Century Britain*. London, 1972.
Thane, Pat. "Non-Contributory Versus Insurance Pensions, 1878-1908," in *The Origins of British Social Policy*. London, 1978.
———. "Women and the Poor Law in Victorian and Edwardian England." *History Workshop* 1978 (6): 29-51.
———. "The Working Class and State 'Welfare' in Britain, 1880-1914." *Historical Journal* 1984 27 (4): 877-900.
Thompson, Edward P. "The Political Education of Henry Mayhew." *Victorian Studies* 1967 11 (1): 41-62.
Thompson, Paul. "Liberals, Radicals, and Labor in London, 1880-1900." *Past and Present* 1964 (27): 73-101.
———. *Socialists, Liberals, and Labor: The Struggle for London, 1885-1914*. London, 1967.
Tobias, J. J. *Urban Crime in Victorian England*. New York, 1972.
Tomes, Nancy. " 'A Torrent of Abuse': Crimes of Violence between Working Class Men and Women in London, 1840-1875." *Journal of Social History* 1978 11 (3): 328-45.
Topalov, Christian. "Understanding Unemployment: Scientific Vocabulary and Social Reform in Britain, France, and the United States, 1880-1910." A paper presented at the University of Virginia on 27 January 1995.
Treble, James. *Urban Poverty in Britain, 1830-1914*. London, 1979.
Vincent, A. W. "The Poor Law Reports of 1909 and the Social Theory of the Charity Organisation Society." *Victorian Studies* 1984 27 (3): 343-63.
Vorspan, Rachel. "Vagrancy and the New Poor Law." *English Historical Review* 1977 92 (362): 59-81.
Walkowitz, Judith. *City of Dreadful Delight*. Chicago, 1992.
———. "Jack the Ripper and the Myth of Male Violence." *Feminist Studies* 1982 8 (3): 543-74.
———. "Male Vice and Feminist Virtue: Feminism and the Politics of Prostitution in Nineteenth Century Britain." *History Workshop* 1982 (13): 79-93.
———. *Prostitution and Victorian Society*. New York, 1980.
Walvin, James. *Victorian Values*. Athens, Ga., 1987.
Waters, Chris. *British Socialists and the Politics of Popular Culture, 1884-1914*. Stanford, Calif., 1990.
Webb, Robert K. *Modern England*. 2nd Edition. New York, 1980.
Wechsler, Robert. "The Jewish Garment Trade in East London, 1875-1914." Ph.D. Dissertation, Columbia University, 1979.
Weiler, Peter. *The New Liberalism*. London, 1982.
Wiener, Joel. *Papers for the Millions: The New Journalism in Britain, 1850-1914*. New

Bibliography

York, 1988.
Wiener, Martin. *English Culture and the Decline of the Industrial Spirit, 1850-1980.* New York, 1981.
Williams, Gertrude. *The Coming of the Welfare State.* London, 1967.
Williams, Karel. *From Pauperism to Poverty.* London, 1981.
Williamson, Jeffrey. *Did British Capitalism Breed Inequality?* Boston, 1985.
Willis, Kirk. "The Introduction and Critical Reception of Marxist Thought." *Historical Journal* 1977 20 (2): 417-59.
Wilson, Charles. "Economy and Society in Late Victorian Britain." *Economic History Review* 1965 18 (1): 183-98.
Wilson, Elizabeth. *Women and the Welfare State.* London, 1977.
Winch, David. *Economics and Policy: A Historical Study.* London, 1972.
Wohl, Anthony S. "The Bitter Cry of Outcast London." *International Review of Social History* 1968 13 (2): 189-245.
———. "The 1880s: A New Generation." *Nineteenth Century Studies* 1990 (4): 1-22.
———. *The Eternal Slum.* London, 1977.
———. "The Housing of the Working Classes in London, 1815-1914," in *The History of Working Class Housing.* Totowa, N.J., 1971.
———. "Octavia Hill and the Homes of the London Poor." *Journal of British Studies* 1971 10 (2): 105-31.
Wolfe, W. *From Radicalism to Socialism.* New Haven, Conn., 1975.
Woodroofe, Kathleen. "The Making of the Welfare State in England." *Journal of Social History* 1968 1 (4): 303-24.
Wright, T. R. *The Religion of Humanity: The Impact of Comtean Positivism on Victorian Britain.* New York, 1986.
Yelling, J. A. *Slums and Slum Clearance in Victorian London.* London, 1986.
Yeo, Stephen. "A New Life: The Religion of Socialism in Britain." *History Workshop* 1977 (4): 5-56.
Young, Ken and Patricia Garside. *Metropolitan London: Politics and Urban Change, 1837-1981.* London, 1982.

Index

Adler, Hermann, 149
Alber, Jens, 5
Aliens Bill (1894), 149
Anarchism. *See* Socialism
Anti-Sweater, 150
Arnold, Matthew, 7
Arnstein, Walter, 3
Artisans' Dwellings Act (1875), 121
Asquith, Herbert Henry, 95, 124, 162
Atlee, Clement, 181
Australian Relief fund, 102
Aveling, Edward, 91

Balfour, Arthur J., 95, 170
Barnett, Henrietta, 64
Barnett, Samuel A., 4, 58, 66-67, 80-81, 129, 161, 167
Baumann, Arthur, 149, 151
Beer, Samuel H., 5
Bentham, Jeremy, 6, 129, 176
Besant, Annie, 100-101, 105
Besant, Walter, 41-42, 45, 66-68, 106, 144-45
Beveridge, William, 6, 181
Bismarck, Otto von: social reforms of, 118, 166
Black, Clementia, 106
Blackley, William, 162, 164-68
Blatchford, Robert, 84-85
"Bloody Sunday" (13 November 1887), 25, 32, 34-35
Booth, Bramwell, 142
Booth, Catherine, 71, 142
Booth, Charles: and *The Life and Labour of the People in London*, 3, 6, 46-48, 51-53, 95, 99, 151; reform proposals of, 48-49, 162-63, 167-70
Booth, William, 71; and his *Darkest England* scheme, 72-74
Bosanquet, Charles B. P., 58-59
Bosanquet, Helen Dendy, 28, 52
Bowley, Arthur L., 19
Brabazon, Reginald. *See* Meath, Reginald Brabazon, Earl
Bradlaugh, Charles, 115, 128
Brand, Henry, 156
Briggs, Asa, 2
Bryant, Theodore, 100-101
Bryant and May Match Factory, 100-101
Bryce, James, 75
Burns, John, 34-35, 42, 89, 102-3, 107-8, 137
Butler, Josephine, 7, 142

Campbell-Bannerman, Henry, 124
Chadwick, Edwin, 6, 129
Chamberlain, Joseph, 95, 120, 173; and reform, 6, 10, 89-90, 111, 122-24, 126-27, 129-31, 138, 155-56, 161-62, 165-66, 169-70; and the empire, 13; and the "Condition of England," 22-23
Champion, Henry Hyde, 34, 96, 102-3, 110-11
Charity: ill-administration of, 58-62; and district visiting, 61-64; role of women in, 63-64; and "People's Kitchens," 64; and homeless

shelters, 65; and "fallen women," 65; and the mission movement, 65-67; and open spaces, 68; and model dwellings, 68-71; and the Salvation Army, 71-72; and William Booth's *Darkest England* scheme, 72-74; and metropolitan medical charities, 74-75; and the City of London Parochial Charity Fund, 75, 167
Charity Organisation Society (COS), 7, 28, 52, 68; philosophy of, 58-61, 82; aid provided by, 60; and indiscriminate charities, 60-61; and district visiting, 61-63; and model dwellings, 71; and the Salvation Army, 71; and William Booth's *Darkest England* scheme, 73-74; and metropolitan medical charities, 74-75; and the London Parochial Charity Fund, 75; and Poor Law out relief, 75-78, 81; and opposition to old age pensions, 81; and the Poor Law workhouse, 81, 171; and colonization, 145
Charles II (of England), 133
Cheap Trains Act (1883), 157
Christian Socialism. *See* Headlam, Stewart; Socialism
Churchill, Randolph, 42, 120-23
Churchill, Winston, 6
City of London Parochial Charity Fund, 75
Clark, George Kitson, 2, 7
Cobden, Jane, 134-35
Cobden, Richard, 98
Collier, Robert, 137
Columbine, W. B., 4
The Commonweal, 92
Compton, William George Spencer Scott, Earl, 158
"Condition of England" Question, 21, 26-32, 36, 45-53, 175
Criminal Law Amendment Act (1885), 142
Cross, Richard A., 135, 155-57

Daily News, 30
Degeneration, impact of: on the economy, 22-24; on the military, 24-25; on politics, 25; and socialism, 112; and *laissez-faire* economics, 125-26; and social reform, 172-73
Democratization, impact of. *See* Social reform
Derby, Edward George Stanley, 14th earl of, 58
Dicey, Albert V., 5, 173
Dickens, Charles, 7
Dilke, Charles, 107, 111
Dilke, Emilia, 107
Disraeli, Benjamin, 13, 120-21, 150
Disused Burial Grounds Act (1884), 68
Dock Strike Relief fund, 102
Donajgrodzki, A. P., 7
Dunraven, Windham Thomas Wyndham-Quin, earl of, 12

The Economist, 123, 127, 157, 163, 166
Education Act (1870), 124
Edward VI (of England), 133
Edward VII (of England), 169
Elizabeth I (of England), 1, 133
Employers and Workmen Act (1875), 120
Employers' Liability Act (1880), 124
Engels, Friedrich, 92, 98
Evans, Eric, 5

Fabian Society. *See* Shaw, George Bernard; Socialism; Webb, Beatrice Potter; Webb, Sidney
Factory Act (1833), 118
Factory Act (1874), 120
Factory and Workshop Act (1878), 150
Factory and Workshop Act (1895), 125
Fair Trade League, 33
Fawcett, Henry, 76
Firth, Joseph F. B., 129-32
Flora, Peter, 6
Food and Drug Act (1875), 120
Forster, William E., 58, 124
Fourier, Charles, 177
The Free Life, 173
Froude, James Anthony, 12

General Dockers' Union, 102
George, David Lloyd, 6, 42, 170, 176
George, Henry: and the "single tax,"

Index

87-89, 173
Giffin, Robert, 18-19, 26
Gissing, George, 19, 24, 40, 85
Gladstone, Margaret, 107
Gladstone, William E., 58, 76, 107, 110-11, 122-25, 128, 161, 173
Glasgow Improvement Act (1865), 156
Gordon Riots (1780), 33
Gorst, John, 120-23
Goschen, George J., 19, 58, 76
Grahame, Cunningham, 35
"Great Depression in Trade and Agriculture," 14-18, 20-21, 26, 44-45, 175
Green, Thomas Hill, 6, 177-78
Grey, Edward, 95
Guild of St. Matthew, 87

Haldane, Richard, 10, 95, 125-26
Harcourt, William, 83, 124, 130
Hardie, James Keir, 42, 108, 110-11
Harkness, Margaret, 39, 130
Harris, Frank, 125, 158
Harris, Jose, 5-6
Harrison, Brian, 7
Hatton, Joseph, 41
Hay, J. Roy, 5
Headlam, Stewart, 7, 86-87
Heasman, Katherine, 7
Heidenheimer, A. J., 5
Henderson, Arthur, 42
Henderson, Edmund, 33
Henry I (of England), 133
Henry VIII (of England), 1, 133
Hill, Octavia, 7, 58, 60, 62, 68, 70-71
Himmelfarb, Gertrude, 6-7, 51, 53, 180
Hobhouse, Leonard Trelawney, 125-26
Hobson, John A., 6, 21, 82, 87, 89, 106-7, 125-26, 147-48
Hogarth, Janet, 107
Holland, Lionel, 170
Hughes, Hugh Price, 86
Huxley, Thomas Henry, 73
Hyndman, Henry M., 34, 36, 89-93, 96, 114

Independent Labour Party. *See* Socialism
Industrial Freedom League, 173
Irish Land Act (1870), 124
Irish Land Act (1881), 124

"Jack the Ripper": response to murders of, 25, 31-32, 43-44
James I (of England), 133
James, Henry, 37
Jeune, Mary, 74
Jones, Gareth Stedman, 5, 34, 36, 51

Keynes, John Maynard, 6, 181
Kidd, Benjamin, 115
Kingsley, Charles, 86
Kipling, Rudyard, 13

Labour Elector, 110-11
Labour Leader, 110, 170-71
LaFone, Henry, 102-3
The Lancet, 155
Levi, Leon, 20, 54
Liberal Party. *See* Social Reform
Liberty and Property Defense League, 173
The Liberty Review, 173
The Link, 100
Local Government Act (1888), 123, 131-32, 146
Loch, Charles Stewart, 59, 169, 171
London: and the dock strike, 25, 32, 49, 100-104; and the gasworkers' strike, 25, 32, 49, 104-5; studies of poverty in, 27-29, 47-49, 51-52; demoralization of the poor in, 28-29; irreligion in, 29, 55-56; as the focus of the "Condition of England" Question, 32-33, 37-38, 40, 43-44; riots and demonstrations in, 32-36; segregation of classes in, 37-38, 71; overcrowding in, 39, 71, 152-54, 156, 158; crime in, 39, 43; prostitution in, 39-40; condition of labor in, 40-41, 44-45, 99, 101-8, 129, 147-52; death rate in, 42; sanitary improvements in, 42-43; and the City of (financial district), 43, 75, 130, 132-33, 167; negative impressions of the East End of, 43-44, 66; unemployment in, 44-45; positive views of the East End of, 44-46; parks in, 68; unions in, 98, 100-105; apathy in, 98, 129; and the matchgirls' strike, 100-101; under-representation of, 129-

30; and municipal government reform, 129-39; county council of, 130-39; political shift in, 131; and the (London) Progressive Party, 132-37, 139; and the water companies, 135-36; and the gas companies, 136; and the (London) Moderate Party, 136-39; immigration to, 147-50; and the Jews, 148-50; and slum clearance, 153-56; rising rent in, 154; and working class trains, 156-57; and working class housing, 156-58; lack of sanitary inspectors in, 159; and public works, 161-62
London County Council. *See* London; Social reform
London Government Act (1899), 139
London Ratepayers League, 173
London Street Tramways Company, 136
Louise, Princess (of England), 58
Lubbock, John, 138
Lynd, Helen, 5
Lyons, Lewis, 150

MacDonald, Ramsey, 107
MacKinnon, Mary, 45
Mallock, William, 111-14, 173
Mann, Tom, 73, 89, 102-3, 109-10
Manning, Henry Cardinal, 58, 68, 103-4, 145
Mansion House Relief Fund (1886), 60-61, 133
Marshall, Alfred, 6, 24, 80, 114-15, 144
Marx, Eleanor, 91
Marx, Karl, 89-92, 96, 114
Massingham, Henry, 128
Matthews, Henry, 34-35
Maurice, (John) Frederick Denison, 86
Mayhew, Henry, 51
Mearns, Andrew: and "The Bitter Cry of Outcast London," 27-29, 31, 39-40, 42, 117
Meath, Reginald Brabazon, Earl, 54, 68, 118, 145-46
Metropolitan Association for Improving the Dwellings of the Industrious Classes, 71
Metropolitan and National Nursing Association, 64
Metropolitan Board of Works, 71, 131, 155
Metropolitan Open Spaces Act (1881), 68
Metropolitan Poor Act (1867), 76, 80
Metropolitan Public Gardens Association, 68
Middle Class Defense Organization, 173
Midwinter, Eric, 5
Mill, John Stuart, 6, 176-77
Mines Act (1842), 118
Morley, John, 30, 124
Morning Chronicle, 51
Morris, William, 7, 36, 91, 93, 95, 114
Morrison, Arthur, 41-42, 45
Mulhall, Michael, 19
Municipal Reform League, 129
Musson, Albert Edward, 15

National Association for the Promotion of State-Aided Colonization, 145
National Insurance Act (1911), 176, 180
National Union of Gas Workers and General Labourers, 104
National Vigilance Association, 142
Nevison, Henry, 99
The New Age, 128
New Imperialism, 12-13, 26
New Journalism, 30-31
New Political Economy, 119-20
Nightingale, Florence, 64

O'Connor, Thomas Power, 30
Old Age Pensions Act (1908), 53, 167, 180
O'Neill, James, 5
Owen, David, 5
Owen, Robert, 177

Paine, Thomas, 176
Pall Mall Gazette, 27-31, 101, 142-43
Parochial Charities Act (1883), 75
Passenger Act (1855), 146
Paterson, Emma, 107
Peabody, George: and the Peabody Trust, 69-70
The People, 161

Index

People's Palace, 67
People's Press, 73
Perkin, Harold, 178-79
The Personal Rights Journal, 173
Place, Francis, 98
Poor Law Amendment Act (1825), 161
Poor Law Amendment Act (1834), 76-77
Poor Law, English: and outdoor relief, 76-78; abolition of proposed, 78-79; and pauper children, 79-80; and the aged, 80; and indoor relief, 81, 171; and emigration, 146; and the "labour test," 160
Poor Law Union Rateability Act (1865), 76
Poor Law, Viennese, 81, 167
Potter, Beatrice. *See* Webb, Beatrice Potter
Pretyman, John Radclyffe, 79
Primrose League, 145
Primrose League Gazette, 123
Progress: defined, 9; international threats to, 13-14, 24, 26; in the economy, 15-16; in working class standards of living, 16-19, 21, 25-26, 48, 114-15, 175, 179; dangers of, 20-21; critics of, 21-25, 27-28; deniers of, 22-26; inhibited by alcohol, 42, 55; threatened by overcrowding, 69
Public Health Act (1875), 120
Public Works Act (1883), 160

Rae, John, 15, 126
Ranyard, Ellen, 64
Redistribution Act (1885), 9
Reform Act (1832), 9
Reform Act (1867), 9, 118
Reform Act (1884), 9, 36, 124
Reform League, 177
Reynold's Newspaper, 73
Ridge, William Pett, 96
Roberts, David, 2
Rosebery, Archibald Philip Primrose, earl of, 13, 132
Rowntree, Joseph, 143-44
Rowntree, Seebohm, 3, 6, 32, 50-52, 171
Ruskin, John: and Victorian social reform, 7, 58, 86

Salisbury, Robert Cecil, marquess of, 34, 58, 95; and reform, 31, 120-23, 131, 138-39, 149, 156-58, 170
Salvation Army: relief provided by, 71-72, 102; *Darkest England* scheme of, 72-74
Sandhurst, Margaret, 134-35
Sankhdher, M. M., 5
Saturday Review, 57
Schloss, David, 151
Seeley, John Robert, 12
Sellers, Edith, 167
Shaftesbury, Anthony Ashley Cooper, earl of, 28, 58, 126, 159, 172
Shaw, George Bernard, 36, 40, 89, 93-95
Sherwell, Arthur, 143-44
Sims, George R., 180
Smiles, Samuel, 69
Smith, Hubert Llewellyn, 23
Social Democratic Federation. *See* Hyndman, Henry M.; Socialism
Social reform: and the "New Liberalism," 6, 111, 124-28; and democratization, 9-11, 22, 26, 91, 119, 166, 173; and emigration and immigration, 12, 14, 145-51; and the Conservative Party, 110-11, 120-23, 135, 170, 175; and the Liberal Party, 110-11, 123-29, 175, 180; and the "death" of *laissez-faire*, 117-18, 178; spurred by fears of national decline, 119; and municipal government reform, 129-39; and the (London) Progressive Party, 132-37, 139, 155; and the (London) Moderate Party, 136-39; and "social purity," 141-44; and education, 144-45; and sweated labor, 150-52; and the "dangerous trades," 152; and housing, 152-60; and public works, 160-62; and old age pensions, 162-72, 180; opponents of, 172-74; and Thomas Paine, 176; and John Stuart Mill, 176-77; and Thomas Hill Green, 177-78
Socialism: and the Social Democratic Federation, 33-34, 89-91, 114; and Robert Blatchford, 84; and Oscar Wilde, 84; promises of, 84-

85, 90; advent of, 85, 114; as a system of ethics, 85-86; and Judaism, 86; and Christianity, 86; and land nationalization, 88; and the Christian Socialists, 86-87, 113; and Henry George, 87-89, 113-14; and the Socialist League, 91-92; and anarchism, 92-93; confused with social reform, 93-94; and the Fabian Society, 93-96, 114; and the passivity of labor, 96; and the Independent Labour Party, 96, 108-11, 114, 131, 175; critics of, 111-15; and immigration, 149; and housing reform, 159; and Charles Fourier, 177; and Robert Owen, 177
Socialist League. *See* Morris, William; Socialism
South Metropolitan Gas Company, 104
Spencer, Herbert, 173
The Star, 30, 73, 101
Stead, William T., 30-31, 142-43
Steuart, John Alexander, 25
Street Offences Act (1959), 142

Ten Hour Act (1847), 118
Tennyson, Alfred Lord, 13, 38
Thorne, William, 104
Tillet, Ben, 73, 102-3
The Times (London), 57, 73-74
Torrens, William, 153, 155-56
Toynbee, Arnold, 4, 119, 127-28, 157, 164
Toynbee Hall, 66-67, 161
Trade Union Congress, 108, 149
Trades Union Act (1875), 120
Trafalgar Square, 32-35, 128
Trevelyan, Charles, 24, 61-62, 75
The Trumphet, 173

"Unemployed" Riot (8 February 1886), 32-34
Unemployed Workmen's Act (1905), 50, 179-80
Unemployment: in Britain, 14-15; in London, 44-45. *See also* "Great Depression in Trade and Agriculture"

Vagrant's Act (1824), 142

Victoria (of England), 58, 179

Warren, Charles, 34-35
Webb, Beatrice Potter, 36, 40, 93, 95, 102, 107
Webb, Sidney, 36, 83-84, 89, 93-95, 128, 137, 167
Welfare State: sixteenth and seventeenth century "origins" of, 1; early Victorian "origins" of, 2; late Victorian "origins" of, 2-8, 175-76, 178-81; defined, 179
Wells, Herbert George, 89
Wemyss, Francis Charteris, earl of, 10, 173
White, Arnold, 145-46, 161
Whitmore, Charles A., 138
Wilde, Oscar, 84
Williams, Ernest E., 12
Williams, Gertrude, 5
Williams, J. W., 166-67
Williams, Jack, 34
Wohl, Anthony, 2-4, 36, 158-59
Women's Industrial Council, 107
Women's Trade Union Provident League, 107
Wood, George, 19
Working class: respectability within, 11, 19-20, 45-46; health of, 20; threats to character of, 24; necessity of a healthy, 24; demoralization within, 28-29, 37-42, 54-58, 141; irreligion of, 29, 55-56; militancy of, 32; riots and demonstrations of, 32-36; prostitution within, 39-40; lack of culture of, 41, 66; use of alcohol by, 42, 46, 51, 54-55, 58; crime within, 56; passivity of, 96, 98, 114; anti-socialist sentiment within, 96-97; and "sweated labor," 99, 105, 107-8; and the trade union movement, 97-98, 100-107, 175; and the employment of women, 105-8; and profit-sharing, 115; and marriage, 141; savings of, 163, 171
Working Class Housing Act (1885), 158-59
Working Class Housing Act (1890),

156
Workmen's Compensation Act (1897), 50

York: studies of poverty in, 32, 50-52, 171

About the Author

ROBERT F. HAGGARD is Assistant Professor on the general faculty at the University of Virginia.